FUNDAMENTALS
OF LOGIC

FUNDAMENTALS
OF LOGIC

JOEL KUPPERMAN, Ph.D.

Assistant Professor
Department of Philosophy
University of Connecticut

ARTHUR S. McGRADE, Ph.D.

Assistant Professor
Department of Philosophy
University of Connecticut

A COLLEGE COURSE GUIDE

DOUBLEDAY & COMPANY, INC., GARDEN CITY, NEW YORK

1966

Material from *Aristotle's Syllogistic—From
the Standpoint of Modern Formal Logic* by
Jan Lukasiewicz is reprinted by permission of
the publisher, The Clarendon Press.

Preface

This book makes logic simple in the sense that it reduces its principles, and the problems surrounding them, to their clearest essentials. We have consistently tried to avoid frills in presentation, jargon, or an apparatus of footnotes. Wherever possible, problems have been presented in down-to-earth terms, with copious use of examples.

This does not mean, however, that this book is guaranteed to be easy. Some of the problems connected with logic, even when stated with maximum clarity, are not entirely easy to grasp. Some logic books get around this difficulty by ignoring the problems most closely related to the nature of logic. But it is our view that logic can have great value as a discipline only if it stimulates the thinking of its student. The study of logic should toughen up the reasoning powers. Consequently, however simply logic is presented, the student ought to expect to have to think hard. The harder he thinks, the more value he will derive from his study.

As a result of our attempt to present the most meaningful problems connected with logic, parts of this book contain discussion of the philosophy of logic, as well as explanations of techniques used in logic. In particular, we have included some discussion of recent findings in linguistic philosophy which shed light on the justification of logical procedures, and also on the uses of logic. We also have discussed a number of the philosophical issues surrounding the problems of induction. We have tried to preserve a uniformity of philosophical approach throughout the book. However, it is worth telling the reader that primary responsibility for the first and fifth chapters and all of the third chapter except for section 3.1. rests with the first-named author, and that primary responsibility for the second and fourth chapters and section 3.1. of the third chapter rests with the second-named author.

We should like to express our thanks to Betty Jo McGrade, who read parts of the manuscript and made helpful suggestions, and also to our helpful editors at Doubleday, Vicki Fay and Denise Rathbun.

Contents

FUNDAMENTALS
OF LOGIC

Chapter 1

Introductory

1. The nature of logic

Quite naturally, any survey of a subject is likely to begin by stating what the subject is. A study of geography may begin by stating that geography is the study of the areal differentiation of the earth's surface. The American College Dictionary offers several definitions of logic, the first of which is "the science which investigates the principles governing correct or reliable inference." This is good for a short definition. But, as the reader will see in the course of this work, it is characteristic of logicians and philosophers to worry about the nature of the concepts which define their own work. The geographer, having given his definition of geography as the study of the areal differentiation of the earth's surface, will in general no longer spend his time worrying about the definition of geography: instead he will study the areal differentiation of the earth's surface. The logician, on the other hand, may very well continue to investigate the nature *of* logic as part of his investigations *in* logic. The logician may make a discovery which will lead him to try to redefine the nature of logic, whereas it is hard to imagine a geographer trying to redefine the subject of geography as a result of discovering that a boundary has been wrongly described.

All this is by way of saying that the nature of logic is by no means a cut and dried matter. It is an issue on which extremely intelligent and prominent philosophers have had sharp disagreements. Any really full statement of the nature of logic is bound to be partisan with regard to some issues outstanding, and also to beg at least some questions. Nevertheless we shall try to give the reader some broad idea of what most generally is meant by "logic," and what may be expected from the study of logic.

There are three main points that we shall make about the nature of logic. They are: (1) that logic is generally classified as a part of philosophy; (2) that most of what is taught in logic courses is concerned with systems of inference, as distinguished from philosophy in general, which is most usually concerned with analysis or reconstruction of basic concepts; and (3) that most of what is taught in logic courses is in fact what is called "formal logic," which is distinguished from a good deal of ordinary reasoning by its systematization and by the precision of its language. Having sketched the road immediately ahead, we shall now try to explain these three points. In particular, we shall explain in detail what philosophy is, what inference is, and just what the distinctive features of formal logic are.

1.1. Logic as a part of philosophy

The first point was that logic is generally classified as a part of philosophy, whose other parts include ethics, metaphysics, theory of knowledge, and philosophy of science. There are signs that this classification is being undermined, and that professional work in logic is being taken up by more and more mathematicians and by fewer and fewer philosophers. But for the time being logic is taught as a subject in philosophy departments, and most of the people who teach courses in logic and write about logic are trained also in other branches of philosophy.

Philosophy is extremely hard to define, for reasons which have already been suggested: the nature of philosophy is itself a philosophical issue. But the outsider may be struck by certain characteristic features of philosophical activity. We shall describe these, which will help to clarify the peculiarity of logic as compared to the rest of philosophy.

First of all, philosophers argue with one another a great deal; and often the arguments seem to lead to no widely agreed-upon conclusion. Indeed, some philosophers would claim that more enlightenment is provided by the course of the arguments than by the solutions proposed. Philosophy, they would say, offers the opportunity for hard and clear thinking; and in a world in which so many widely sought-after pleasures turn out to be deceitful, or to imply suffering and boredom, philosophy offers unique satisfactions. Be it as it may, it seems a fact that many philosophical questions never get settled and yet that arguments about these questions continue to provide valuable insights.

Secondly, it is noticeable that philosophy usually maintains an independent role with regard to facts provided by physics, biology, or psychology. Philosophers often refer to facts as examples in their arguments, or use them as grist for their mills; but on closer examination it seems that facts rarely or never *decide* philosophical arguments. This distinguishes philosophy sharply from the sciences. If two scientists have a scientific disagreement, usually they can conduct an experiment, or at least suggest future experiments, which will settle the matter. But in general, philosophical issues are not settled by experiments.

Some philosophers have suggested, as a way of accounting for this, that what philosophy provides is a way of talking or thinking. Obviously the merits of a way of talking or thinking about facts cannot be decided in any straightforward way by experiments. One can always apply one's way of talking to the results of experiments, no matter what the results are, and thus continue in the same philosophical vein. In most cases the most that experiments might conceivably do in discrediting a philosophical theory is to provide facts which it is *awkward* to speak of in the way provided by that theory. In fact when philosophical theories are discarded, it is usually because they have been found awkward, rather than that they have been proven wrong.

A third obvious point about philosophy, which has already been referred to, is that philosophers very often are engaged in analysis or reconstruction of concepts. The reader should realize, by the way, that concepts are correlative with language. When we speak of examination of concepts we mean examination of general words in language, and vice versa. For example, a philosopher who analyzes the concept of knowledge is in effect deciding what we ordinarily mean, in various contexts, by the word "know." A good example of this is A. J. Ayer's book *The Problem of Knowledge*, which could be spoken of as an examination of the concept of knowledge, or alternatively as an analysis of the use of the word "know" in various contexts.

In much the same way, a philosopher whom we would speak of as reconstructing the concept of knowledge is in effect providing a meaning for the word "know" which he considers superior to our ordinary use of the word. Some philosophers, for example, have tried to say that we cannot know anything unless we are able to prove it. This involves an attempted reconstruction of our concept of knowledge. It also involves using the word "know" in a different way from the way in which we normally use it. (In ordinary usage we are said to know all sorts of things which we cannot prove, such as that Tibet exists.)

Sometimes of course a philosopher will both analyze and reconstruct: e.g., he might analyze our ordinary concept of knowledge and at the same time try to tidy the concept up. Which of the two functions, analysis or reconstruction, is more proper for philosophy is itself a philosophical issue. There are some philosophers who feel that all that philosophy should do is to analyze our ordinary concepts, and that any attempt to alter and reconstruct these concepts represents anxiety-producing "speculation." There are other philosophers who believe that philosophy should provide us with a distinctive way of looking at things, which involves providing us with new, reconstructed forms of old concepts. In between, there are philosophers who believe that analysis is the most important function of philosophy, but that a philosopher should be allowed to do a little reconstruction if it is firmly tied to his analysis.

In any event, it is noticeable that the concepts with which philosophers are concerned usually are both basic and abstract. For example, philosophers concerned with mathematics often are found examining the concept of a proof, which is basic to the whole nature of mathematics; they rarely if ever are found examining the concept of a triangle. Philosophers of science concentrate on the most basic concepts or the concepts most crucial to the development of science. For example, the English philosopher David Hume is famous for his analysis of the concept of cause. Alfred North Whitehead is well known for a philosophical analysis of the concept of simultaneity, which is crucial in questions related to the theory of relativity. In general philosophy, one is more likely to find philosophers investigating concepts like those of knowledge and reality than, say, those of pretending or of lamps.

There are of course exceptions to this historical tendency of philosophy to deal with abstract and basic concepts. Existentialist writers often quite deliberately gear their writings to the problems implicit in concrete human situations. There also is a long tradition, dating back to Socrates, which assigns to philosophy the task of deciding which ways of life are good and which ways of life are bad. When modern philosophers write about ethics, usually they are concerned with analyzing or reconstructing the concepts involved in our thinking about ethics. But in traditional ethics, when philosophers discussed the question of "What is the good life?" they were sometimes concerned neither with examining nor with altering our normal concepts of goodness, but simply with arriving at value judgments within the framework of these concepts.

Enough has been said at this point to give the reader some idea of the variety within philosophy, and also of the different philosophical theories which can be proposed as to the nature of philosophy. Philosophers who believe firmly in analysis will speak of philosophy as a semiscientific way of getting at the truth about our language and the structures of our thinking. Philosophers who believe in reconstruction of concepts sometimes speak of philosophy as a semipoetic way of constructing a new and striking picture of reality. (The philosopher's new concepts give us a new picture.) Philosophers impressed by work such as Whitehead's on simultaneity sometimes speak of philosophy as the examination of the foundations of the sciences and of knowledge in general. It is sometimes claimed that philosophy will systematize all of our knowledge by connecting the fundamentals of various branches of knowledge. Some existentialists appear to believe that the proper object of philosophy is to teach us how to make life meaningful. What seems true is that each of these theories of the nature of philosophy fits what at least one or two philosophers are trying to do.

1.2. *Logic as concerned with inference*

None of the theories that we have just mentioned fits logic. Logic has aims far different from teaching us how to lead our lives. Logic is not primarily concerned with analysis or reconstruction of concepts. It is true that in a logic class someone may discuss, for a while, the concept of proof or the concept of inference. In general, a course in logic will involve some analysis or reconstruction of concepts, and the examination of the fundamentals of reasoning. But the bulk of what is taught in elementary logic courses is different. It consists of actual systems and techniques of inference. For example, a good deal of most elementary logic courses involves learning the rules of the syllogism. Only by an extreme stretch of language could someone explaining the syllogism be held to be analyzing concepts in the sense in which someone discussing the nature of knowledge is analyzing concepts.

On the analogy of such recognized subjects as philosophy of science, philosophy of history, and philosophy of art, we might speak of the philosophy of logic. The philosophy of logic involves analysis or reconstruction of such fundamental logical concepts as "proof," "implies," "derive from," etc. In general, a little of what is taught in elementary logic courses is philosophy of logic; but most is simply logic. The student, that is, learns rules involved in inferences and in formal proofs. His attention is directed primarily not toward understanding the concepts of "inference" and of "proof," but toward inferring and proving things. The distinction here is *not* that logic is practical and that the philosophy of logic is not. Any sort of philosophy has practical use in terms of strengthening the student's tendency to shape his life with thoughtfulness and clarity. The distinction, rather, is that learning how to construct syllogisms and truth tables, and in general learning most of what is taught in elementary logic courses, does not require any deep analysis of the nature of concepts used; nor does it require any sort of inventiveness in shaping these concepts. What we have called the philosophy of logic, on the other hand, does involve such careful analysis or development of fundamental logical concepts.

The same general point about logic study can be put in a cruder way. The student in a logic course may find that the mental activity expected of him on the whole bears a closer resemblance to what is involved in a geometry course than it does to what is involved in other sorts of philosophy courses. Learning logic, as well as learning geometry, involves learning rules, and becoming able to apply these rules in carrying out inferences.

Of course the common denominator of logic and geometry is that both center around inference. We shall now provide an analysis of inference. (As the reader can see, this book contains philosophy of logic as well as logic.) The nature of inference can best be explained by way of an account of the different sorts of basis we can have for making a statement. Inference is one sort of basis, and its character can be explained partly by means of contrast with other sorts of bases for making statements.

In general, we like to have a basis for making statements. Indeed normally, if we have no basis for what we say, we are liable to be accused of not knowing what we are talking about. But it is quite obvious that there are different kinds of basis that a statement can have. If someone asks us how we know X, for example, we might say, "Someone told me X," or, "I read X in a newspaper." We might distinguish between firsthand bases and secondhand bases. If, for example, we justify our claiming X by saying, "I read X in a newspaper," a questioner can very well inquire as to the basis the newspaper had for X. If the newspaper got X from a Mr. A, the questioner can inquire as to Mr. A's basis for X. If X does have some ultimate basis, rather than being something which originated by being said arbitrarily or foolishly, then *someone* must have more basis for saying X than that he has been told it by someone else. In other words: if a statement that we make secondhand did not have its ultimate origin in an arbitrary utterance, then someone must have a firsthand basis for it.

Let us analyze the cases in which someone has a firsthand basis for saying X. There are three main types of firsthand basis. In one type, X has a basis in that it expresses what we experience or remember. For example, if we say that it is snowing, our basis for this may be that we see it snowing. If we say that it snowed yesterday, our basis for this may be our recollection that it snowed yesterday.

Another type of firsthand basis involves a relation to our awareness of correct language. X has a basis of this type if it expresses what is true by definition, or is true by virtue of more elaborate conventions of language. For example, if we say that every triangle has three sides, our basis for this is our awareness that the definition of "triangle" includes having three sides. If we say that every rich man is well off, our basis for this is our awareness that (even though "rich" is not defined as well off) we would not call a man rich if he was not well off.

The third type of firsthand basis involves our relating a statement not directly to our experiences or our awareness of language, but instead to another statement (or statements) from which we derive it. This is inference. For example, when we say that it is snowing, we might give as our basis, "We haven't looked to check whether it is snowing. But we can hear snowplows moving about, so it seems very likely that it is snowing." In this case we are not *directly* expressing our experience when we say, "It is snowing." Instead we give a basis by providing a related statement, "Snowplows are moving about," from which we derive "It is snowing." Of course the related statement in the example does directly express our experience, but that is beside the point. The point is that the statement "It is snowing" did not directly express our experience, but instead was given a basis in terms of another statement from which it was derived.

In much the same way, if we say that the sum of the angles of a triangle equals 180 degrees, we might give as our basis the statements which comprise the axioms of Euclidean geometry, from which we assert that the statement is derivable.

The above explanation should help the reader to understand what is meant when it is said that logic is concerned with inference. Logic is not concerned with the sort of basis we provide for a statement when we relate it directly to experience; and (on the whole) logic is not very concerned with the sort of basis we provide for a statement when we relate it directly to our awareness of correct language. Logic *is* concerned with cases in which we give a basis for a statement by relating it to another statement (or statements) from which we derive it. This is what we mean when we say that logic is concerned with inference.

"*How* is logic concerned with inference?" a reader may ask. The answer lies in pointing out that when someone gives a basis for a statement his basis can be criticized. When, on the basis of our visual experiences, we say that it is snowing we might be criticized, for example, as having used the wrong word. ("The right word for what you saw was 'hail.'") Or we may not have looked closely enough to be sure that it was snowing. We may say that all triangles have three sides of equal length, under the impression that this is what is meant by "triangle"; and our basis in awareness of the language may be criticized.

In the case of statements arrived at by inference, there may be two main sorts of criticism. First, the related statement which is supplied as a basis may be argued to be wrong. For example, it may be that there were *not* snowplows moving about (we heard wrongly), so that we really did not have a good basis for saying that it was snowing.

Secondly, the critic might complain that the statement that we made is not really derivable from the statement we gave as a basis. He might claim, for example, that just because snowplows are moving about there is no reason to suppose that it is snowing. If we claim that the earth is flat on the basis of certain observed facts, he might claim that these facts do not provide a basis for saying that the earth is flat. And so on. In general, when we say X on the basis of Y, the quality of our inference can be challenged: it can be alleged that the truth of Y (if it is true) does not justify us in saying X.

Logic is concerned with quality of inference, and not in general with the truth of the statements from which the inference proceeds. Logic is con-

cerned with quality of inference in two ways. First, logic provides tools for
evaluating the quality of inferences—at least of some inferences. And even
when an inference is not of a type dealt with in logic courses, we would
normally say that questions as to its quality ("Is it a justifiable, or valid,
inference?") are in some sense logical questions. Secondly, logic trains the
student to make good inferences. To put it another way: logic provides rules
for good inferences. These rules can be used to criticize inferences—to
show whether they are justified or unjustified. They also can be *followed*, in
constructing good inferences.

The same general point can be put in yet another way, which has the
advantage of introducing some basic terminology. Typically a logical argument consists of a statement or statements called *premises,* together with a
statement or statements called *conclusions,* which it is asserted follow
from (or could be maintained on the basis of) the premises. For example,
take the argument

        (1) Socrates is a man.
        (2) All men are mortal.
Therefore (3) Socrates is mortal.

(1) and (2) are the premises. (3) is the conclusion, which is asserted to follow from the premises. Now the question that the logician typically asks is
"Is the inference *valid?*" That is, "Would one be entitled to assert the conclusion on the basis of those premises?" The reader should realize that this
does not directly involve examining the *truth* of the premises and conclusion. In fact the premises and conclusion might all be false and yet the inference be valid. For example, the inference given above is valid, and would
count as valid even if in fact "Socrates" had been the name of an angel
rather than of a man, or if it had turned out that not all men are mortal.
An inference is valid as long as it would be reasonable to assert the conclusion *if* the premises are true. All the logician is concerned with is this reasonableness. Whether the premises are in fact true is in general not the concern
of the logician.

To say that the logician is concerned with reasonableness rather than
with facts is another way of putting the point made earlier: that what the
logician is concerned with is the quality of inferences. We also made the
point earlier that the logician is concerned not only with criticizing the reasonableness of inferences, but also with inculcating reasonableness.

Thus far we have explained, in a number of ways, that logic is concerned
with inferences, and that it is concerned with the quality of inferences. This
still does not adequately distinguish logic from geometry. After all, in geometry one makes inferences (from axioms); one is concerned with the

quality of inferences and with making good inferences. Is geometry then logic?

The answer is both a partial "yes" and also "no." The word "logic" is used in more than one way. Sometimes the word "logic" is used in such a way that any judgments of the quality of inferences count as logic. In this broad sense, one would say that the part of geometry which is directly concerned with the quality of the geometrical inferences indeed does come within the realm of logic. In much the same sense, philosophers sometimes speak of "the logic of science" or "the logic of aesthetics," meaning the study of the standards of quality of the thought processes by which scientists or art critics arrive at some statements on the basis of other statements. One could just as well speak of "the logic of geometry," and say in general that any branch of knowledge which involves inference has (in virtue of this) its own specialized logic. In this broad sense of "logic," logic is quite diverse and has parts related to various disciplines.

However, in terms of what is meant by "logic" when a course is advertised in a university catalogue as a course in logic, the answer is "no." Normally a course in logic will not teach a student how to construct geometrical proofs, although it will help to strengthen his mental powers which are related to the ability to construct geometrical proofs. In the same way, normally a logic course will contain only the most simple of remarks about the professional reasoning processes of scientists. Very little of "the logic of science" is normally taught in courses labeled "logic."

What this amounts to is perhaps a practical restriction. It is impossible to teach someone rules which will enable him to reason well with regard to every conceivable situation or problem which might arise. In a semester or two of university teaching, it is impossible to teach a student much more than the most general principles of constructing good inferences. Therefore teachers of logic, rather than attempting the peripheral tasks of teaching students specialized rules of constructing good inferences in geometry, science, or aesthetics, will leave this instruction to teachers of geometry, science, or literary criticism.

What we are saying is that not all of logic (in the broad sense) is studied in logic courses. In fact very little of logic (in the broad sense) can be studied in logic courses. For practical reasons the logic course narrows its scope. We have already indicated one aspect of the narrowing process. The logic of the special sorts of inference associated with specific disciplines (e.g., geometry and science) is left out of logic courses. The inferences studied in logic courses are only of the most general kind: inferences which occur in everyday thinking, or which represent a type which might occur in connection with a number of different disciplines.

However, it is not even the case that all inferences which occur in everyday thinking are liable to be studied in a logic course. There is a further narrowing process, which we can indicate by saying that most of what is studied in logic courses is formal logic. We shall now explain what formal logic is, and why logic courses usually concentrate on the study of formal logic.

1.3. The nature of formal logic

A preliminary description of formal logic might be this: formal logic is concerned with inference which can be systematically treated, and in which words and symbols are treated as being precisely defined. We shall now try to explain these two salient characteristics of formal logic.

First, let us contrast two specimens of valid inference.

A. Socrates is a man.
   All men are mortal.
   Therefore Socrates is mortal.

B. Socrates is a man.
   Socrates is married.
   Therefore Socrates has a wife.

These two inferences may seem at first to be of very similar types. But in fact A would generally be classified within the realm of formal logic, as involving a reasoning process which can be readily systematized. B, on the other hand, in general would not be treated within formal logic: its reasoning cannot be readily systematized.

The difference becomes clear if we ask how, in A and B, we are justified in arriving at the conclusion on the basis of the premises. In the case of A, the answer that a logician would give would be: "By the form of the argument." He could not give the same answer in the case of B.

We can produce the form of an inference if for terms like "Socrates," "man," and "married" we substitute X, Y, and Z, etc.: in doing this we must be sure to use the same letter in places where a term is repeated, and not to use the same letter for two different terms. In A, for example, we can substitute X for "Socrates," Y for "man," and Z for "mortal." The form of A then emerges as

X is a Y.
All Y's are Z.
Therefore X is a Z.

It will be explained at length later in the book how it is that *any* inference which can be reduced to the form above counts as valid. For the time being we might simply point out that this is so. For example, "Socrates is a goose; all geese eat leaves; therefore Socrates eats leaves" counts as a valid inference. (The reader will remember our earlier remarks that an inference can be valid even if both the premises and conclusion are false. To say that an inference is valid is to say that if the premises are true, one would be justified in asserting the conclusion on their basis. And quite plainly if Socrates were a goose, and all geese ate leaves, one would be justified in asserting that Socrates ate leaves.) Any inference, about anything whatsoever, which has the form in question is thereby valid. It is because of this that if anyone asks us why the inference about Socrates' mortality is valid, we can answer, "Because of the form."

If we look at B, we see that the situation is quite different. Let us rephrase the concluding sentence as "Therefore Socrates is someone who has a wife." If we substitute X for "Socrates," Y for "man," Z for "married," and W for "someone who has a wife," the form of B emerges as

X is a Y.
X is Z.
Therefore X is W.

It is *not* the case that any inference in the above form is valid. For example, "Socrates is a man; Socrates lives in Chicago; therefore Socrates is someone who is eight feet tall" is not a valid inference. Even if Socrates were a man living in Chicago, this would by no means justify us in saying that he was eight feet tall. Since it is not the case that any inference in the form of B is valid, we cannot say that B is valid because of its form. It is valid for some other reason.

Actually B is valid because of the meanings of "man," "married," and "wife." The conclusion follows from the premises because we could define a married person as someone who has a spouse, and our word for the spouse of a man is "wife." Once we realize this, we can understand why not all proofs in the same form as B are valid. The validity of B depends on the meanings of "man," "married," and "wife." When we reduced B to its form we replaced these terms by letters, and these did not convey those semantic relationships among the meanings of the terms which made B valid.

One way then to put the difference between A and B is to say that B is valid because of the meaning of its terms. Logicians have pointed out that inferences like A, on the other hand, are valid because of the meaning of the logical connectives (words like "is" and "all"). We can see this by the very fact that any inference of the same form (i.e., having the same pattern of logical connectives, and of repetition of words) is valid.

A more general way of putting the difference between A and B is this. Because the validity of A is a matter of its form, in learning about A's validity we in effect learn about the validity of a wide assortment of inferences. The logical knowledge involved in A carries over to inferences about sheep, stars, electrons, glasses of whisky: in fact to inferences about anything, providing that the inference has the same pattern of logical connectives and repetition of terms that A has. The logical knowledge involved in B, on the other hand, carries over merely to other inferences involving "man," "married," and "wife." If we want to construct inferences which are comparable to B, but which deal with other topics, we have to analyze the meanings of various special terms. Building a logical knowledge in this way is a piecemeal process.

Without discussing at this stage the various types of formal logic, we can remark that there are some types of valid arguments in formal logic whose validity does not depend on the pattern of logical connectives and of repetition of terms. But in the cases of these arguments, too, the principles which make the arguments valid can readily be generalized so as to apply to inferences on a wide variety of topics.

This is, then, a major difference between formal logic and the rest of logic. Formal logic consists of inferences whose justification can be treated systematically, by means of principles which can be readily applied to inferences on a wide variety of topics. Inferences like B, the justification of which depends on the meanings of words related to its topic, do not find a place in formal logic.

The reader already should be able to see one reason why in general most of what is taught in logic courses consists of formal logic. We remarked earlier that one could scarcely give an adequate account of the bulk of logical processes in a mere semester or two of college work. By concentrating on formal logic, a teacher can cover a maximum amount of ground in a given amount of time. Within a short time he can enable the student systematically to construct inferences on a wide variety of topics. If, on the other hand, a teacher concentrates on reasoning of the sort exemplified by B, and tries to give a complete explanation of why the reasoning is valid, he will cover limited ground.

Another reason why logicians concentrate on formal logic is that traditionally knowledge has been thought to consist of general principles. The more general the principles, the more important the knowledge. The focus of scientific advance, for example, has generally been considered to be in that direction. As we have shown, formal logic is distinguished by the generality of the principles which it involves. Consequently, someone whose ideals of knowledge were influenced by traditional thinking might very well feel that formal logic offers the best sort of logical knowledge.

There is a third reason why logicians concentrate on formal logic: the principles of formal logic lend themselves to very precise development. We want to discuss this reason in some detail. Earlier we remarked that there are two important general characteristics of formal logic: that the inferences it dealt with could be systematically treated, *and* that in these inferences words and symbols are treated as being precisely defined. We want to explain now what this precision consists of.

The first point to make is that a good deal of work in formal logic is carried on in symbols. That is, the inferences in a book of formal logic are liable to be stated in terms of p, q, X, and various logical signs for equivalence, conjunction, etc., instead of in terms of "Socrates," "man," "mortal," "is," "all," etc. Instead of saying that "Socrates is a man; all men are mortal; therefore Socrates is mortal," the formal logician is likely to say, "$(x) (Fx \supset Gx) \cdot Fs$ implies GS." As his work progresses he is likely to forget about Socrates, humanity, and mortality entirely; and at the same time, more special symbols are likely to be introduced.

One striking thing about the symbols in a logical text is that they mean exactly what the logician wants them to mean. It is said that not even the emperor at Rome could change the meaning of a word in ordinary, general language. (It is at least true that he could not do so overnight.) A logician, on the other hand, creates and controls the meanings of his symbols. Because of this, sets of logical symbols are sometimes spoken of as "artificial languages." English, French, German, etc., by contrast are natural languages. It would be hard to say that anyone controls English, French, or German in the way in which a logician controls the meaning of his equivalence and conjunction signs, etc.

One result of the controlled character of logical symbols is that they are as precise as logicians want to make them: which in fact means that they are entirely precise. To take just one dimension of this precision: every time a logician uses the symbol p or q, by convention it means exactly what it did in every previous use. The meaning of every symbol that a logician uses is fixed.

By comparison natural languages are vague. One dimension of this vagueness is that words have different meanings in different contexts. For example, if I say that a delinquent teen-ager is a scoundrel, I am saying something different from what I am saying when I say that Stalin was a scoundrel. It is not at all certain that I would consider the delinquent teen-ager a scoundrel in *that* sense in which I consider Stalin a scoundrel.

There are two things that we should remark upon in connection with the above example. One is that our language would be impoverished if we used the word "scoundrel" only in cases in which the person referred to was quite comparable to Stalin. This is what recent philosophers have meant when they have pointed out that our vague natural languages are richer and more useful than a precise language would be.

The second thing is this. The reader might be inclined to think: "Of course what is involved in our calling the delinquent teen-ager a scoundrel is the same as what is involved in calling Stalin a scoundrel. The difference is one of degree." But a little thought will show that this is wrong. The things that we convey when we call the delinquent teen-ager a scoundrel are different (in character) from the things that we convey when we call Stalin a scoundrel. It is not as if the delinquent teen-ager murders fewer people, or murders them to a lower degree. As applied to the two different people, the word "scoundrel" communicates two different sets of things. In the case of Stalin it sets our minds to secret police and legal murders; in the case of the delinquent teen-ager it might set our minds to rudeness, street disturbances, and possibly petty theft.

A closely related (and famous) point is made by Wittgenstein in *Philosophical Investigations*. In discussing the concept of "game," he points out that no definition can be given which would fit our ordinary use of the word. That is: there is no set of characteristics which is such that everything which we would call a game has this set of characteristics, and nothing which we would not call a game has it. Games are quite diverse. There is not *very* much in common among football, chess, and ring-around-a-rosy.

Let us suppose that we try to find a common denominator among games which will provide us with a definition. We might come up with a phrase like "playful activity proceeding according to a definite pattern." But this phrase fits musical performances and also marching, neither of which would normally be called games. And for that matter, also, it is by no means sure that championship football or chess played for high stakes is playful. Thus it appears that the phrase could serve neither as a definition of "game" nor as part of a definition. To take another example of the difficulties here: suppose that someone suggests the quality of having more than one side, and involving the possibility of victory and defeat, as part of the nature of games. Certainly most games do have this quality. But ring-around-a-rosy does not. Wars on the other hand do have this quality, and yet we would not normally call them games, except metaphorically.

In fact it is impossible to define the word "game." We learn to use the word, not through definitions, but rather through being given examples of games, and being made to understand that activities which are very like these examples will count as games. For example, as children we are told that football is a game; and we realize that lacrosse is a game, too, since it is like football in the respect of being playful activity which fits a definite pattern, and in a number of other respects. War and marching, on the other hand, are not games because they are not similar enough to anything which might be pointed out as an example of a game. Wittgenstein sums up the point by remarking that games, instead of fitting a definition, exhibit a crisscrossing pattern of similarities. The respects in which football resembles chess are different from the respects in which football resembles ring-around-a-rosy.

We can now explain how it is that natural languages are vague. Most general words in the language are like "game" (or "scoundrel") rather than like, say, "triangle" (which can be defined, and does have a precise meaning in virtue of its very close connection with a technical discipline). "Game" is vague in three respects. First, a lot of very different sorts of things count as games. Chess is very different from ring-around-a-rosy, and both are different from playing with dice. There may be cases in which someone speaks of a game, and we can have very little idea of just which sort of activity he is talking about. Secondly, not only can "game" not be defined, but also (as it turns out on further investigation) it is impossible even to specify precise rules as to what counts as a game and what does not. Thirdly, the concept of "game" has a border area. It is quite clear that basketball and cribbage are games, and it is quite clear that street brawls and banking are not. But what about a case in which a child tosses up a ball into the air and tries to catch it? Or ritual fighting? Or cases in which someone is washing dishes for money, but gives himself a point for every very clean dish, and subtracts two points for every dish which he breaks? We can imagine at least some cases along these lines in which we would be uncertain whether to label the activity in question a "game" or not. This is what we meant by "borderline cases."

As we said, most general words in the language are like "game." They are vague, in a way in which a symbol controlled by a logician will not be vague. Thus we see how the vagueness of natural languages contrasts with the precision of artificial languages.

Now that we have made this contrast, the reader may wonder how the logician who constructs inferences with A, B, and C can, if he wishes, also use the terms "Socrates," "man," and "mortal." How can he interpret "A is a B; all B's are C; therefore A is C" as "Socrates is a man; all men are mortal; therefore Socrates is mortal"? How can one substitute imprecise words for precise symbols, and not bring about a difference?

The answer sometimes given is that our ordinary vague language may approximate what would be a precise language, and that consequently one can substitute words in a natural language for logical symbols as a matter of approximation. A correct reasoning process in formal logic will approximate a correct reasoning process in ordinary language, and consequently the logician can use one process to cast light upon the other.

An answer which perhaps is a bit better is this. In some contexts we can treat words like "man" and "mortal" as if they were precise. The vagueness does not have to get in our way. To put it in another way: in a great many cases the vagueness of the words used in ordinary reasoning simply is not a relevant difference between it and the corresponding reasoning in symbols. The more important of the reasons why logicians rely heavily on symbols rather than words is the increased generality of symbols, although precision also is a factor.

The practical point here is one which will become familiar to the reader as he works in logic. As he applies techniques of formal logic to reasoning in ordinary language, he will just have to be careful. In some cases the vagueness of a word involves a shift in meaning as the word is used in two different contexts. In such a case a piece of ordinary reasoning which *seems* to fit a valid pattern in formal logic may in fact be invalid. In other sorts of cases, however, one may find a word used repeatedly with very little shift in meaning. If there is no relevant shift in the meaning of words, one can assume that a piece of ordinary reasoning which fits a valid pattern in formal logic is in fact valid. Sound linguistic sense is required in order to detect whether relevant shifts in meaning occur or not.

We have already given an example of this second sort of case—in which there is no relevant shift in meaning. When we say, "Socrates is a man; all men are mortal; therefore Socrates is mortal," normally there would be no relevant shift in meaning between the two occurrences of "man" or the two occurrences of "mortal." In virtue of this, and also of the fact that the inference fits the valid form "*A* is a *B;* all *B*'s are *C;* therefore *A* is a *C*," we say that the inference concerning Socrates' mortality is valid.

We might illustrate as follows the sort of case in which there are relevant shifts in meaning. Imagine a biologist who divides all organisms of any complexity into plants and animals. Mushrooms, he tells a student, are plants. Later on, the student sees a patch of mushrooms and describes it to a friend by saying, "The ground was quite covered with plants." The friend pictures green, leafy things, and is annoyed to find only mushrooms. Not only does he feel annoyed, but he also feels deceived.

If we construct an inference, "The ground was covered with mushrooms; mushrooms are plants; therefore the ground was covered with plants," it certainly resembles a valid inference. After all, "The hall was crowded with good citizens; good citizens are people; therefore the hall was crowded with people" is valid. But the difference, and the source of difficulty, is that the word "plant" is used in more than one way, and that more than one sense of "plant" might be involved in the inference that we have just given. There is a precise biologist's sense in which all complex organisms which are not animals are plants. Also there is a more everyday use in which one tends to speak of green, leafy things, and perhaps also cacti, as plants, but tends not to speak of oak trees and mushrooms as plants. If, in the inference given, one starts from the biologists' definition and expects to prove the presence of green, leafy things or cacti, one will be disappointed.

In contrast to this, neither "citizen" nor "crowded with," in the inference about the hall being crowded with people, shifts in meaning. But again one can get a sense of how one has to be careful in ordinary reasoning if one substitutes "full of" for "crowded with." The inference then reads, "The hall was full of good citizens; good citizens are people; therefore the hall was full of people." Someone could very well feel gingery about the validity of the inference in this new form. One might, after all, describe a hall as "full of good citizens" if the hall was half full but it was very notable that everyone there was a good citizen. In other words, the phrase "full of," in "The hall was full of good citizens," has connotations of "predominantly containing," which would prevent us from treating it as identical in meaning with "crowded with." But "full of," in "The hall was full of people," *is* more or less identical in meaning with "crowded with" (unless of course one is writing a science-fiction story in which Martians play a part). Thus, in the inference which led us to say that the hall was full of people, there was a relevant change in meaning in a key phrase, and we cannot assume that the inference is valid.

At this point we have said enough to have delineated the character of formal logic. To sum up the points made: there are two qualifications which an inference would normally have to meet in order to be counted as part of formal logic. One is that the inference can be treated in relation to a very general principle of reasoning: i.e., if the inference is valid, it can be treated as embodying the principle; if it is invalid, it can be treated as violating it. The other qualification is that the symbols or words in the inference can be treated as being steady in their meanings. An example of an inference which meets both qualifications is the one about Socrates' mortality. The inference about Socrates' wife failed to meet the first qualification, and the inference about the ground being covered with plants failed to meet the second.

As we have said, most of what is commonly taught and written under the heading of "logic" is formal logic. This book is no exception. Most of this book consists of formal logic. In the next part of this chapter we shall discuss the basic types of formal logic. This will provide the distinction between the reasoning examined in the second and third chapters of this book, on one hand, and the reasoning examined in the fourth chapter, on the other.

2. The division of formal logic

At this point we have distinguished formal logic from logic in general. The main point that we wish to illustrate now is that formal logic is divided into two branches: deductive and inductive. In order to explain, however, what the differences between deductive and inductive logic are, we shall have to go back to the foundations of our subject and develop a number of basic concepts. Only after a discussion of, for example, the sorts of ways in which a statement can be true shall we be able to make fully clear the differences between deductive and inductive logic.

2.1. Types of true statement

We might begin by distinguishing two classes of true statements: those that are true primarily because of facts which they describe, and those that are true because they embody conventions of language. An example of the first sort of true statement would be "The earth is round" or "Julius Caesar was assassinated in 44 B.C." That the earth is round is a fact, as is Caesar's assassination. The reader will note that the earth *could* have been other than round (a universe is conceivable in which our planet was flat) and that Julius Caesar *could* have avoided assassination (a universe is conceivable in which Julius Caesar died a natural death). The facts described by the two statements, that is, could have been otherwise. And if the facts were otherwise the statements would be false. In a universe in which the earth was flat, for example, "The earth is round" would count as a false statement.

We can sum it up by saying that this first sort of true statement is *contingent*. We call it contingent because it describes facts, and because facts always could conceivably have been other than they are. The word "contingent" is also applied to false statements which would be true if (alleged) facts described had been the case. To call a statement "contingent" is to say that it describes facts, or alleged facts, and that whether it is true or not depends upon what is the case.

Another technical way of describing the first class of true statements is to say that they are *synthetic*. (Again, false statements like "The earth is flat" also are spoken of as "synthetic." "The earth is round" would be spoken of as "synthetically true"; "The earth is flat" would be spoken of as "synthetically false.") "Synthetic" is not quite synonymous with "contingent." There have been some philosophers, notably Kant, who have maintained that statements of mathematics, and statements in general which describe the structure of our experience, are synthetic but not contingent. However, most philosophers nowadays believe that only contingent statements are synthetic, and vice versa. We shall not go into these issues in this book. It is enough to point out that the word "synthetic" usually is used to mean "descriptive of reality, or of the nature of our experience." "Julius Caesar was assassinated in 44 B.C." is descriptive of reality and therefore synthetic, as is the statement about the roundness of the world. In general we can say (and even Kant would say) that all statements which are contingent are also synthetic. In particular we might point out that any statement which describes facts is both contingent (because the facts could be otherwise) and synthetic (because it describes reality).

The other class of true statements that we shall distinguish is that of statements which are true because they embody conventions of language.

Examples are: "Triangles have three sides"; "If Jones is a father, he must have a child"; and "If Socrates is a man, and all men are mortal, then Socrates is mortal." "Triangles have three sides" is true simply because by a triangle we mean a figure with three sides. If a figure did not have three sides, we would not call it a triangle. In much the same way, if Jones did not have a child we would not call him a father. If Socrates were not mortal, either we would not call him a man (but instead a "demigod," or something on that order) or we would have to say that not all men are mortal. All of the statements in this class are true simply because of the meanings of words.

The differences between the two classes of true statements which we have distinguished are worth stressing. Let us take as an example of the first class "The earth is round," and of the second class "Triangles have three sides." We might point out first that language is a factor in the truth of "The earth is round." *Part* of the reason for its being true is that we mean what we do by "earth," "is," and "round." If the meaning of the word "round" changed to what is now meant by "flat," "The earth is round" would become false.

On the other hand, there is, in a way, a factual element in the truth of "Triangles have three sides." After all, it is fact that by a triangle we mean a figure with three sides. If our language had been different, we might have used the word "triangle" to designate figures with four sides. Thus, that the word "triangle" has a meaning which makes "Triangles have three sides" true is a fact. The statement is true because of that fact.

What we are trying to bring out is that the differences between the two types of statements are more complicated and subtle than they might appear at first. The truth of both types is related to facts (e.g., a fact about the earth, or a fact about the meaning of "triangle"), and also to the meanings of words. The difference is this. *Given* the meaning of words, we would need to make, or be told about, certain observations in order to have a basis for saying, "The earth is round." If we relied only on the meanings of words, we would not know that the earth is round. It is quite consistent with the meanings of "earth" and "round" that the earth should be flat. It is only experience which has told mankind that the earth is in fact round. On the other hand, *given* the meanings of words, we do not need observation or experience to know that triangles have three sides. Once we know what "triangle" means, we do not have to start looking at triangles, or collecting experimental data, to know that triangles have three sides.

One way of putting the difference is to say that, whereas statements of the first class are contingent, statements of the second class are not contingent. Given the meanings of the words, we still can conceive that the universe might have been such that "The earth is round" would be false; but we could not conceive of a universe in which what we would now agree to call a triangle would not have three sides.

Another way of putting the difference is to remark that the two types of true statements are related to facts in different ways. Statements of the first type *describe* facts. "Triangles have three sides," on the other hand, does not describe the facts about the meaning of "triangle." The facts—i.e., that we use the word "triangle" to designate three-sided figures—make the statement true, but the statement does not describe the facts. The reader might become clear about this if he contrasts "Triangles have three sides" with "In English we mean by 'triangle' a figure with three sides." The latter sentence does describe facts; it is contingent, since the facts about the English language which it describes could have been otherwise; and in short it has the same general character as "The earth is round." It belongs in the first class of true statements. It is not true by definition, whereas "Triangles have three sides" *is* true by definition.

The differences between our two classes of true statements can be expressed also in a number of technical terms, which are used throughout the study of logic. For example, we said that true statements of the second class differed from those of the first class in not being contingent. This is sometimes expressed by saying that true statements of the second class are *necessary*, or *necessarily true*. True statements of the second class also differ from those of the first class in not describing reality. Indeed, as we said, they are true simply because of the meaning of their words. For this reason they are spoken of as *analytic*, or *analytically true*.

The reader might wonder at this point whether the two classes of true statements which we have distinguished are exhaustive. Are there any other sorts of true statements? The answer is "maybe." Kant, whom we have already mentioned, claimed that there were statements which were synthetic but necessarily true. Statements of mathematical theorems, he felt, were in this category. Since the two types of true statements which we have distinguished were, respectively, synthetic and contingent, and analytic and necessarily true, the reader can see that these synthetic and necessarily true statements about which Kant speaks would form a third type. There also is the philosophical question of whether ethical statements can be accorded truth and falsity, and (if so) of what sort of truth they might be said to have. In other words, there are some philosophers who would claim that there are more types of true statement than the two which we have distinguished. A great number of contemporary philosophers, on the other hand, would claim that there are only these two types of true statements. Fortunately, we shall not have to try to settle these issues. Whether or not there are more types of true statement than the two which we have distinguished, quite clearly all of the true statements which we shall have to consider in this book will be of one or the other of these two types. In other words, for the purposes of the study of introductory logic, the reader can proceed as if all true statements are either synthetic and contingent or analytic and necessarily true.

2.2. Two types of formal logic: deductive and inductive logic

Having said this, we can now begin to distinguish the two types of formal logic. The best way of introducing the distinction is by mentioning the needs which logic attempts to fill. One need involves becoming clear about the implications of the words and phrases which we use. What are we committed to saying as a result of the meanings of the words which we have used? The other major need involves our need to predict, or make estimates about, reality which we have not experienced. We have never experienced all of the facts in the universe which we would like to know about. What are the unexperienced facts like; what can we estimate about the reality which we have not experienced, on the basis of the reality which we have experienced?

The logic which answers the first need is called *deductive*. The logic which answers the second need is called *inductive*. In spelling out the differences between the two types of logic we shall give examples of both types, and also relate both types to the technical terms whose meanings we have just explained.

We should first remark that while deductive and inductive logic are the two main types of formal logic, there also are inferences that would not be classified within formal logic which nevertheless have a deductive or an inductive character. Of the four examples of deductive reasoning which we shall give, the first and third would not be classified within formal logic, for reasons that were explained in part 1. The second and fourth would be classified within formal logic.

Examples of valid deductive reasoning are:

1. Jones is a father.
   Therefore Jones has at least one child.
2. Socrates is an Athenian.
   All Athenians live by the sea.
   Therefore Socrates lives by the sea.
3. Jones is a habitual drunkard.
   For the last year Jones has been able to do pretty much what he pleases.
   Therefore Jones has drunk at least some alcoholic beverage in the last year (otherwise we could not call him a habitual drunkard).
4. P and Q cannot both be the case.
   P is the case.
   Therefore Q is not the case.

Examples of inductive reasoning are:

1. The sun rose today.
   The sun has risen every day now for as long as we can remember.
   Therefore the sun will rise tomorrow.
2. We have examined a third of the eggs, taken at random.
   Five per cent of the eggs that we have examined are defective.
   Therefore we can assume that about five per cent of the remaining
   eggs are defective.
3. Jones has just taken an oath that he was out of town on May 29th.
   Jones has always, as far as we can determine, told the truth when
   under oath.
   Therefore, probably, Jones is telling the truth when he says that he
   was out of town on May 29th.
4. Let us suppose, for the sake of argument, that Jones was the murderer.
   Murderers very often act the way Jones did on the 28th.
   Therefore, if Jones were the murderer, we would expect him to act
   in the way in which he in fact did act on the 28th.

There are a number of basic differences between the two types of reasoning, which can be illustrated by the examples. However, before we begin
to discuss these differences, we should make one remark about the general
character of inductive inference. Often in inductive reasoning the process of
inference is from facts which we have experienced, or feel sure about, to
other facts which we have not experienced, or feel less sure about. But this
is not always the case. We sometimes try to set up a hypothesis which we
feel uncertain about, and try to see whether we can infer from the hypothesis facts which we know quite well. If the facts can be inductively
inferred from the hypothesis, this strengthens the hypothesis; and we might
then wish to use the hypothesis in order to make predictions. Scientific laws
are often developed in a procedure roughly of this type (although much
more complicated). Example 4 of inductive reasoning presents a rudimentary case of this sort of use of inductive reasoning.

One basic difference between deductive and inductive reasoning is as follows. In deductive reasoning one is engaged in drawing out the verbal consequences of one's premises. Facts may be asserted in the premises, but
in the conclusion one never really states further facts: the conclusion always asserts the same facts as the premises (or at least some of them) but
expresses them in a different way. For example, if one takes it as a fact
that Jones is a father, one is scarcely asserting a new fact when one says
that Jones has at least one child. Traditional logicians often express this

character of deductive reasoning by saying that in valid deductive reasoning "the conclusion is contained in the premises."

In inductive reasoning, on the other hand, one is moving from facts, or hypotheses, to other facts. That the sun will rise tomorrow is a different fact from the fact that the sun rose today and has risen every day now for a long time. That Jones told the truth on this occasion is separate from the facts that he always told the truth on other occasions. In inductive reasoning the conclusion is not "contained in the premises."

Another general difference between the two types of reasoning is that the process of deductive reasoning assumes merely that words have certain definite meanings. For example, if we can assume that the words used in example 2 have their customary meanings, then we can assume that if the premises are true Socrates lives by the sea. In order to know that if Jones is a father he has at least one child, all that we have to assume is that the word "father" has the meaning with which we are all familiar. In cases of inductive reasoning, however, we are assuming more than just matters of the meanings of words. We are assuming that there is some continuing pattern or regularity in reality. We assume, for example, that if the sun has risen regularly, the pattern will be worked out for another day. We assume that the eggs that we haven't looked at will fit roughly the pattern of the eggs that we have looked at. And so on. Indeed the assumption of some sort of continuing pattern in reality represents the only way in which we can infer facts from other facts. If the universe were completely chaotic, we could not know anything more than what was in front of our nose (and there is some philosophical question as to whether we would be able to know that).

This leads us to yet another general difference between deductive and inductive reasoning. We pointed out that inductive reasoning involves inferring facts from other facts (or hypotheses), and relies on patterns in reality. An obvious point is that sometimes patterns are not followed, or are broken. Sometimes what seems on limited experience to be a pattern turns out to be a concord of accidents. In such cases even the most intelligent inductive inference, relying upon the most dependable premises, is liable to lead to false conclusions. This is a basic difference between deductive and inductive reasoning. The usefulness of deductive reasoning is, so to speak, more within our control. If the premises are true, and we are sure that we have been accurate in our reasoning, then we can be sure that the deduced conclusion is true. In inductive reasoning, however, if the premises are true, and we are sure that we have been accurate in our reasoning, the most that we can say is that the conclusion is probably true. This is what logicians traditionally have meant when they have said that in deductive reasoning the conclusion is "certain," whereas in inductive reasoning "the conclusion is only probable."

Yet another way of putting the difference is to say that the statement of a valid deductive inference is analytic and necessary. For example, "If Socrates is an Athenian, and all Athenians live by the sea, then Socrates lives by the sea" is analytic and necessary. We can tell that it is true, that is, solely by examining the meanings of words; and given these meanings of words, we know that it *has* to be true. The statement of a valid inductive inference, on the other hand, would have to be classified as synthetic and contingent. Take, for example, "If the sun rose today, and rose every day that we can remember, it will rise tomorrow." What is being asserted is that the pattern of sunrises will be continued through tomorrow. This is of course to describe reality, which is why the statement is synthetic. It also could conceivably be false: the pattern might be broken tomorrow. Thus the statement of the inference is contingent.

Actually, of course, the relations between deductive and inductive logic are much more complicated than we have explained in this chapter. A good deal more will be said about them in the chapter on inductive logic. However, the reader has, at this point, been told enough to have a good general idea of the differences between the two types of reasoning. If one wanted to give a very broad, oversimple summary of the differences, one would say this. Deductive reasoning is purely analytic. It is concerned with the meanings of terms and with the consequences of these meanings. Inductive reasoning, on the other hand, has a synthetic element. It is concerned with relations among different parts of reality. This synthetic element makes it necessary for science; although, as will be pointed out in the section on induction, a good deal of scientific reasoning is deductive.

Chapter 2

Aristotelian Term Logic:
The Logic of the Syllogism

In this chapter we shall study a branch of deductive logic developed systematically by the Greek philosopher Aristotle. For many centuries this branch of logic was generally thought to be the sum and substance of all logic. Kant could write in 1781 that logic had neither advanced nor retreated a single important step in the two thousand years since Aristotle. We shall see in the next chapter that there are, in fact, other branches or varieties of formal logic. This does not mean, however, that Aristotle's logic is now, finally, out of date. Within its own limits it offers an unrivaled account of deductive inference.

The central topic of Aristotelian logic is a form of inference called the *syllogism*. Like other forms of inference studied in this book, the syllogism has application to an extremely broad range of arguments in ordinary life. Unlike some types of inference which will be discussed in the next chapter, it depends for its validity on relations asserted between the *terms* of which an argument may be composed. We shall begin by explaining this important contrast between *term logic* and *propositional logic*. Then, after indicating more exactly what a term is, we shall discuss the four basic term relations which are asserted in various kinds of syllogisms. This will prepare the way for a discussion of the syllogism itself.

As we said at the very beginning of the last chapter, discoveries *in* logic may affect our ideas as to the nature *of* logic. It is hard to imagine a discovery in geography which would change our conception of what geography itself is, but the ways logicians have worked within the field of logic have often raised questions as to what logic is. In particular, it has often been asked, what is the relation between formal logic and ordinary language? Or, what is the relation between formal logic and our claims about the real world? Historically, the answers given to these questions have been shaped by the kind of work being done within the field of logic. Now through most of this chapter we shall be doing work in logic. But this work will lead us back to some fundamental questions about logic. These questions will be reserved for special treatment at the end of the chapter.

1. Elements of the syllogism: terms and their relations

In contrast with certain other forms of inference, the syllogism depends on "term relations," not primarily on "propositional relations." We shall have something to say about what a term is, and what a proposition is, later. Even before these expressions are defined, however, the difference between term logic and propositional logic can be seen by comparing arguments from each. Indeed, one way to explain what terms and propositions are is by pointing to the contrasts between arguments in which one, rather than the other, is the basic logical unit. Consider, then, the following two arguments. The first is a syllogism; the other illustrates a form of inference (called *modus ponens*) which will be shown valid in the next chapter.

(1) All Greeks are men.
    All men are rational.
    ———————————
    All Greeks are rational.

(2) If it rains, then it pours.
    It rains.
    ———————————
    It pours.

Argument (1) depends for its validity on the "All . . . are . . ." relation asserted to hold between "Greeks" and "men," "men" and "rational," and, hence, "Greeks" and "rational." "Greeks," "men," and "rational" are the terms of the argument. "All . . . are . . ." expresses one of the four term *relations* basic to syllogistic logic. Argument (2) also depends for its validity on a logical relation, but the crucial relation here is not a term relation. "If . . . then . . ." expresses a propositional relation: if such-and-such a proposition is true, then thus-and-such a proposition is also true.

Both of our sample arguments can be represented symbolically, but to make the validity of each most clearly evident, the symbolic unit will need to be different in the two cases. An assignment of code letters at the rate of one per simple proposition exhibits clearly the form of inference involved in argument (2):

(2)′ If *R*, then *P*
     R
     ————
     P

So far as formal validity is concerned, it does not matter *what* propositions are used in an argument of this kind: so long as the *same* proposition is substituted for both R's, and the same proposition is substituted for both P's, the result will be a valid argument. More about this inference form in the next chapter. But notice now that the same sort of code lettering will not work with argument (1). No two propositions in argument (1) are the same, so that a propositional assignment of symbols will give us the rather implausible logical skeleton:

One certainly cannot tell, just from looking at , that the argument it represents is valid. If "G" stood for "Giraffes have long necks," while "M" stood for "Monkeys are cats," and "R" for "Rhinoceroses are good house-pets," the argument would *not* be in any sense valid. To make clear the validity of (1), we must use as our logical unit, not the proposition, but the term. If we assign code letters at the rate of one per term, leaving only the relations between terms to be expressed in full English, we come up with:

(1)′ All *G* are *M*.
  All *M* are *R*.
  ———————
  All *G* are *R*.

So far as formal validity is concerned, it does not matter what *terms* are used in an argument of this kind: so long as we replace our code letters on a one-to-one basis, the result will be a valid argument. "Replacing our code letters on a one-to-one basis" means that we plug in the same term for each occurrence of the same code letter.

In the light of these examples, we can state the contrast between term logic and propositional logic in this way. If the validity of an inference directly depends on what relations are asserted to hold between the terms of the inference, then the inference belongs to term logic. Argument (1) directly depends on the "All . . . are . . ." relation connecting each term of the argument with one of the other terms of the argument. If, on the other hand, an argument depends for its validity only on relations asserted between the statements or propositions of which it is composed, then the inference made is part of propositional logic. Argument (2) depends on the "If . . . then . . ." relation asserted between the propositions "It rains" and "It pours." Accordingly, the type of inference involved in (2) will be shown valid in the first part of the next chapter. In this chapter we shall be concerned only with inferences which, like (1), are based on term relations.

The contrast has important consequences. Although propositional logic presents us with many powerful and beautiful forms of inference (including a way of rigorously deducing the formulas of term logic from a few basic assumptions), we can use the preceding examples to point out an important advantage possessed by term logic. In any argument having the same form as (1) each proposition of the argument will have some reference to reality in common with each of the others. This is brought out in our logical skeleton, for each line of (1)′ has a code letter in common with each of the other lines. This means that the very form of the argument lays down a requirement for a certain unity of content or subject matter. No comparable requirement is imposed by the form of argument (2). The logical skeleton (2)′ does perfectly for the following:

> (3) If rhinoceroses are Jabberwocks, the moon is made
>   of cheese.
>   Rhinoceroses are Jabberwocks.
>   ——————————————————————————
>   The moon is made of cheese.

The fact that rhinoceroses being Jabberwocks "has nothing to do" with the moon being made of green cheese does not affect the formal validity of the argument. The "If . . . then . . ." relation between propositions just does not restrict the subject matter of a simple argument as tightly as the term relation "All . . . are . . ." Although the looseness of "If . . . then . . ." is for some logical and scientific purposes a good thing, the strictness of "All . . . are . . ." can be counted as an advantage to the student seeking to develop mental clarity and sharpness of focus from his work in logic.

Still more could be said about the importance of terms and their relations as the basis of Aristotelian logic. Aristotle marks off each large class of syllogisms by stating the term relations distinctive of that class. Different inferences are possible given different relations of terms. Perhaps enough has already been said, however, to justify a precise treatment of the question "What *is* a term?" To this question, we turn now.

1.1.1. What is a term?

What is a term? Like most questions worth asking, this is not an easy one. We have already said that terms are the basic units in Aristotelian logic, but this is hardly a sufficient answer at the *beginning* of a study of Aristotelian logic. Perhaps, though, we can use the syllogism from page 26 to give one sort of brief answer that will in fact be helpful. One sort of answer to the question "What is a term?" is this. An expression that might meaningfully be substituted for a code letter like G, M, or R in our logical skeleton (1)′ is a term. (A proposition, on the other hand, is an expression that might meaningfully be substituted for a code letter like R or P in (2)′.) Quite a few words and phrases meet this requirement. Substituting "Black Angus," "cattle," and "animal" gives us the valid syllogism "All Black Angus are cattle, all cattle are animals; hence, all Black Angus are animals." Now try "cats," "felines," and "dogs." If you write in these substitutions, you may not be happy with the result. There is something wrong with an argument "proving" that cats are dogs. Still, the individual substitutions make sense. The trouble with the argument is not that it is invalid or meaningless, but that its second premise is false—and when you are given a false premise, no amount of purely logical cleverness will guarantee you a true conclusion. It would be not merely false but nonsense, however, if we tried replacing the code letters with such phrases as "the a an," "$2+2=4$," and "ouch." Expressions like these are not terms.

Supposing that we avoid nonsense substitutions, the results of replacing our code letters on a one-to-one basis is always an argument of exactly the same logical form as our original syllogism about the rationality of Greeks and men, but different substitutions will give us arguments which differ in *content* or *subject matter*. This suggests another important point about terms. Its terms, we may say, are what determine the content or subject matter of a statement or proposition. Expressions like "All . . . are . . ." determine the logical form of an assertion, but we do not actually have a statement or proposition unless we fill in the gaps with terms.

Still another kind of brief answer to the quesiton "What is a term?" would be this. A term is the linguistic expression of a concept. The terms "featherless biped" and "rational animal" refer in a way to the same subject. That is, only men are featherless bipeds, and only men, so far as we know, are rational animals. And yet the two terms are very different. One way of describing the difference is to say that we have quite different ideas in mind when we use them. The fact that these phrases refer to the same things does not make them the same term, for conceptually they differ enormously.

So far we have given a rough three-dimensional account of what a term is. (1) From the standpoint of formal logic, a term is the replacement for a certain kind of code symbol. (2) But terms, unlike the logical symbols they replace, make a direct mention of some subject matter or other. (3) And terms express *how* we look at things, as well as indicating what things we are looking at. These points will be clearer if we put them to work in looking over the following two lists. The items in the left-hand list would

normally be used as terms; the expressions in the other list are not terms.
Let us see why this is so, on the basis of the points we have made.

Terms	Non-terms
1. Furry cats	1. Cats are furry
2. Cats meowing in the moonlight	2. Cats and dogs
	3. All, some
3. USAF (if used simply as an abbreviation for "United States Air Force")	4. Are . . . , Are not . . .
	5. A (as in the logical formula "All A are A")
	6. Ouch

Comparing "Furry cats" with "Cats are furry" brings out an important
point. Terms merely mention things, they make no explicit claims about
them. The term "furry cat" refers to a certain kind of cat but makes no
claim about that kind of cat or about anything else. The term "furry"
might be applied as a description of certain things, yet by itself the term
makes no claim that there is anything which fits the description. But to
state that cats *are* furry is to make a claim. Although the claims made by
many statements are implicit in the terms composing them, no claim is
actually made until and unless a statement is made. To put the point another way, terms, since they merely mention things, cannot be true or false.
A statement, because it makes a claim, is true or false. Even though the
truth of an analytic statement (such as "Furry cats are furry") depends only
on the meaning of its terms, it is only the statement which is true, not the
terms.

We have said that its terms determine what a statement is about. Some
statements are about more than one sort of thing, and they accordingly
have more than one subject term. Compare the term "Cats meowing in
the moonlight" with "Cats and dogs" from our right-hand list. They behave
very differently when we try plugging them into the statement-form "All
A are B." "Cats meowing in the moonlight" does nicely as a single term,
even though it is composed of three other terms. An insomniac might say,
for example, "All cats meowing in the moonlight are worthy of extermination!" Now this statement is not about cats in general, or about meowing
things, or about all things in the moonlight. Rather, the statement has a
single subject, cats meowing in the moonlight. The component terms, "cats,"
"meowing," and "in the moonlight," all work together to indicate this
subject. Now look at "cats and dogs" in the proposition "All cats and dogs
are animals." This proposition looks simpler than the last one, and from a
literary standpoint perhaps it is. Yet the term "cats" and the term "dogs"
do *not* work together here to indicate a single kind of thing; as it happens,

there *isn't* anything which is both a cat and a dog. Instead, "cats" picks out one subject and "dogs" another. From the standpoint of formal logic, the proposition about cats and dogs is definitely more complex than the one about cats in the moonlight meowing. For the purpose of logical analysis, we should read "Cats and dogs are animals" as shorthand for two distinct propositions, "Cats are animals" and "Dogs are animals." "All cats meowing in the moonlight are worthy of extermination" cannot be broken up in this way. We conclude, then, that the phrase "cats and dogs" is not one term; it cannot properly be substituted for one of the code letters in "All *A* are *B*."

Our point about terms having content is brought out in various ways by lines 3, 4, and 5 of our right-hand list. The items in the third and fourth lines affect the meaning of statements in which they occur, but none of these expressions mentions anything by itself. "All" and "some" indicate how much of a subject we are talking about, but they say nothing as to what the subject is. "Are" and "are not," when used as transitive verbs, are also shy of content. In saying, "Cats are furry," we use "are" to assert a connection between the content words "cats" and "furry," but "are" itself has no independent meaning in such a statement.

If we compare "USAF" on our list of terms with *"A"* on our list of non-terms, an extremely basic point emerges. If a letter or a group of letters is used simply as an abbreviation for a specified word or phrase, then it has all the content associated with that word or phrase. If the word or phrase is a term (such as "United States Air Force"), then for logical purposes its abbreviation ("USAF") also counts as a term. "The USAF has many planes" is in this case only a shorter way of *writing,* "The United States Air Force has many planes." In our statement of the logical law, "All *A* are *A*," the letter *A* is not used as an abbreviation but as a *variable.* It is not merely a shorter way of writing a definitely specified term. Rather, *A* is used here to stand for any general term whatever. The claim made by "All *A* are *A*" is that if you substitute *any* one general term for both *A*'s in the formula, the result will be a true statement. Another way of putting the point is to say that "USAF" in our illustration has only one *value*—only one expression, "United States Air Force," may replace it; in the logical law "All *A* are *A*" the variable *A* has many values—any general term may be substituted for it. Its having many values in this way is what makes a code letter a variable. The fact that *A*'s values are terms makes *A*, in our formula, a *term variable.*

In this chapter we shall be using specific terms like "Greek" and "mortal" only in *examples* of different types of proposition and inference. To make our discussion easier to follow, we will choose code letters that tie in with the terms used in the examples. If we are using "All Greeks are mortal" as an example, we encode the sentence as "All *G* are *M*." This does not mean, however, that *G* and *M* are meant simply as abbreviations for the terms of the example. The points we shall make about "All *G* are *M*" will apply to an extremely broad range of statements; the whole range of statements which would result from replacing *G* and *M* with any general terms whatever. This is to say that our code letters will be used, and should be read, primarily as term variables.

"Ouch" is on our list of non-terms for a different reason. The normal function of "ouch" is not to mention anything, but to express a feeling. When we are pained and say "ouch," we are not talking about our feeling but giving vent to it. We *can* talk about our feelings, of course. Some terms refer to feelings ("the pain in my head . . ."), and some descriptive terms have feeling as their content ("my head *ached*"). But it doesn't make sense to refer to the ouch in one's head, or to say that one's head ouched very much last week.

EXERCISES FOR SECTION 1.1.1.

I. Identify the terms of the following statements. If two or more terms cooperate to function as a single term, count only the composite as a term of the statement.
   1. Roses are red.
   2. Roses are red, and violets are blue.
   3. Roses and violets are flowers.
   4. Roses and violets have attractive fragrances.
   5. Some roses are white.
   6. Every rose in the southeast corner of Aunt Jane's garden is white.
   7. Most roses are red, but some of those in Aunt Jane's garden are white.
   8. On the other hand, three bushes elsewhere in Aunt Jane's garden have yellow roses.
   9. Ah me, this is indeed a fragrant flower.
   10. Three is a prime number.
   11. This is a difficult exercise, but a profitable one.
II. Construct logical skeletons for the preceding statements, using variables for terms. Mark off distinct propositions by enclosing each in parentheses.

Two rules should be followed in substituting code letters for terms:

   A. If the same term occurs more than once in the same statement, use the same code letter for each of its occurrences.
   B. Do not use the same code letter to represent more than one term of a single statement.

1.1.2. Kinds of terms

There are many ways of classifying terms. A poet or novelist might classify them, as well as other words, on the basis of their emotional impact, putting ordinary words in one group, exotic expressions in another, and so on. A scientist, primarily interested in gaining knowledge of the natural world, might classify terms in accordance with the things they mention, putting chemical terms in one category, psychological terms in another, perhaps reserving a special place for terms useful in many sciences, such as "cause," "correlation," and the like. As logicians, we must ignore the affective nuances of words, important as these are in literature, for the validity of an inference has nothing to do with the charm of its language. The fact that terms mention things is of great interest to us, even as logicians; but, unlike the scientist, we are unable to divide them according to *which* things they mention—that is not our job. There are, however, two ways of sorting terms which are appropriate to our subject and generally useful.

(1) *Singular and general terms.* A term is singular if it is used with the intention of referring to just one thing. Proper names and definite descriptions are the clearest examples of singular terms. The normal purpose of a proper name, such as "John Jones," is to pick out one individual. This purpose is sometimes defeated—when, for example, there is more than one person named John Jones in a theater where "John Jones" is paged. The term is still singular, for it was *meant* to refer to one and only one individual. Similarly, a description consisting of general terms preceded by the definite article "the" (or by "this," "that," etc.) is usually intended to refer to one and only one thing. Such expressions are called *definite descriptions.* "The man next door" has the form of a definite description, and would thus be classified as a singular term. It fails in its purpose if in fact there are two men next door.

A general term, often called a *universal*, mentions a *kind* of thing. It may thus be used to designate any of possibly many things of the same kind. This is clear enough in the case of terms like "man" and "sweet." There are many men, and "man" can be used to designate any or all of them. There are many sweet things, and "sweet" can be used in describing all or some of them. But what about "man next door," if there turns out to be only one man next door? We say in this case that the term is still general. So far as *it* is concerned, there might be many men next door. To put it another way, "man next door" refers to any and every man next door—whether one or one hundred; it would not fail to refer to one man next door even if he was the only one. "*The* man next door" *would* fail as a definite description if one man next door was *not* the only one. What counts in both cases is the intent with which a word or phrase is used. If a term is meant to pick out one individual, it is a singular term; if it is meant to cover any of possibly many individuals of a certain kind, it is general.

What we do or should mean by "one thing" or an "individual" is an extremely difficult point. Determining what it is to be an individual is one of the persistent problems of philosophy. Abstract terms, like "heat" and "justice," and class names, like "man," give trouble here. It seems as if we can talk about heat as singular. "Heat is produced by molecular motion" makes sense. And yet it is not easy to find any single thing answering to the name. There are, of course, many hot things, but apart from them, what, if anything, is "the" property heat? As for class names, we often do use them in a singular way. "Man is a species of animal" clearly does not mean that John Jones and his friends are, all by themselves, a species of anything. They are animals, to be sure, but not species. What sort of "man," then, *is* a species?

Perhaps we can say this much, negatively. To use a singular term does not imply that the thing referred to by the term has an absolute physical or metaphysical simplicity from every point of view. And conversely, the fact that a thing is complex in some respects need not keep us from referring to "it" as an individual. The expression "this sheet of paper" is quite an ordinary singular term. It is clear, however, that a sheet of paper has many spatial parts (left side, right side, top, and bottom), many words printed on it, and so on. We have, then, a philosophical problem. Stated crudely, the problem is, "Is 'the' paper one thing or many things?" Instead of attempting to solve this problem, we shall fall back upon our earlier definition of a term as the expression of a concept. A concept is a way of looking at things. Let us say, therefore, that looking at the paper as a single thing yields a singular term; looking at "its" parts affords a basis for applying general terms. "The" one, single man next door can be treated as an individual in spite of having two arms, two legs, and so on. We leave for a higher branch of philosophy the questions of how "the" paper is related to the sum of its parts, and how the man next door is related to his arms and legs.

(2) *Positive and negative terms.* Every term may be thought of as a means for dividing up reality into two large classes: on one hand, things mentioned by the term; and on the other hand, everything else. If we think of the term itself as a label for one of these classes, we can construct a corresponding negative term as a label for the "everything else" in the second class. Two terms related in this way may be called contradictories of each other. "Voter," for example, has as its contradictory "nonvoter." The point is that everything in the world can be classified as either a voter or a nonvoter, but not both; the two terms divide the world between them. One contradicts the reference of the other by picking out all that it does not cover,

and nothing that it does cover. Everything is either a voter or a nonvoter, but nothing is both, or at least not with respect to the same sort of voting in the same election.

Still, it is at least a bit whimsical to say that the number 3 is a nonvoter. The reason it is odd to describe 3 in this way is, of course, that no number *is* a voter. Accordingly we would wonder what someone was up to if he said that 3 is a nonvoter, for he certainly is not telling us anything distinctive about that particular number. Some logicians, including Aristotle, would want to restrict the application of "nonvoter" to things of the same general class as "voter" applies to. This is a good rule to follow if you want to avoid such statements as "3 is a nonvoter." Call something a non-*A* only if some things of the same class are normally or usually *A*'s. "3 is a nonvoter" makes poor sense because no numbers *are* voters. But if someone is an adult citizen of a democracy, we feel we are being told something quite distinctive about him if it is said, "He is a nonvoter." Most people in his situation are, or have been, could be, or should be, voters, and on any of these grounds we may feel we are learning something about a person when we are told that *he* is a nonvoter.

Contradictories should not be confused with *contraries*. Two terms are contrary to each other if they cannot both be truthfully applied to the same subject at the same time. Thus "hot" and "cold" are contraries, for no one thing can be both hot and cold in exactly the same way at exactly the same time. The same can be said for the pairs of terms "wise" and "unwise," and "welcome" and "unwelcome." But it may be the case that *neither* of a pair of contraries applies, and this is the difference between contraries and contradictories. Some guests are neither unwelcome nor (especially) welcome, some people are of a middling degree of knowledge, while some bodies are lukewarm. On the other hand, a term and its contradictory split up reality between them: one or the other applies to everything. Even if we restrict the application of a negative term to things of a kind to which the corresponding positive term may normally be applied, still at least that kind of thing is divided exhaustively. This is not so with contraries. Exactly the same kind of thing may be hot, cold, or lukewarm.

EXERCISES FOR SECTION 1.1.2.

I. Classify the following terms as singular or general.
1. Baseball (as in "He threw a baseball onto the field.")
2. Baseball (as in "Baseball is our national game.")
3. Team in first place in the American League during some part of 1963.

4. Best center fielder in all baseball.

5. Three (as in "He scored a three or a four on each of the first nine holes.")

6. Three (as in "Three is a prime number.")

7. Autumn (as in "Come visit us some autumn, when the leaves are falling.")

8. Autumn (as in "O wild west wind, thou breath of autumn's being.")

9. The elephant (as in "The elephant is a mammal.")

10. The elephant (as in "The elephant in our zoo is very friendly.")

II. Which of the following pairs of terms are pairs of contradictories, and which are pairs of contraries? Assume that the terms are applied only to things to which it makes good sense to apply them.

1. good–bad.

2. possible–impossible.

3. animal–plant.

4. true–false.

5. known to be true–known to be false.

1.2.1. The meaning of "proposition," "statement," and "sentence"

Our syllogism about all Greeks being rational was based on a series of "All . . . are . . ." relations among the terms "Greeks," "men," and "rational." Now any assertion that "All *A*'s are *B*'s" states a type of *proposition* basic to classical logic. In the next few pages we shall study this and the three other types of proposition basic in classical logic. We must first try to be clear, however, as to what propositions are and how they are related to certain other factors in human knowledge. It should be noted that "proposition" and the related words "statement" and "sentence" have a variety of meanings in ordinary and logical usage, and that any choice of definitions is subject to intense philosophical dispute. We shall try, however, to approximate the most typical everyday usages, while assigning distinct enough meanings so that these key words can be used later in discussing some basic questions about logic.

When a person says that something is or is not the case, or may or may not be, must or must not be, ought or ought not to be, the case, he asserts a proposition. For practical purposes, a proposition is anything that meaningfully completes the expression "He said that ———." A *statement* can be defined as an act of speaking or writing in which some claim or proposal is made which can be called true or false. In other words, a statement is the act of asserting a proposition, and a *proposition* can be defined as the claim made in a statement, a claim which is either true or false, depending upon the facts or upon the meaning of the terms in which it is stated.

It is an essential mark of a proposition or statement that we can sensibly ask about it, "Is it true or false?" The relevance of this question distinguishes propositions fairly sharply from other expressions, such as exclamations, commands, requests, and questions. It does not make sense to ask "true or false" about any of the following expressions, for example: "Hurrah for Pooh!" "Let's think clearly," or "What is a proposition?"

The great difficulty in being clear about propositions lies in correctly relating them to (1) the thoughts they express, (2) the things they are about, and (3) the words in which they are embodied. We shall say something about each of these complicated relationships before proceeding to the various specific propositional types of classical logic.

(1) *Propositions and thought.* We described a term as the linguistic expression of a concept. In a similar way, propositions can be described as the linguistic expressions of beliefs, opinions, or mental judgments. Indeed, in everyday life we sometimes speak of propositions as if they were mental or prelinguistic things. A person sometimes thinks of something to say without actually saying it, and in this sense, at least, we can have a proposition "in mind" as well as in (written or spoken) words. For purposes of logical analysis, however, propositions cannot usefully be discussed except insofar as they are given definite linguistic expression. Furthermore, the logician is interested in propositions as such or in their own right, not as symptoms of the nature or state of mind of the persons who produce them. The psychological factors involved in the production of propositions belong to the science of psychology.

(2) *Propositions and facts.* Every statement expresses a judgment or belief *about* something—call it a subject-matter or reality. Indeed, we try to "state facts" about as often as we "state propositions," and some writers on logic have accordingly treated the expressions "fact" and "true proposition" as identical. This is perhaps an unnecessarily odd use of "proposition," for the properties of propositions studied in logic are not the same as the facts studied in the natural and social sciences. It is of great interest to logicians that propositions do or can bear on real things, but what these things are or are like is outside the scope of logical analysis. The situation with propositions is like that discussed earlier in the classification of terms (section 1.1.2.).

(3) *Propositions and language: sentences.* A proposition can be thought of as the meaning of a statement: it is the claim a statement means to make. It is difficult to deal logically with meanings that are not expressed in any language at all, yet a proposition is clearly not identical in every way with the language in which it is embodied. For different words can be used to say the same thing, and contrariwise, the same words can be used to say

many, quite different things. The commonest illustration of the first point is the identity of meaning of expressions from different languages. *"Il pleut"* is normally used to say in French what we say in English with "It's raining." It may even be the case that different statements in the same language "say the same thing," that is, make the same claim about things. If so, we should count them as statements of the same proposition. The second point, that the same words can be used to say quite different things, can be illustrated in extreme form by the sentence "At this very moment, I am alive," which can never be used twice to state the same proposition. Either the moment or the "I" must be different in any two occurrences. At the other extreme, a sentence can be used for some other purpose than expressing any proposition at all. *"Il pleut,"* is a French sentence used in this paragraph to make a point in logic, not to comment on the weather.

It will be useful, therefore, to distinguish sentences from propositions in the following way. A declarative sentence is a group of words—that is, a pattern of sounds or visible marks—that can appropriately be used in stating propositions. A sentence will *be* a proposition insofar as it amounts to a definite, specific claim about things, that is, insofar as it is actually being used for its normal purpose. Grammatically or verbally different sentences will be considered "the same"—logically speaking—when they can reasonably be interpreted as making identical claims. Using "proposition" and "sentence" in this way avoids identifying logical meaning with the sounds and visible marks of language, while not committing us to the view that propositions are by nature disembodied beings which normally exist apart from any language at all.

We need not always use "sentence," "statement," and "proposition" with full precision. Strictly speaking, the concrete examples used in this book consist merely of sentences, not of statements or propositions. Just as we did not use the French sentence *"Il pleut"* to make a claim about the weather, in the same way we have never once in this book actually asserted that all Greeks are men, or even that all men are rational. Rather, we have been using *sentences* such as "All Greeks are men" to make points in logic. Since, however, most of the logical points apply to these sentence insofar as they *can* appropriately be used to state propositions, we shall have no qualms about referring to them *as if they were* statements or propositions. That is, we shall refer to the sentences in our examples sometimes as statements or, more often, as propositions.

On a few occasions (notably in 2.2.4. and in Chapter 4) full precision will be needed. On these occasions we shall refer to the points made in the last few paragraphs.

1.2.2. *Basic propositional forms:* **A, E, I,** *and* **O**

Aristotelian logic is the logic of four basic term relations. The assertion of any one of these relations amounts to a distinctive type of claim, or proposition. The following rather homely sentences are, in their normal usage, such clear examples of our four types of basic proposition that each can be considered a prize specimen of the form it illustrates.

  I. All Holsteins are cattle.

  II. No Holsteins are Herefords.

  III. Some cattle are Holsteins.

  IV. Some cattle are not Holsteins.

Let us consider first what the propositions normally stated by these sentences have in common, and then how they differ.

Common properties. (1) Each has exactly two terms (see 1.1.1. for an explanation of why "are," "are not," "all," "no," and "some" are not counted as terms).

(2) One of the terms in each proposition is used as a *subject,* indicating what the proposition is about, while the other term functions as a *predicate,* indicating what the proposition says about its subject.

(3) In each proposition the subject term is "quantified" as either universal or particular. I and II are claims about all of their subject; III and IV are claims about some of their subject.

(4) In each proposition we either affirm or deny that the predicate applies or belongs to, or includes, the subject. No ifs, ands, ors, or buts are injected. It is not said that the predicate may or may not apply to the subject, nor, on the other hand, that the predicate must or must not apply. In each proposition we simply assert, without qualification, that the predicate does or does not belong to the subject.

Any proposition with all of these properties has one of the four basic forms studied in classical logic.

Differences. Our sample propositions differ in content, in quantity, and in quality. (1) They are composed of different terms. Important as this difference would be if we were interested in Herefords and Holsteins, it does not matter to us as formal logicians. Any *general* terms might have been used; the propositional form would have remained unchanged no matter what content was used to illustrate it.

(2) A difference that does matter to us is the difference in *quantity* between I and II, on one hand, and III and IV, on the other. To mark this difference, the former are called *universal* propositions, the latter are called *particular.* To classify statements as universal or particular, we must be able

to answer the question "Does this statement make a claim about part of some subject, or does it make a claim about the whole subject?" If we ask this question about the statement that no Holsteins are Herefords, it is clear that, as to quantity, this statement belongs with "All Holsteins are cattle." For on the basis of "No Holsteins are Herefords," we can say of *each* and *every* Holstein, "It's not a Hereford." So much for the quantifiers "all" and "no." Two points should be borne in mind about "some." First, although "some" ordinarily suggests "more than one," it does not have this meaning in classical logic. Second, in classical logic, "some" does not mean "only some, not all." Normally, of course, we do not say "some" if we are fully prepared to say "all," and in some everyday situations "some" is intended as a direct denial of "all" ("All women are fickle," he said. "Oh no," she replied. *"Some* women are fickle."). But we do not always use "some" in this way. We may be willing to make a claim about part of a subject and simply not know about the rest of it. In such cases we certainly do not mean to deny "all" when we say "some." In real life, then, "some" has different meanings in different contexts. In logic, however, we want such words to have a constant meaning. The meaning assigned to "some" in classical logic justifies the following paraphrases of III and IV. "At least one member of the cattle family is a Hereford, and I am not denying that they all might be," for III. And for IV, "At least one bovine is not a Hereford, and I am not rejecting the possibility that no cattle are Herefords."

(3) The only other difference we need to notice now is the difference between affirming and denying. I and III each affirms a predicate of a subject, while II and IV each denies that a predicate belongs to a subject. Another way of stating this difference is to say that I and III claim that their subjects are wholly or partially included by, or contained in, their predicates, while II and IV claim that their subjects are wholly or partially excluded by, or from, their predicates. The difference between affirmation and denial is called a difference of *quality*.

If we consider both quantity and quality, we see that each of our prize specimens has a different form from each of the others. The four basic term relations of Aristotelian logic are those of one term's (1) belonging to all, or (2) belonging to none, or (3) belonging to some, or (4) not belonging to some, of another term. The four propositional forms in which these relations are asserted are called, in the listed order, *universal affirmative, universal negative, particular affirmative,* and *particular negative.* It is customary to label these forms with vowels drawn from Aff**I**rmo and n**E**g**O**, Latin for "I affirm" and "I deny." Universal affirmative propositions, such as "All Holsteins are cattle," are called **A** propositions. Universal negatives, such as "No Holsteins are Herefords," are **E** propositions. The particular affirmative, "Some cattle are Holsteins," is an **I** proposition, while the particular negative, "Some cattle are not Holsteins," is an **O** proposition.

The following diagram sums up all that we have said thus far:

	AFFIRMATIVE	NEGATIVE
UNIVERSAL	**A** All *A* are *B*.	**E** No *A* are *B*.
PARTICULAR	**I** Some *A* are *B*.	**O** Some *A* are not *B*.

In a later part of this chapter we shall consider in detail several important logical relationships which hold between corresponding **A**, **E**, **I**, and **O** propositions. It may help to convey the "feel" of these propositional forms if we indicate some of these relations briefly here.

A and **O** propositions composed of the same terms are *contradictories*. This means that one of them must be true and the other false. For example, the **A** proposition, "All men are mortal," is true if, and only if, the **O** proposition, "Some men are not mortal," is false. Another way of stating this relationship is to say that each of the two propositions is equivalent to the direct denial of the other. **O** could be *defined* as "not-**A**." Alternatively, **A** could be defined as "not-**O**." **E** and **I** propositions are also contradictories. To assert the **E** proposition that no cats are dogs is the same as denying the proposition that some cats *are* dogs. In the same way, if you are willing to say, "Some cows are brown," you should also be willing to say, "It is false that no cows are brown." **E** could be defined as "not-**I**," and **I** means the same as "not-**E**."

Corresponding **A** and **E** propositions are *contraries* in classical logic. This means that they cannot both be true, though both might be false. Neither "All cows are brown" nor "No cows are brown" is true (some cows are, and some aren't). If one of these universal claims *were* true, however, the other would have to be false. It is impossible that all of a given subject should both have and not have the same predicate applicable to it in the same way at the same time. Accordingly, if you are willing to assert one universal claim (affirmative or negative) about a subject, you should be ready to deny the opposite universal claim (negative or affirmative).

The **I** and **O** term relations of Aristotelian logic yield pairs of propositions which are *subcontraries*. Corresponding particular propositions (an **I** and an **O**) cannot both be false, though, as in the case of brown cows, both may be true. Given some cows to talk about, we must concede either that some of them are brown or that (at least) some of them are not brown. Accordingly, if you are ready to *deny* one particular claim about a subject (an **I** claim or an **O** claim), you should be willing to assert the opposite particular claim (**O** or **I**).

Finally, particular propositions follow (as *subalterns*) from corresponding universal propositions of the same quality. That is, **I** follows from **A**, and **O** follows from **E**. If you are willing to make a claim about all of a given subject, you should be willing to make the same claim (affirmative or negative) about some of the same subject. If all men are mortal, then some of them are mortal; and "Some cats are not dogs" seems a modest enough conclusion to draw from the universal negative "No cats are dogs."

The logical relations among corresponding **A**, **E**, **I**, and **O** propositions are traditionally presented in a *square of opposition*. Another way of summing these relations up is to list the simple inferences which are possible given the truth or falsity of various propositions of these types. Here is the classical square of opposition:

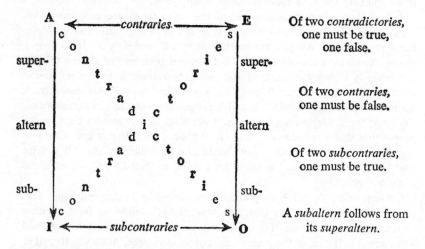

Of two *contradictories*, one must be true, one false.

Of two *contraries*, one must be false.

Of two *subcontraries*, one must be true.

A *subaltern* follows from its *superaltern*.

Assuming that the same terms are used as subject and predicate in all cases, the Aristotelian square of opposition justifies the following simple inferences:

If **A** is true, then **I** is true, **E** is false, and **O** is false.

If **A** is false, then **O** is true.

If **E** is true, then **O** is true, **A** is false, and **I** is false.

If **E** is false, then **I** is true.

If **I** is true, then **E** is false.

If **I** is false, then **E** is true (and hence **A** is false), **O** is true.

If **O** is true, then **A** is false.

If **O** is false, then **A** is true (and hence **E** is false), **I** is true.

The preceding inference relations among **A, E, I,** and **O** propositions reveal a great deal about the classical interpretation of such expressions as "All . . . are . . . ," "No . . . are . . . ," "Some . . . are . . . ," and "Some . . . are not . . ." In our opinion, the classical interpretation of these phrases comes very near the meaning they have in most everyday uses. (Our only important reservation is with regard to "some," which almost always means "more than one" in ordinary life, and usually means "not all.") In some areas of modern logic, however, a very different meaning is given for each of these key phrases, and on the basis of this modern interpretation, some arguments which would be analyzed as valid inferences by classical logicians come out as clearly invalid. Indeed, only those inferences within the square of opposition which proceed from a given proposition to the denial of its contradictory have valid modern counterparts. We shall explain the modern interpretation of "all" and "some" in 2.2.4., and shall deal at the end of the chapter with the problem of choosing the appropriate interpretation for these expressions in various contexts.

To complete our account of **A, E, I,** and **O,** we should notice that two of these term relations, **E** and **I,** are *symmetrical*. This means simply that you can reverse the order of subject and predicate in propositions of these types without affecting the truth or falsity of what you have said. If no lions are tigers, then no tigers are lions, and in general if a proposition of the form "No A's are B's" is true, then the corresponding "No B's are A's" must also be true. And **I** is also symmetrical. If some E's are F's, then some F's must be E's: if some roses are red, it must be the case that some red things are roses. **A** and **O** are nonsymmetrical; all roses are flowers, but not vice versa; and some flowers are *not* roses, but from this it hardly follows that some roses are not flowers.

EXERCISE FOR SECTION 1.2.2.

Label the following as **A, E, I,** or **O.** In each case, which word or words constitute the subject? The predicate?

1. Some men who fly through the air are not pilots.
2. Some men who are flying are not pilots.

3. No animals who are not men are pilots.
4. All passengers are animals.
5. Some passengers are men.
6. Some animals who are not men are passengers.
7. Some passengers in airplanes are poodles.
8. No passengers are cases of crackerjacks.

1.2.3. A-E-I-O *and ordinary language*

In the next few pages we shall discuss sentences which can ordinarily be treated as statements of **A, E, I,** or **O** propositions, even though their linguistic form differs in some way from that of our prize specimens. Our discussion will not be exhaustive, but it should give you a start toward applying the classical forms correctly in analyzing real-life arguments. Bear in mind that no matter what the wording of a statement is, you can treat it as **A, E, I,** or **O** in logical form if you can answer "yes" to three questions about it: (1) Does the statement apply a predicate to a subject? (2) Is the predicate applied to some of the subject or to the whole subject (you must be able to say which)? (3) Does the statement either simply affirm or simply deny that the predicate belongs to the subject? These questions are easier to answer about some statements than about others. We begin with some easy cases.

(1) *Attributive predicates.* "All Holsteins are bovine" is equivalent to "All Holsteins are bovines." "Some trees are green" means the same as "Some trees are green things." In general, the grammatical difference between a predicate adjective and a predicate noun makes no difference logically. This does not mean that being a "thing" is the same as being a property or quality. It means merely that the difference can usually be ignored for purposes of analyzing ordinary statements and arguments.

(2) *Verb copulas.* "Are" and "are not," in our four forms, are *copulas.* Their function is to connect terms, but they themselves are not terms. In many sentences this connecting function is performed by a word which is part, or all, of the predicate. "All fishes swim" can be treated as "All fishes are swimmers," or, less elegantly, as "All fishes are things that swim." For our purposes, "No birds bark" is the same as "No birds are barkers," while "Some people complain about everything" comes out the same as "Some people are complainers about everything."

Here we would like to introduce a piece of symbolism which will prove useful in this and the following chapter. We propose to replace the expressions "All . . . are . . . ," "No . . . are . . . ," "Some . . . are . . . ," and "Some . . . are not . . ." with the symbols **A, E, I,** and **O,** in writing some propositions and formulas. This device is especially handy in writing propositions with verb copulas. "All fishes swim" can be written, **"A** fishes/ swim"; "No birds bark" can be written, **"E** birds/bark"; "Some people complain about everything" comes out as **"I** people/complain about everything." We can also use these symbols in writing other kinds of sentences. "All Holsteins are bovine" can be written, **"A** Holsteins/bovine." "Some trees are green" may be set down as **"I** trees/green." "No Holsteins are Herefords" becomes **"E** Holsteins/Herefords." "Some cattle are not Holsteins" and "Some men are not Greeks" are written, respectively, **"O** cattle/Holsteins" and **"O** men/Greeks."

(3) *Singular subjects*. Strange as it may seem, propositions with singular subjects behave more like universal than like particular propositions, and should normally be analyzed accordingly. That is, it is better to treat "Socrates is mortal" as an **A** proposition rather than as an **I** proposition, while "Socrates is not a barbarian" should usually be analyzed as an **E**, never as an **O**, proposition. If we recall that **A** and **E** are used to make claims about all of a subject, while **I** and **O** express claims about parts of subjects, some of the strangeness of this treatment of singular subjects disappears. In "Socrates is mortal" we are not, after all, talking only about some part of Socrates. And when we deny that Socrates is a barbarian, the denial covers what *could* be described as "the whole Socrates," for we do not mean that his little toe may be barbaric, though his head is not. Accordingly, if we limit our choice of propositional forms to **A, E, I,** and **O,** it is clear that **A** and **E** must be used to express affirmations and denials about singular subjects.

We have said that propositions with singular subjects should be treated *as* universals, rather than as particulars. There are times when we must recognize that they are not universals but form a distinct class of propositions. We have seen, for example, that "Some *A* is *B*" follows from "All *A* is *B*," if general terms are substituted for the variables *A* and *B*. Substituting a singular subject leads to nonsense in such inferences. It hardly makes sense even to say, "Some Socrates is mortal," let alone to infer such a proposition from "Socrates is mortal." The whole point of a singular term is to pick out an individual, and *logically* speaking, an individual does not *have* parts. For example, we do not establish that Socrates is mortal by rejecting a series of **O** propositions about the mortality of his parts. For logical purposes, "Socrates" is not the same as "All (of) Socrates(' parts)."

To sum up the last two paragraphs: strictly speaking, propositions with singular subjects are neither universal nor particular. For many purposes they can be treated as universals, but you must use good sense to avoid some occasional awkward results of treating them in this way. "Socrates is a man; all men are mortal; hence, Socrates is mortal" is a valid argument, but we must have the good sense not to go on from "Socrates is mortal" to "Some Socrates is mortal." To make it somewhat easier to avoid this sort of mistake, we shall put a small *s* by any **A** or **E** used to represent a singular proposition. This will be a sign that some inferences which can be made from a genuine **A** or **E** proposition cannot be made from the proposition at hand. "Socrates is mortal" can thus be written, "**A**$_s$ Socrates/mortal," the *s* by **A** being an indication that the proposition is singular, rather than universal. "John Jones is not a doctor" comes out as "**E**$_s$ John Jones/doctor."

One final complication. Terms which are singular in grammatical form sometimes are not singular logically. "The *A*" sometimes means "All *A*." For example, "The buffalo is a prairie animal" would seem to be a statement about all buffalo. The difficulties mentioned in the last two paragraphs do not arise here, for it makes good sense to say, "Some buffalo are prairie animals." But compare this with two propositions which look very similar: "The buffalo enjoyed the peanuts Johnny gave him at the zoo" and "The buffalo is vanishing from the American scene." Johnny's buffalo is evidently a single, individual animal, and the predicate, "enjoyed the peanuts . . . ," applies to him as to a straightforwardly singular subject. But when we say, "The buffalo is vanishing from the American scene," we do not mean by this that "vanishing" applies either to all individual buffaloes or to just one individual buffalo: on the basis of this statement, we do not expect to find any particular buffalo that will do a vanishing act before our very eyes. What is vanishing—that is, coming to have fewer members as the years go by—is a *class* or species of things. Statements about a class or species as such should definitely not be confused with statements about all or some of the members of the class. "The buffalo is a prairie animal" can be written, "**A** the buffalo/prairie animal," or, better, as "**A** buffalo/prairie animal." On the other hand, "The buffalo enjoyed the peanuts . . ." should be written, "**A**$_s$ the buffalo/enjoyed the peanuts . . ." And to represent "The buffalo is vanishing . . ." most precisely, we recommend "**A**$_s$ the buffalo species/vanishing . . ."

(4) *Lack of a quantifier.* "Women are fickle" is, quantitatively, an *indefinite* proposition, at least for our purposes. In everyday life, of course, a quantifier is often understood without being stated. What you must do is try to determine whether a statement is intended to cover all of its subject or part of it. In case of doubt, "some" is the conservative interpretation, while "all" is the interpretation which leads to the logically strongest conclusions.

(5) *Circumstantial quantifiers.* Some sets of words behave very much like the classical **A**, **E**, **I**, and **O**. Consider, for example, the time expressions "always," "never," "sometimes," and "sometimes not." A proposition containing "always" is likely to be related to a "never" proposition in the same way as an **A** proposition is related to an **E**. To make this clearer, one can rewrite the "always" proposition with "times" as a universally quantified subject. "The poor ye have always with you" thus becomes "All times are times when you have the poor with you" or "**A** times/times when you have the poor with you." These revisions certainly do not improve the literary qual-

ity of the statement, but they reveal an important logical feature: the feature, namely, that this proposition has as its contrary and contradictory the propositions "Ye never have the poor with you" and "Sometimes ye do not have the poor with you." The same sorts of features are revealed by revising "Jones never loses" to read "No time is a time when Jones loses" or "**E** times/times when Jones loses." The revised version has, as its clear contrary, "**A** times/times when Jones loses" ("Jones always loses"), and as its contradictory, "**I** times/times when Jones loses" ("Jones sometimes loses").

The following sets of words, among others, can be dealt with in the same way as "always," "never," "sometimes," and "sometimes not": (1) "everywhere," "nowhere," "somewhere"; (2) "everybody," "nobody," "somebody"; (3) "in all circumstances," "in no case," "under some conditions."

In ordinary language we sometimes stack up quantifiers at such a rate that **A, E, I,** and **O** can hardly do justice to the resulting propositions. "All men always do what they think best" is, so to speak, a doubly universal proposition. In treating it as an **A** proposition, however, we can focus on only one quantifier at a time. We can analyze this example either as a statement about all men or as a statement about all times. Classical logic does not give us a propositional form which takes full logical account of both quantifiers in a single reading.

(6) *Other quantifiers.* "Any" and "every" can be read as "all," and "none" can be read as "no." Some nuances of meaning are lost sight of in these translations, but they are not nearly so important as the distinctions ignored in translating all partial and numerical quantifiers as "some." The following, for example, is a valid inference which looks like a syllogism: "Most dogs are mongrels, and most dogs are gentle; hence, some mongrels are gentle." Yet since the only distinction of quantity taken account of in our four forms is the distinction between whole and part, we must translate "most" as "some," and this destroys the validity of the inference. Some dogs might be mongrels, and some might be gentle, but it does not follow from *these* premises that any particular dog is both. It is with some regret, therefore, that we must propose "some" as a translation for all of the following: "a," "a few," "most," "quite a few," "nearly all," "75 per cent," "1,932," etc. Classical logic is not a fully adequate substitute for arithmetic.

Points (4), (5), and (6) can be summed up in this way. The difference between a claim about all of a given subject and part of it is in many ordinary situations a crucial difference. Accordingly, the propositional forms of classical logic are applicable to an extremely broad range of actual statements and arguments, for they capture the difference between whole and part and allow us to pursue its logical consequences systematically and precisely. They do this even in some cases where the words "all" and "some" do not appear (5). For these benefits, however, a price is paid. We must, first, be prepared to *make* the whole-part distinction before we have a proposition suitable for classical forms of inference. In some cases (4), this is difficult, for people do not always state clearly whether their claims cover all of a subject or only some of it. But, second, the distinction between all and part of a subject is the *only* distinction of quantity allowed us in **A-E-I-O** analysis. Thus in some cases (6), we would miss important quantitative distinctions if the classical propositional forms were our only instruments of analysis. As we shall see in the next chapter, one of the most striking features of modern logic is the freeing of quantification from some of these restrictions.

(7) *Exceptives and exclusives*. Propositions like *"None but* the brave deserve the fair" and "Every metal *except* mercury is a solid" are called *exceptive* propositions. The best line to take with negative exceptives ("none but") is to treat them as **A** propositions with subject and predicate reversed. Thus, "None but the brave deserve the fair" becomes "All who deserve the fair are brave." The subject of the negative exceptive becomes the predicate of the corresponding **A** proposition, while the subject of the **A** proposition is the predicate of the exceptive. Be cautious about interpreting negative exceptives as claims about all of their *subjects*. "None but females are mothers" does indeed make a universal claim about its *predicate*. We capture this in our **A** translation, "All mothers are females." But the exceptive was not intended to make a universal claim about its subject. It does not commit us to "All females are mothers." To sum up, "None but *A*'s are *B*'s" should be read as **A** b/a. It does *not* imply **A** a/b.

Affirmative exceptives, such as "Every metal except mercury is a solid," normally involve three distinguishable claims. Our example sentence offers a concise way of making the claims "Mercury is a metal," "Mercury is not a solid," and "Every metal other than mercury is a solid." In general, "Every *A* except *B* is *C*" means "*B* is *A*, and *B* is not *C*, and *A*'s other than *B* are *C*." If we use "*A*–*B*" to represent "*A*'s other than *B*," we can fit affirmative exceptives into our usual symbolic apparatus. Singular affirmative exceptives, such as our mercury example, have the form "A_s b/a, and E_s b/c, and **A** a—b/c." "All students except freshmen were invited" comes out as "**A** f/s, and **E** f/i, and **A** s—f/i," if we use f for "freshmen," s for "students," and i for "were invited."

Propositions like "Friends alone are faithful" and "Only a fool contradicts himself" are called *exclusive* propositions. They should ordinarily be treated in the same way as negative exceptives. That is, our examples may be revised to read, "All who are faithful are friends," and, "All who contradict themselves are fools."

(8) *Other exponibles*. An *exponible* proposition is one which appears to be a simple subject-predicate proposition, but can in fact be expounded, or unpacked, as the *joint* assertion of more than one simple proposition. "Every metal except mercury is a solid" is normally exponible as "Mercury is a metal, *and* mercury is not a solid, *and* all metals other than mercury are solids." Another example was given in 1.1.1. We noted that "All cats and dogs are animals" is equivalent to the two propositions "All cats are ani-

mals" and "All dogs are animals." When we assert that all cats and dogs are animals, we mean to assert *both* of the propositions that can be unpacked from it. Propositions with compound predicates can also stand unpacking. "Cats are soft and furry" should be read as "Cats are soft, *and* cats are furry."

Not every proposition which looks compound is compound. To translate "John and Mary are married" as "John is married, and Mary is married" is to miss the important point that the couple are married to each other. "Jack and Jill went home together" is similarly misunderstood if we translate it as "Jack went home, and Jill went home," for this translation lacks all togetherness. We must recognize in such cases that we have only one claim to deal with, rather than the joint assertion of two claims, but that the claim is a *relational* claim about the elements of an internally complex subject. Both of our examples are, roughly speaking, **A** propositions. "John and Mary" form an internally complex subject; the point in applying the predicate "married" is to assert a relationship between the elements of the subject. In the same way, "Jack and Jill" (together) form an internally complex subject for the relational predicate "went home together."

(9) *Propositions better left for the next chapter: Hypotheticals and disjunctives.* When we introduced **A, E, I,** and **O** propositions in 1.2.2., we pointed out that every statement having one of these forms involves a simple assertion or denial, "with no ifs, ands, ors, or buts." The unqualified application of a predicate to a subject defines a proposition as *categorical*. While **A, E, I,** and **O** are not the only types of categorical propositions, they are extremely well-chosen representatives of the broader family. At least part of the meaning of any other categorical can be preserved by translation into one of our four forms. In the preceding paragraphs we have shown how this work of translation can be carried on. We shall conclude our discussion of propositions by considering two families of propositions which are *not* categorical and which accordingly cannot be handled by an **A-E-I-O** analysis.

"If he doesn't get home by six, he'll miss dinner" is a *hypothetical* proposition. It asserts one predicate of a subject only on the condition that another predicate is asserted first. That is, in our example, the predicate "will miss dinner" is not asserted without qualification, but only *on the condition that* he doesn't get home by six. Note, however, that the condition is not itself asserted of the subject. It is not said, in other words, that he *will* get home late. Accordingly, it is not said categorically that he will in fact miss dinner. What is asserted is a *connection* between his possible late arrival and his possible missing of dinner. There is simply no way of fitting this entire proposition into one of our four forms. ("He who gets home late misses dinner" is about the closest we can come.)

"He is either a man or a mouse" is a *disjunctive* proposition. Neither "man" nor "mouse" is asserted categorically, and we would miss the point of the statement if we treated it as applying a single complex predicate, "man-or-mouse." It is essential to the meaning of the proposition that "man" and "mouse" be considered as distinct predicates, *one or the other* of which belongs to the subject.

Aristotle was well aware of the existence of such propositional forms. Indeed, he discusses a few types of inference involving them. Nonetheless, we shall do best to leave hypothetical and disjunctive propositions out of the picture in this chapter, for we are here concerned with inferences belonging to term logic. Although term relations are important in determining when it makes sense to assert a hypothetical or disjunctive proposition, their behavior in inference is better studied in propositional logic. Instead of presenting an Aristotelian treatment of hypotheticals and disjunctives here, we shall treat "If . . . then . . ." and ". . . or . . ." in part 1 of the next chapter as expressing propositional relations.

EXERCISE FOR SECTION 1.2.3.

Analyze as **A, E, I,** or **O** propositions whenever possible, and identify all logical subjects and predicates.

1. All men by nature desire to know.
2. Everyone in the room except Gruff laughed.
3. Only the wise man is truly free.
4. Five men went up the mountain; four came down.
5. Man is a rational animal.
6. People are funny.
7. Jones can take a vacation whenever he likes.
8. Jones does not take vacations.
9. Jones never takes vacations.
10. His mother gave Johnny an apple or an orange.
11. Johnny and his brothers all like apples and oranges.
12. Cats and dogs are enemies.
13. Ninety-nine out of every one hundred women prefer mink.
14. Although the cost of excellence is sometimes high, it is never too high.
15. A man walked into the house next door.
16. The man who pays attention to the evidence is likely to draw the right conclusion.
17. All but a few swallows had left by December.
18. The man who walked into the house next door had no companions.
19. Only a few swallows had left by December.
20. If Jones comes back soon, then Smith will be surprised, but if Smith is surprised, then either Green won't pay back Black or some geese will turn purple.

2. The syllogism

Certain types of inference involving hypothetical or disjunctive propositions are commonly known as (hypothetical or disjunctive) syllogisms. The type of inference with which Aristotle was most concerned, however, and for which he regarded the name "syllogism" (a synthesis or connection of reasons or statements) as most appropriate, involves reasoning from two categorical premises to a categorical conclusion. It is with this family of inferences—categorical syllogisms—that we shall become acquainted in the present chapter.

Our treatment of the syllogism has three main parts. In the next few pages we shall explain what a categorical syllogism is. Then, in 2.2., we shall consider several techniques for determining whether a given syllogism is valid or invalid. Both 2.1. and 2.2. will be formal in character, though we shall offer concrete examples every step of the way. In 2.3., however, our whole concern will be with the application of syllogistic inference forms to the broadest possible range of everyday situations. Our treatment of inference will thus parallel our treatment of propositions. We shall begin by presenting a few important patterns from formal logic, using prize specimens from ordinary life to illustrate them. We shall conclude by considering ways of applying these patterns to items from ordinary discourse which do not at first glance seem to fit them very closely.

2.1. The categorical syllogism—what it is

Every categorical syllogism is an inference from two categorical premises to a categorical conclusion, but not every such inference is a categorical syllogism. What marks off the syllogism from other types of inference is the way in which term relations asserted in the premises are used to justify the syllogistic conclusion. Every categorical syllogism is an *inference through a middle term*. That is, in a categorical syllogism the relations of two terms to a third term are used as the basis for asserting some relationship of the two terms to each other. The third term is called the "middle" because it is, so to speak, a middleman bringing the other two terms together. To put the point more elegantly, the middle term "mediates" the relations of the other two terms to each other. Through the good offices of the middle term, the "extremes" make some sort of definite contact with each other. Even the best mediator in real life is not always able to achieve a friendly relation between the "extremes" he has to deal with. It is the same in logic. That is, some types of valid syllogism have negative conclusions. It is often an advantage to reach a definite result, however, even if it is a negative one. In a valid syllogism the relations of the extremes to the middle provide a basis for inferring that the extremes *must* be related to each other in a certain definite way.

The points made in the last paragraph will be clarified by an example or two. First consider our old stand-by about Greeks being rational. It is a prize specimen of the most important of the 256 types of categorical syllogism.

<table>
<tr><td>(1) All Greeks are men.
All men are rational.
<hr>All Greeks are rational.</td><td>In symbols: (1) A Greeks/men
A men/rational
<hr>A Greeks/rational</td></tr>
</table>

In (1), "men" is the middle term, "Greeks" and "rational" are the extremes. What makes the argument a syllogism is this. The **A** relationship between the extremes is asserted on the basis of **A** relationships between the extremes and the middle. From their stated relations to the middle, it follows necessarily that the extremes are related in a certain way to each other. Although it is natural to state these term relations in a series of three propositions, the distinctive character of syllogistic inference will perhaps be seen more clearly from the following diagram. We assign each term in the preceding argument a circle. If a relation between two terms is asserted in the argument, we connect the two circles by a line. We arrange the circles so that the subject of a relationship appears below its predicate. We indicate *what* relations are asserted by labeling the lines with block capitals. Our picture of (1) comes out like this:

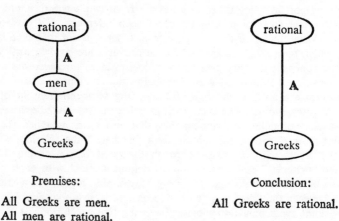

Premises:

All Greeks are men.
All men are rational.

Conclusion:

All Greeks are rational.

The middle circle drops out in the conclusion, but the line we finally draw, connecting the extremes in the conclusion, is deductively justified by the lines in the premises which connect each extreme with the middle. In the argument we bring "Greeks" and "rational" together by way of "men."

We said that the middle term does not always produce an affirmative relation between the extremes. Here is a syllogism with a negative conclusion:

(2) All spaniels are dogs.	(2) **A** spaniels/dogs.
No dogs are cats.	**E** dogs/cats.
No spaniels are cats.	**E** spaniels/cats.

The inferred relation between spaniels and cats, although negative, is definite; the inference is logically necessary. In this sense we can say that the extremes are "connected"—negatively connected—by the middle term, "dog." The **A** relation between "spaniels" and dogs" and the **E** relation between "dogs" and "cats" permit us to infer an **E** relation between "spaniels" and "cats." Our new drawing technique gives us this portrait of (2):

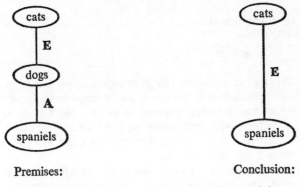

Premises:

All spaniels are dogs.
No dogs are cats.

Conclusion:

No spaniels are cats.

Before laying out the basic varieties of categorical syllogisms, we shall present some arguments which are *not* syllogisms. Pointing out why these arguments are not syllogisms will complete our general account of what a syllogism is.

(3) Socrates is a Greek.
All Greeks are men.
All men are rational.

Socrates is rational.

(4) John is married to Mary.

Mary is married to John.

(5) If Bossy is a cow, then she's an animal.
Bossy is a cow.

She's an animal.

Argument (3) is syllogistic, but not *a* syllogism, for it involves four term relationships rather than three. We shall deal with (3) as a *compound* syllogism in section 3.5.

Argument (4) is valid because "married to" is a two-way, or *symmetrical,* relational predicate (which means that "A is married to B" is a sufficient basis for deducing that "B is married to A"). Thus term relations are indeed involved in this argument, but not the sort of term relations asserted by A, E, I, and O propositions.

Argument (5) looks a bit like a syllogism. Indeed, given the information in the premises of (5), we could construct a syllogism proving the same conclusion:

(6) All cows are animals.
Bossy is a cow.

Bossy is an animal.

But this differs a great deal from (5) as to logical form. The form of (5) is "If *B*, then *A; B;* therefore *A*," where *B* and *A* stand for propositions. Even though it is based on the same information as (5), (6) has the contrasting logical form, "*A c/a, A_s b/c;* therefore A_s *b/a*," where *c, a,* and *b* stand for terms. This illustrates again (see 1, page 26) the point that the categorical syllogism depends on term relations.

The drawing technique developed a few pages ago will be helpful in laying out the various types of simple (that is, three-term) categorical syllogisms. Leaving the syllogistic conclusion aside for a moment, we find three general possibilities for arranging the terms of the premises; we give an example to illustrate each possibility, italicizing the middle term in each example:

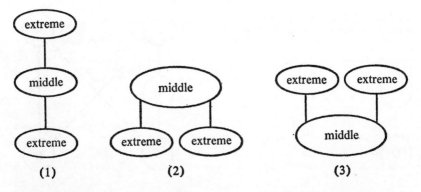

All Greeks are *men*. All collies are *dogs*. All *Holsteins* are cattle.
All *men* are rational. No cats are *dogs*. No *Holsteins* are Herefords.

Remember that the vertical positioning of our circles is meant to indicate the subject-predicate positions of the terms involved. In other words, reading from left to right, our drawings suggest that the middle term can either (1) be predicated of one extreme, while the other extreme is predicated of it, (2) be predicated of each extreme, or (3) have both extremes predicated of it. Thus, if the position of the middle term were our sole basis for classification, we would have to recognize three basic *figures* or shapes for the categorical syllogism.

Since the Middle Ages an additional factor has been taken into account in determining figure. This is the factor we set aside at the beginning of the last paragraph, namely, the conclusion of the syllogism. If we add this factor now, we can see that the first figure splits in two. For the extreme which is predicated of the middle in the premises will appear as the predicate of the conclusion in some syllogisms, and as the subject of the conclusion in others. According to tradition, syllogisms of the latter type are assigned to a distinct figure, the fourth. Labeling each extreme and writing in the conclusion will make the difference between the first and fourth figures clear. An example of a valid syllogism of the type is given beneath each picture:

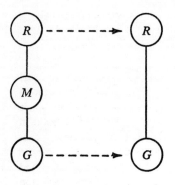

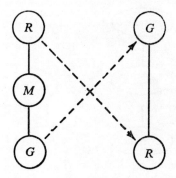

All Greeks are men.
All men are rational.

All Greeks are rational.
First Figure

All Greeks are men.
All men are rational.

Some rational beings are Greek.
Fourth Figure

Each of our four figures has sixty-four *moods,* depending on what combination of **A, E, I,** and **O** relations is asserted. In the premises of a syllogism, each extreme is connected with the middle. Each of these two connections can be an **A, E, I,** or **O** relation. Accordingly, we have 4×4, or 16, possible combinations of premises in each figure. But on the basis of any one of these combinations, any of four relations **(A, E, I,** or **O)** might conceivably be asserted in the conclusion. Accordingly, there are 16×4, or 64, moods in each of our four figures, or 256 possible types of categorical syllogism. (We hasten to say again that not nearly all of the 256 are valid forms of inference.) The two syllogisms considered on pages 52 and 53 are both first figure, but they differ in mood, for the one about Greeks being rational consisted entirely of **A** propositions, while the one about spaniels not being cats had an **A** premise, an **E** premise, and an **E** conclusion. The following (invalid) syllogism has the same *mood* as the argument about Greeks, but it is second *figure* rather than first.

All dogs are animals.
All cats are animals.

All cats are dogs.

If we solve a minor technical problem first, we can use figure and mood labels to identify perfectly the logical form of any categorical syllogism. What the technical problem is will be clear from a comparison of the following first-figure syllogisms:

(A) All married men are husbands.   (B) All husbands are married.
    No husbands are wives.   No wives are husbands.
    _____   _____
    No married men are wives.   No wives are married.

Argument (A) is a valid syllogism. (B) is obviously invalid, since it leads from true premises to a false conclusion. Clearly, then, we do not want to identify (A) and (B) as having the same form. If we compare them more closely, we see what the difference is. In (A), the **A** relationship is between the *subject* of the conclusion and the middle term, while the **E** premise concerns the *predicate* of the conclusion and the middle term. In (B), on the other hand, the **A** relation is between the predicate of the conclusion and the middle term, while the **E** premise concerns the subject of the conclusion and the middle. The difference stands out plainly if we draw both arguments, leaving all irrelevant features out of the picture:

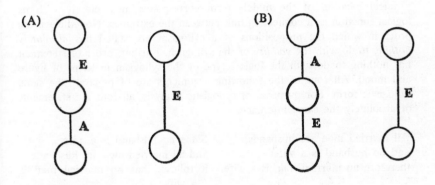

(A)   (B)

The customary solution to the problem is this. We simply agree to list the three term relations of a syllogism in a *standard order* when we wish to designate the mood of the syllogism. We list *first* the **A, E, I,** or **O** relation asserted between the middle term and the *predicate of the conclusion*. We list *second* the relation asserted between the middle term and the *subject of the conclusion*. We list *third* the term relation asserted in the conclusion. The predicate of a syllogism's conclusion is traditionally called the *major term* of that syllogism, the subject of the conclusion is called the *minor term* of the syllogism, and the two premises of the syllogism are named accordingly: the premise composed of the major term and the middle is called the *major premise,* while the premise composed of middle and minor terms is called the *minor premise.* Our agreement as to the order in which we shall list propositions for purposes of mood identification amounts to this, then: we list first the **A, E, I,** or **O** form of the major premise, then the form of the minor premise, and finally we list the form of the conclusion. If we apply this convention to arguments (A) and (B) above, we can easily distinguish their logical forms. (A) comes out as first-figure **EAE**, while (B) can be described as first-figure **AEE**. The main reason for making the labeling distinction is, of course, that first-figure **EAE** syllogisms are valid, while first-figure **AEE** syllogisms are not.

It cannot be stressed too much that the *labeling* order adopted in the last paragraph has no regular connection with the *statement* order of actual syllogistic arguments. Argument (A) is **EAE** in mood, despite the fact that the **E** premise is stated after the **A** premise. In our opinion, the logical form of first-figure syllogisms is *presented* more clearly if first the subject of the conclusion is connected with the middle, and the middle is then connected with the predicate of the conclusion. This order of statement (minor premise, then major premise) has the great virtue of putting the *logically* middle term in the middle of the *stated* premises; in this way the physical location of the middle term corresponds most closely with its logical function as a connecting link between the extremes. Nonetheless, the order in which the propositions of a syllogism are stated has *absolutely nothing* to do with the *validity* of the syllogism. Further, order of statement has nothing to do with the logical type of the syllogism in terms of figure and mood. All four of the following arguments are of precisely the same syllogistic form. For purposes of syllogistic analysis, all four are statements of absolutely the same inference.

All married men are husbands,
and no husband is a wife;
therefore no married man is a wife.

Since no husband is a wife,
and all married men are husbands,
it follows that no married man is a wife.

It must be true that no married men are wives,
since all married men are husbands,
and no husband is a wife.

No husbands are wives;
hence, no married man is a wife,
since all married men are husbands.

If we adopt the labeling procedure described in the last paragraph, we identify all of these arguments as first-figure **EAE**. Our means of identification is this. We first look for the conclusion. This, in each of our four cases, is the proposition that no married men are wives. We call this the conclusion, not because it is *stated* last, (sometimes it *isn't* stated last), but because it is asserted *on the basis of* other propositions. This is indicated by the expressions "hence," "it follows that," and "therefore." Once we have identified the conclusion of a syllogism, the rest is easy. We look for the premise which contains the predicate of the conclusion, and then for the premise composed of the middle term and the subject of the conclusion. The first of these, the major premise, is in all four cases the **E** proposition that no husbands are wives. We list this first, and then the minor premise, which is the **A** proposition, "All married men are husbands." Finally we list the **E** conclusion. We come up with first-figure **EAE**, in every case.

EXERCISE FOR SECTION 2.1.

Identify the figure and mood of each of the following syllogisms. (Bear in mind that not every syllogism is a valid syllogism.)

1. Boys aren't girls, and all Little Leaguers are boys; it follows, therefore, that no Little Leaguers are girls.
2. Palominos aren't mules, since mules aren't horses, and palominos are.
3. All sparrows are birds, and all parrots are birds; hence, no sparrows are parrots.
4. No nightingales are sparrows; all nightingales are songbirds; hence, no songbird is a sparrow.
5. All dogs are animals; hence, so are all Dalmatians, for all Dalmatians are dogs.
6. All brave men fight, for no coward fights, and no brave man is a coward.
7. All waves crest, but undertows don't crest; hence, undertows aren't waves.
8. Everyone who is really absent-minded is a college professor, and no well-informed person is really absent-minded; hence, we may be sure that no well-informed person is a college professor.
9. No well-informed person is a professor, for every professor is absent-minded, and no one who is absent-minded can be well informed.
10. It is true that no dogs are cats, but they (dogs) must all be animals, for all cats are animals.
11. Most dogs are animals, and all collies are dogs; hence, some collies are animals.
12. No tigers are lions, and thus, since all lions are animals, some animals are not tigers.
13. All boiling water bubbles, and some boiling water is salty; hence, some salty things bubble.
14. It's necessarily true, by definition, that all English novelists are novelists, and, as we all know, some novelists are not men; it follows, therefore, in case anyone needs proof, that at least some men are not English novelists.

15. Some sailboats are not rowboats, for some canoes have sails, though none is a rowboat.

16. Some fish are flounder, and no birds are fish; hence, some birds, at least, are not flounder.

17. All steaks are delicious, but they are all expensive, too; hence, sad to say, some delicious things are expensive.

18. Granted that some animals aren't collies; but it's also true that some dogs aren't collies; from this it follows that all dogs are animals.

19. No one who is playing the piano wears mittens; it follows of necessity, therefore, that some who are cold are not piano players, since at least some of those who wear mittens are cold.

20. All English words are of Indo-European derivation, but some Hungarian is not Indo-European; hence, some Hungarian is not English.

2.2.1. *Establishing validity by reduction to the first figure*

Not all of the 256 types of syllogism are valid forms of inference. Some, indeed, are bound to lead you to false conclusions from true premises (AAE in the first figure will do this), the worst thing a form of inference can do. Others will lead you from true premises to conclusions which might, consistently with the premises, be true or false (AAA in the second figure, for example). In the next several pages we shall consider methods for judging correctly whether or not a particular syllogism, or type of syllogism, is valid. Unless a syllogism *guarantees* true conclusions from true premises, we reject it as deductively invalid.

From a formal logician's point of view, the most satisfactory way of establishing the validity of one form of inference is to *deduce* that form of inference from some other form already accepted as valid. There are, in all, twenty-four types of valid syllogism (each of which is referred to as a *valid mood*). As it happens, the validity of twenty-two of these can be deduced from the validity of the two types presented near the beginning of 2.1. In other words, if we can see the validity of these two moods without proof, we shall be able to prove deductively that the other twenty-two moods must also be valid. At the end of our chapter on symbolic logic, we shall show this method at work in a completely rigorous formal system. In the present chapter we shall indicate briefly how the universal moods of the first figure can be used to establish the validity of several other moods.

Since the Middle Ages it has been customary to give names to the valid moods in each figure. Our argument about Greeks being rational was an instance of *Barbara*. The vowels in the name indicate the mood (though not the figure) of the syllogism. The order of the vowels corresponds with the standard labeling order: major premise, minor premise, conclusion. Since our argument about the Greeks was composed of three **A** propositions, the vowels of its name are all *a*'s. We assume from direct inspection that Barbara is valid. Let us see where this gets us. If we change the order of the premises to conform to the standard labeling order, our example of Barbara will look like this:

> **A** men/rational
> **A** Greeks/men   A case of BARBARA
> _____
> **A** Greeks/rational

One way of explaining the validity of Barbara is to say that whenever three terms are so related that the first includes all of the second, and the second includes all of the third, it follows of necessity that the first includes all of the third. In our example, "rational" covers all men in this way, "men" includes all Greeks, and accordingly, "rational" must also be affirmed of all Greeks. Suppose now that "men" had only been said to include *some* Greeks. What would follow? It would follow that "rational," too, must belong to at least some Greeks, that is, to at least those Greeks who are men. We have, in other words, a *particular* mood of the first figure, *Darii:*

> **A** men/rational
> **I** Greeks/men   A case of DARII
> _____
> **I** Greeks/rational

The other universal mood of the first figure is called *Celarent*. Celarent was illustrated in our inference about spaniels not being cats (again, we have transposed the premises to correspond to the standard labeling order):

> **E** dogs/cats
> **A** spaniels/dogs   A case of CELARENT
> _____
> **E** spaniels/cats

In accepting Celarent as valid, we assume without proof that whenever three terms are so related that the first is totally excluded from the second, but the second totally includes the third, then the first must of necessity be totally excluded from the third. "Cats" is totally excluded from "dogs," but "dogs" includes all spaniels; accordingly, "cats" must be totally excluded from "spaniels." Suppose now that the third term had only been said to be partially included in the middle. What would follow? We could conclude only that it partially *ex*cluded the first term. If we were only willing to say that *some* spaniels are dogs, we could only conclude that some spaniels are *not* cats. We have, in other words, another particular mood of the first figure, *Ferio:*

$$\frac{\begin{array}{l}\textbf{E } \text{dogs/cats} \\ \textbf{I } \text{spaniels/dogs}\end{array}}{\textbf{O } \text{spaniels/cats}} \quad \text{A case of FERIO}$$

From Barbara, Celarent, Darii, and Ferio we can proceed by extremely simple steps to most of the other valid moods (two, as we shall see, give difficulty). To justify these steps formally, we must accept three intuitively plausible forms of immediate inference. The first is that **E** propositions which differ only in the order of their terms can be freely substituted for each other. For example, "No dogs are cats" can be freely substituted for "No cats are dogs," and vice versa. It seems clear that these are both statements of the same fact, the fact, namely, that cats and dogs are completely distinct kinds of things. Accordingly, whenever one of these propositions can be inferred, so can the other; and whatever can be inferred with the aid of one of them can also be inferred using the other. Let us see what can be done on the strength of this principle.

To begin with, we can "convert" the **E** premise of Celarent, or the conclusion, or both the **E** premise and the conclusion. By substituting "**E** cats/dogs" for "**E** dogs/cats," we produce a case of *Cesare,* a valid mood of the second figure:

$$\frac{\begin{array}{l}\textbf{E } \text{cats/dogs} \\ \textbf{A } \text{spaniels/dogs}\end{array}}{\textbf{E } \text{spaniels/cats}} \quad \text{A case of CESARE}$$

If we use our original **E** premise, but convert the conclusion of Celarent, we reach *Camenes,* a valid mood of the fourth figure.

$$\frac{\begin{array}{l}\textbf{E } \text{dogs/cats} \\ \textbf{A } \text{spaniels/dogs}\end{array}}{\textbf{E } \text{cats/spaniels}} \quad \text{A case of CAMENES}$$

Note that our case of Camenes is not stated in standard labeling order, for by reversing the subject and predicate of our conclusion we have made "cats" the *minor* term of the syllogism, while "spaniels," which was the minor term in our Celarent, is the *major* term of the new inference. To get the major and minor *premises* into standard labeling order, we must transpose them. An *m* in a mood name indicates that the premises of that mood must be transposed (the *m* is for *mutare*) to achieve a direct tie-in with the appropriate first-figure mood. Written in standard labeling order, our Camenes comes out as:

> **A** spaniels/dogs
> **E** dogs/cats   Camenes in standard labeling order
> ———————
> **E** cats/spaniels

If we convert both the major premise *and* the conclusion of Celarent, we reach *Camestres* in the second figure. (We transpose the premises to achieve a standard order statement of Camestres.)

> **A** spaniels/dogs
> **E** cats/dogs   A case of CAMESTRES
> ———————
> **E** cats/spaniels

Thus, simply by converting the order of the terms in various **E** propositions, we have derived three valid moods from Celarent, two of them in the second figure and one in the fourth figure. It is no accident, by the way, that the name of each of these begins with **C**. The initial letters of the medieval names indicate the first-figure mood from which the named mood can be most simply derived.

We shall now derive three additional moods from Darii. For this purpose we assume that **I** propositions, like **E** propositions, can be converted. We assume, in other words, that "Some men are Greeks" can be freely substituted for "Some Greeks are men," and that "Some rational beings are Greeks" can be used for "Some Greeks are rational." On this basis, we can convert either the minor premise, or the conclusion, or both the minor premise and the conclusion, of Darii. Making these changes in the listed order, and transposing premises where necessary, we reach:

> **A** men/rational
> **I** men/Greeks   A case of DATISI
> ———————
> **I** Greeks/rational

> **I** Greeks/men
> **A** men/rational   A case of DIMARIS
> ———————
> **I** rational/Greeks

> **I** men/Greeks
> **A** men/rational   A case of DISAMIS
> ———————
> **I** rational/Greeks

Datisi and Disamis are third figure, Dimaris fourth figure. In the modern derivation of syllogisms which will be presented at the end of the next chapter, Datisi and Barbara are the only two moods assumed valid without proof. From them, along with two *laws of identity* ("All A are A," and "Some A are A"), all the laws of conversion and all the other valid moods of the categorical syllogism can be rigorously deduced.

Thus far we have derived six second-, third-, and fourth-figure moods from Celarent and Darii in the first figure: three from Celarent and three from Darii. By the same method it is possible to derive three additional moods from Ferio. We leave this as a problem for you in the exercises.

In discussing the *square of opposition* in 1.2.2., we noted that in classical logic a universal claim implies a particular claim of the same quality. For example, "**A** men/mortal" implies "**I** men/mortal," and "**E** cats/dogs" implies "**O** cats/dogs." This general principle, that universal propositions imply corresponding particulars, allows us to derive nine additional valid moods. We can apply the principle in two directions, so to speak. First, from a valid mood with a universal conclusion, we can derive a mood with the corresponding particular conclusion. For example, from Barbar*a* we can derive Barbar*i*:

> *Barbara*
>
> | | | |
> |---|---|---|
> | **A** men/rational | **A** men/rational | |
> | **A** Greeks/men | **A** Greeks/men | A case of BARBARI |
> | **A** Greeks/rational $\rightarrow$ | **I** Greeks/rational | |

Similarly, every valid mood with an **E** conclusion gives us a valid mood with an **O** conclusion. From Celar*ent*, for example, we can derive Celar*ont*:

> *Celarent*
>
> | | | |
> |---|---|---|
> | **E** dogs/cats | **E** dogs/cats | |
> | **A** spaniel/dogs | **A** spaniels/dogs | A case of CELARONT |
> | **E** spaniels/cats $\rightarrow$ | **O** spaniels/cats | |

Moods like Barbari and Celaront are said to have *weakened conclusions,* for they involve drawing a particular conclusion when a universal claim is warranted by the evidence contained in the premises.

We can apply the principle, that universals imply particulars, in another direction. If we have a valid mood containing a particular *premise* (**I** or **O**), we can derive another valid mood by substituting the corresponding universal proposition. Moods reached in this way are said to have *strengthened premises,* the point being that more evidence is contained in the premises than is necessary for drawing the desired conclusion. For example, the second **A** premise in *Darapti* is not needed in order to draw the **I** conclusion. Darapti is reached by substituting an **A** proposition for the **I** premise of Datisi.

A men/rational
A men/Greeks   A case of DARAPTI
─────────────
I Greeks/rational

In some cases, strengthening a premise in one mood will yield exactly the same result as weakening the conclusion of another mood. Strengthening the **I** premise of Ferio gives us Celaront, for example. This is not always the case, however. The second **A** premise in Darapti cannot do any more work for us than the **I** premise in Datisi; in both cases, we can only draw a particular **(I)** conclusion. Similarly, strengthening the major premise of Dimaris, in the fourth figure, does not make it possible to draw a stronger conclusion than the **I** conclusion already in Dimaris itself. In contrast, strengthening the **I** premise of Ferio *does* make it possible to draw a stronger conclusion; we would have the premises of Celarent, and could accordingly draw a universal conclusion.

By the methods illustrated in the last few paragraphs, we can account for all but two of the twenty-four valid moods. *Baroco* and *Bocardo* still remain. These are the moods mentioned earlier as giving difficulty. Aristotle's way of deriving these moods from Barbara is strikingly different from any of the tactics we have so far considered. It will be clearer if we first set out examples of the three moods involved. Our examples of Baroco and Bocardo will involve false propositions, but that of course has no effect on the *validity* of these forms of inference. What counts for validity is that an inference form should never lead us *from* truth *to* falsity. If there is falsity in our premises, we should not be surprised if there is falsity in our conclusions.

Barbara	BAROCO	BOCARDO
A men/rational	**A** men/rational	**O** Greeks/rational
A Greeks/men	**O** Greeks/rational	**A** Greeks/men
A Greeks/rational	**O** Greeks/men	**O** men/rational

We establish Baroco and Bocardo as valid by *trying* to make them out as *in*valid. This leads in each case to a flat contradiction. Specifically, denying the conclusion of a syllogism in Baroco or Bocardo leads to the denial of one of the premises of the same syllogism. If we wish to assert the premise, therefore, we must also be willing to assert the conclusion, which is to say that the original syllogism was valid.

If Baroco were *in*valid, it might lead us from true premises to a false conclusion. Let us see what follows, then, if we assume that the premises we have given for Baroco are true and the stated conclusion false. If "O Greeks/men" is false, then, by the square of opposition, "A Greeks/men" must be true. But if we combine "A Greeks/men" with "A men/rational," the major premise of Baroco, we have the premises of a syllogism in Barbara leading to the conclusion "A Greeks/rational." This, however, is the direct denial of "O Greeks/rational," the minor premise of our Baroco. We began by assuming that both premises stated for Baroco were true. By denying the conclusion of Baroco, we have now been able to show that one of the premises is false. Clearly, "O Greeks/rational" cannot be both true *and* false. We assert, accordingly, that Baroco is valid, for the assumption that its premises are true and its conclusion false has led us to a contradiction.

The same approach does nicely for Bocardo. Denying the conclusion gives us "A men/rational." From "A men/rational" and "A Greeks/men" we reach the conclusion (again by Barbara) "A Greeks/rational." "A Greeks/rational" is, however, the contradictory of "O Greeks/rational," the major premise of our Bocardo. The assumption that a syllogism in Bocardo is *in*valid (that its premises might be true and its conclusion false) has led us to a contradiction. We assert, accordingly, that Bocardo is valid.

The technique applied in reducing Baroco and Bocardo to Barbara is called *reductio per impossibile,* reduction by means of the impossible—the impossibility referred to being the contradiction resulting from the joint acceptance of Barbara and rejection of Baroco or Bocardo. This technique can be used to give somewhat more rigorous proofs of Darii and Ferio than those given earlier. If we begin with the case of Ferio on page 62, for example, we can justify the inference by (1) denying its conclusion, thus obtaining "A spaniels/cats," and (2) combining this with "E dogs/cats" (the major premise of our Ferio) to deduce "E spaniels/dogs," which contradicts the minor premise of our original inference. The syllogism used here is, of course, Cesare from the second figure. We must accept Ferio, therefore, if we accept Cesare, for to accept Cesare while rejecting Ferio has led us to a contradiction. Reduction *per impossibile* thus gets us from Ferio back to Cesare. But Cesare itself can be derived, as we have seen, from Celarent in the first figure. Accordingly, we must accept Ferio if we accept Celarent.

EXERCISES FOR SECTION 2.2.1.

I. Try reducing the syllogisms in the exercise on page 59 to valid moods of the first figure. That is, start from the syllogism given, and work back to a valid first-figure syllogism by appropriate conversions and transpositions. (This will be impossible, of course, when the syllogism is invalid.)

II. Three of the syllogisms in exercise I reduce to Ferio. Construct examples of two other types of syllogism which can also be derived from Ferio.

III. Reduction *per impossibile*.

  1. Reduce Ferio itself to a universal mood of the first figure, using the technique of reduction *per impossibile*.
  2. Both Disamis (third figure) and Festino (second figure) can be reduced to Celarent (first figure) *per impossibile*. Show how this can be done, using the terms "good," "existing," and "beautiful" as, respectively, the minor, middle, and major terms of Disamis, and as the major, minor, and middle terms of Festino.

2.2.2. Establishing invalidity by example

A few pages ago we declared that only twenty-four of the 256 moods of the categorical syllogism are valid. By now we have established that these twenty-four *are* valid, but we have yet to show that the remaining 232 are not. In the next few paragraphs we shall discuss one of the simplest methods for showing *in*validity.

The method is to try to construct a specific argument whose premises are obviously true and whose conclusion is false. If it is possible to construct such an example for a given mood of the syllogism, then the mood is deductively invalid, for a deductively valid form of inference is one which *never,* in any instance, leads from true premises to false conclusions. A single case in which this occurs is thus sufficient to show that a mood has some flaw.

Aristotle used this method himself. So far as modern, purely formal logic is concerned, it is not an ideal method. A logician constructing a purely formal system wants to avoid introducing concrete terms into his work. A theoretically superior means of showing invalidity is to *deduce* it, as we deduced the validity of the valid moods in 2.2.1. This can indeed be done. If two moods are rejected as invalid on the basis of direct inspection, it is possible to demonstrate the invalidity of the other 230. The chain of demonstrations involved here is, however, long and complicated. And in practice, the construction of concrete, obviously invalid examples can be crushingly effective, as the following story shows.

Wiseacre and Knownothing were candidates for mayor of Barbaraville. The chief issue of their hotly fought campaign was the desirability of fluoridation for the town's water supply. Each candidate assailed the other's position on this issue at every opportunity. Wiseacre was in the habit of arguing: "Everyone in town who's too stupid ever to try anything new is against fluoridation. Knownothing is against fluoridation. Clearly, my friends, Knownothing is just too stupid ever to try anything new." Knownothing's logic was curiously similar, though his terms were different. *He* argued that "Everyone in town who's silly enough to go off the deep end about every scientific fad that comes along is in favor of fluoridation. Wiseacre is in favor of fluoridation. Clearly, Wiseacre is just one of those silly people who go off the deep end about every new fad that comes along." Those citizens of Barbaraville who were trying to decide the issue on its merits were perplexed. The premises of both arguments were incontestably true: all the faddists in town *were* for fluoridation, and all those who resisted change of any sort *were* against it. For whom was one to vote, if the suggested conclusions did indeed follow from the stated premises? Then, one day late in the campaign, a local logician, Sylas Gism, pointed out that it was possible to construct an argument quite similar in form to those of Wiseacre and Knownothing which led from obviously true premises to an absurdly false conclusion: "Wiseacre is a candidate for mayor of Barbaraville. Knownothing is a candidate for mayor of Barbaraville. Therefore Knownothing is Wiseacre." Since he was an honest logician, Gism pointed out that his argument did not have *exactly* the same form as those of the candidates (both of his premises, and both terms of his conclusion, were singular). He then proposed an argument which was strictly identical in logical form to those which had been used in the campaign: "All cats are animals. Fido, the firehouse dog, is an animal. Therefore Fido is a cat." The good citizens of Barbaraville saw from this parallel example that both Wiseacre and Knownothing had been using horribly invalid arguments. Accordingly, they elected Sylas Gism, the logician, mayor. What *we* see from the story is that **AAA,** second figure, is an invalid mood of the categorical syllogism. If it were true that Acb and Aab implied Aac, it would be absolutely impossible to construct an argument of this form whose premises were true and whose conclusion was false.

2.2.3. Testing for validity by rules

From a practical standpoint, the simplest way of testing a syllogism for validity is to ask whether it violates any of the *rules* discussed in the next page or so. As it happens, no valid syllogism violates any of these rules, while every invalid syllogism violates at least one of them. We shall comment in detail only on those rules which are most frequently violated in ordinary life. We shall show, in discussing Rule 7, exactly what was wrong with the political arguments considered in 2.2.2.

Rule 1. If one premise is negative, the conclusion must be negative.

Rule 2. If the conclusion is negative, one of the premises must be negative.

Rule 3. If *both* premises are negative, no conclusion follows. The first three rules are called *rules of quality.*

Rule 4. If one premise is particular, the conclusion must be particular.

Rule 5. If both premises are particular, no conclusion follows. Rules 4 and 5 are *rules of quantity.* Many modern logicians would add a rule of quantity paralleling Rule 2: if the conclusion is particular, one of the premises must be particular. The same issues are at stake here as in the controversies over the classical square of opposition (1.2.2.). Some light will be shed on these issues in 2.2.4.

The first five rules apply without regard to figure. A syllogism of mood **OOA** violates four of them no matter what its figure. We might accordingly call these *mood rules.* Among them they rule out fifty-two of the sixty-four moods in each figure. One of the remaining moods must be rejected in all figures in accordance with Rule 6. Each of the remaining eleven moods is valid in at least one figure.

The next two rules are known as *distribution rules.* Before stating them, we must explain what distribution is.

A term is said to be *distributed* in a proposition if the proposition makes or implies a claim about everything mentioned by the term. For example, the *subjects* of *universal* propositions are *distributed,* since the whole point of a universal proposition is to make a claim about all of a subject. By the same token, the *subjects* of *particular* propositions are *undistributed.* All that an **I** or an **O** proposition claims is that its predicate belongs or does not belong to *some* of its subject. If we recall the immediate inferences used in reducing second-, third-, and fourth-figure syllogisms to valid moods of the first figure, we see at once that the *predicates* of *affirmative* propositions are undistributed. Both **A** and **I** "convert" to **I**. From "All men are mortal" it follows that *some* mortals are men, and "Some men are mortal" is exactly equivalent to "Some mortals are men." **E** converts fully, so that "No cats are dogs" involves a universal claim about dogs as well as cats. Accordingly, the predicates of **E** propositions are distributed. Strange to say, **O** predicates are also distributed. The universal claim is buried quite deep here, but perhaps we can bring it to light. It amounts to this. When we say that some cows are not brown, we are excluding *those* cows (whichever ones they may be) from the *whole class* of brown things. If we had some way of picking out just those cows that are not brown, we could say, of them, *"None of these cows is brown."* Conversely, we would say, *"No* brown things are among these cows." An **O** proposition thus does involve a claim about all the things mentioned by its predicate, the claim being that nothing covered by the predicate is included in one part, at least, of the subject. We conclude, then, that the *predicates* of *negative* propositions, as well as the *subjects* of *universal* propositions, are distributed. The following table shows all. Distributed terms are circled and labeled with a *D*.

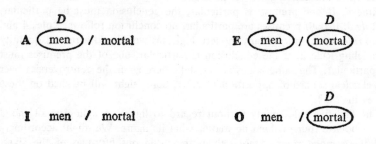

We can now state the two distribution rules for categorical syllogisms.

Rule 6. Any term distributed in the conclusion must be distributed in the premises. Distributing a term is making or implying a universal claim. If no such claim is involved in the premises, there is no basis for it in the conclusion. Violations of this rule are called *illicit processes of* (1) *the major term or* (2) *the minor term,* depending on which term is distributed in the conclusion but not in the premise. Since we are all eager to jump to conclusions at one time or another, violations of Rule 6 are frequent. At least some people, some of the time, would be taken in by arguments like the following:

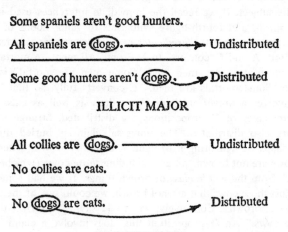

Rule 7. The middle term must be distributed at least once. Violators of this rule are said to commit the fallacy of *undistributed middle*. This is probably the most frequently committed of all formal fallacies. It is the logical "principle" underlying most guilt-by-association arguments. It seems to have a profound psychological plausibility, in spite of the fact that it can lead us from plain facts to absurd conclusions.

We have already given examples illustrating this fallacy. The arguments that "proved" Wiseacre to be a faddist and Knownothing to be against anything new both depended upon undistributed middles. As we saw in 2.2.2., roughly the same form of argument led from the propositions that Wiseacre and Knownothing were both candidates for office to the surprising conclusion that Wiseacre was Knownothing. And exactly the same form of argument was used to show that the firehouse dog, Fido, is a cat. Instead of adding further examples, we shall explain here precisely why the fallacy is a fallacy. We hope that this explanation will be effective logical medicine for preserving the world from at least a few undistributed middles.

The trouble with an undistributed middle term is that it does not really function as *a* term. If each premise involves a claim only about a part of the middle, there is no guarantee that the claim made in one premise has anything to do with the claim made in the other. It might be that one extreme is related to one part of the middle, while the other extreme is related to some quite distinct part of it. In such cases the middle might as well be two terms. To illustrate this situation, we shall draw a heavy line down the middle of a circle representing the middle term in the Wiseacre-Knownothing arguments. The line is to indicate that entirely separate parts of the middle term's range of reference *may* be involved in the claims made by the two premises.

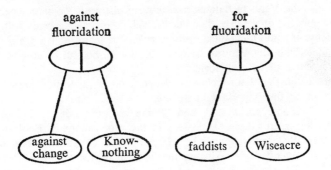

To make the point still clearer, we provide an imaginary X ray of the middle term in our example about Fido.

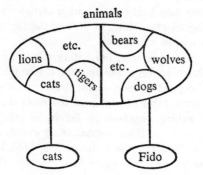

animals

EXERCISE FOR SECTION 2.2.3.

Identify the rule or rules violated by each of the invalid syllogisms in the exercise on page 59.

2.2.4. Boolean algebra and Venn diagrams

The Venn technique for testing inferences for validity is mechanical drawing applied to logic. If you follow three simple rules for drawing a picture of the premises of a syllogism, then, if the syllogism is valid, you will find that you have already drawn the conclusion. And if drawing the premises does not involve drawing the conclusion, then the syllogism is invalid.

Although the Venn technique is strictly mechanical, we shall begin our explanation of it at a fairly theoretical level. The drawing rules will make better sense if some theoretical basis is given for them, and a grasp of the theory underlying the Venn technique will also be helpful in understanding certain features of modern logic.

Theoretically, the Venn technique depends on a nineteenth-century reinterpretation of the important expressions "All . . . are . . . ," "No . . . are . . . ," "Some are . . . ," and "Some . . . are not . . ." The new interpretation relates these expressions to the propositions of Boolean algebra, a formal system invented by George Boole (1815–64), one of the founders of modern logic. Whether the Boolean interpretations of "All . . . are . . ." and the rest achieve a close fit with our ordinary usage of such expressions is a controversial question which we shall take up at the end of this chapter. Our purpose now is to explain the Venn technique, not to criticize or justify its basic theoretical assumptions. With this aim in mind, we shall simply state the new interpretations of the expressions in question, and note the logical consequences.

Our discussion in the next few paragraphs will draw on the distinction made in 1.2.1. between sentences and propositions. To save ourselves the trouble of constantly repeating such phrases as "The expressions 'All . . . are . . . ,' 'No . . . are . . . ,' 'Some . . . are . . . ,' and 'Some . . . are not . . . ,' " we herewith draw a distinction between **A, E, I,** and **O** propositions and **A, E, I,** and **O** *sentences.* By an **A** sentence, we mean a written or spoken expression, such as "All men are mortal," which contains the *words* "All . . . are . . . ," and which might be used to state a proposition. As we have seen earlier, *which* proposition a sentence states is not determined completely by the words composing it. The context in which a sentence is used sometimes indicates that the sentence is meant to express one kind of proposition, sometimes another, sometimes no proposition at all. By an **A** *proposition,* we mean an **A** sentence *interpreted* as having the *meaning* normally ascribed to such sentences in classical logic. The point of the distinction is that the classical and Boolean interpretations of identical sentences treat those sentences as expressions of quite different claims or propositions. On a classical interpretation, for example, a simple "All . . . are . . ." sentence (an **A** sentence) expresses an affirmative claim about the whole of some given subject, while a simple "Some . . . are . . ." sentence (an **I** sentence) expresses an affirmative claim about some undetermined part of a given subject. In each case the content of the claim is specified by a distinct term, the predicate. We shall see that the Boolean reading of such sentences is quite different. Even prize specimens of the classical propositional forms can be given new, Boolean readings.

We begin with **I** and **O** sentences. On the Boolean reading, every **I** or **O** sentence asserts the existence of at least one thing of a certain kind. "Some cows are brown," for example, is said to assert that there exists at least one thing which is both brown and a cow. Another way of stating the Boolean interpretation is this. "Some cows are brown" asserts that the *class* of things which are both cows and brown has at least one member. Still another way of putting the Boolean reading is to say that "Some cows are brown" *denies* that the class of brown cows is *null* (empty). Our three Boolean versions of the **I** sentence, "Some cows are brown," are all intended to mean the same thing. The last version, however, comes closest to the standard symbolic representation used in Boolean algebra. Using B and C for "brown" and "cow," we write, in Boolean notation:

$$BC \neq O$$

In general, the Boolean proposition corresponding to an **I** sentence combines the subject and predicate of the sentence into a single complex term and then asserts that that complex term refers to something existing in the world. More precisely, the Boolean *inequation* denies that the complex term does *not* refer to anything, by denying that the class of things the term refers to is null.

O sentences are also to be read as denying that certain classes are empty. For example, "Some cows are *not* brown" is to be read as a denial that the class of *non*-brown cows is empty. That is, if we construct a complex term from "cow" and the *contradictory* of "brown," we can read, "Some cows are not brown," as asserting that that complex term refers to something existing in the world. (See 1.1.2. for a discussion of terms and their contradictories.) We can indicate the contradictory of a term by writing a bar above the term, or above the code letter standing for the term. We can thus write, "Some cows are not brown," in Boolean notation, as:

$$B\overline{C} \neq O$$

We can read the preceding sentence either as a denial that the class of non-brown cows is empty, or as an assertion that there exists at least one non-brown cow.

A and **E** sentences are to be read as assertions that certain classes *are* empty or, in other words, as denials that there exist any things of a specified kind. For example, "All men are rational" is read as denying the existence of any *non*rational men, or as asserting that the *class* of nonrational men is empty. "No men are rational," on the other hand, is a denial that there exist any rational men, an assertion that the class of rational men is null. We can thus rewrite:

"All men are rational"   as $\overline{\text{Rational}}$ men$=O$"
"No men are rational"   as   "Rational men$=O$"

Putting the last few paragraphs together, we come up with the following list of Boolean counterparts to the classical interpretations of **A, E, I,** and **O** sentences:

Instead of "**A** men/rational"   read,   "$\overline{\text{Rational}}$ men$=O$"
    "   " "**E** men/rational"   "   "Rational men$=O$"
    "   " "**I** men/rational"   "   "Rational men$\neq O$"
    "   " "**O** men/rational"   "   "$\overline{\text{Rational}}$ men$\neq O$"

If we use small *a* and *b* as code letters for general terms in the classical formulas, we can achieve a more compact comparison. We omit quotation marks for clarity.

$$A ab \qquad A\overline{B}=O$$
$$E ab \qquad AB=O$$
$$I ab \qquad AB\neq O$$
$$O ab \qquad A\overline{B}\neq O$$

You may ask at this point whether it makes any logical difference which set of symbols you use. So far as mere symbols are concerned, the answer is "no." The Boolean notation is slightly more cumbersome than the notation we have been using, but this difference is trivial from the standpoint of formal logic. What really counts is not the symbols, but the meaning behind the symbols. Or in other words, what counts ultimately for logical purposes are the propositions expressed (the claims made) by our two sets of sentences, rather than the symbols used to express those claims. Now we pointed out, when we introduced the symbols **A, E, I,** and **O,** that certain words used in ordinary language with a variety of meanings are given single, fixed meanings in classical logic. "Some," for example, often means "not all" in ordinary life; it *always* means "at least some part" of a subject in classical logic. Our chief purpose in introducing a special symbol for "some" was to highlight the fixed and specific meaning that the word is given in classical logic. By the use of this symbol, we have been able to write *sentences,* such as "**I** cows/brown," which were clearer expressions of the *meaning* given *by classical logic* to such ordinary sentences as "Some cows are brown." The logical *sentence,* $B\neq O$, on the other hand, is a way of expressing clearly the meaning given *by Boolean algebra* to the same ordinary sentence, "Some cows are brown." What this boils down to is that classical logic and Boolean algebra give us different accounts of what we mean (which claim or proposition we are expressing) when we say, "Some cows are brown." At the end of this chapter we shall take up the question of which interpretation comes closer to what we *do* mean. Now, however, we would like to point out that the two interpretations really are very different from each other. This is revealed by differences in what they imply.

The fundamental difference is that, on the Boolean analysis of **A, E, I,** and **O** sentences, one can never, under any circumstances, deduce an **I** or an **O** sentence from any combination of **A** and **E** sentences. From *"All* men are mortal," for example, it no longer follows that *some* men are mortal, and from "No cows are purple" we can no longer infer *"Some* cows are not purple." A moment's reflection on the last few paragraphs will show why these inferences are invalid on the Boolean reading of the sentences involved. If "All men are mortal" is taken to mean only that there *aren't* any *non*mortal men, we certainly cannot conclude from this sentence that there *are* any *mortal* men. In the same way, from the proposition that there do *not* exist any cows that *are* purple, we have no right to conclude that there *do* exist any cows that are *not* purple. In general, then, $A\overline{B}=O$ does not imply $AB\neq O$, and $AB=O$ does not imply $A\overline{B}\neq O$. As we shall see, this lack of connection between universal and particular sentences of the same quality means that nine syllogisms which are valid in classical logic (the nine with weakened conclusions or strengthened premises) come out invalid on a Boolean interpretation of the sentences normally used to express them. Fortunately for practical purposes, there is an easy way to retrieve the nine lost moods in most ordinary cases. We need only assert that the major, minor, and middle terms of our syllogisms are not null. If we are prepared to add this assertion to our original premises, all the usual consequences follow. This, however, does not lessen the enormous *theoretical* difference between classical and Boolean readings of the same sentences.

And now here are the drawing rules for the Venn picture test for syllogistic validity.

(1) A term or class is to be drawn as an enclosed area.

(2) The assertion that a class is empty is drawn by shading the area representing the class.

(3) The assertion that a class is not empty is drawn by placing an X somewhere inside the area representing the class.

If you follow these rules in drawing the premises of a syllogism, then, if the syllogism is valid on a Boolean reading, you will find that you have already drawn the conclusion. And if drawing the premises does not involve drawing the conclusion, then, on a Boolean reading, the syllogism is invalid.

A few examples will show the ease and beauty of the technique. Let us start with "cats." In accordance with Rule 1, we draw a circle.

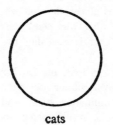

cats

If we wish to deny that there are any cats, we shade the circle, following Rule 2:

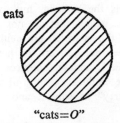

"cats=O"

To show that there *are* cats, we follow Rule 3:

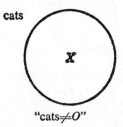

"cats≠O"

To draw **A, E, I,** and **O** sentences, we need a subject circle and a predicate circle. As we have seen, the Boolean reading of such sentences involves combining subjects and predicates to make up complex terms. Accordingly, we overlap our two circles, thus:

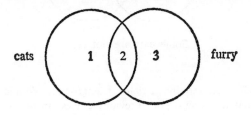

The overlapping of the two main areas gives us three distinct classes to work with. The area marked 1 will be used to say that there are, or are not, *non*-furry cats. Area 2 is the domain, null or not null, of furry cats. Area 3 is for furry things, if any, that are not cats. The area outside both circles could be used for things which are neither cats nor furry, but this rather indefinite class does not concern us here. We can now draw the Boolean versions of **A, E, I,** and **O** sentences with "cats" as subject and "furry" as predicate. (We could also, but will not, use this background to draw sentences with "furry" as subject and "cats" as predicate.)

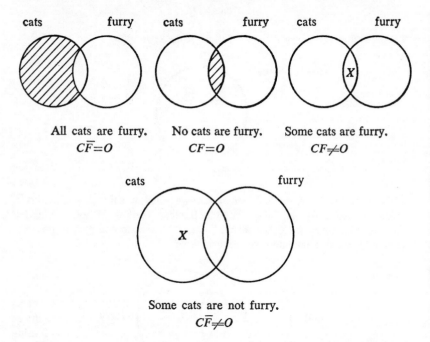

All cats are furry.
$$C\overline{F}=O$$

No cats are furry.
$$CF=O$$

Some cats are furry.
$$CF\neq O$$

Some cats are not furry.
$$C\overline{F}\neq O$$

Drawing syllogisms requires a richer background. We add a third circle, taking care that it overlaps both previous circles. In this way we shall be able to take account of every combination of **A, E, I,** and **O** sentences we may encounter. We add "animal" as a third term. The list below the diagram identifies each of the seven areas we shall be using in our drawings of syllogisms composed of the three terms "cats" (*C*), "furry" (*F*), and "animals" (*A*).

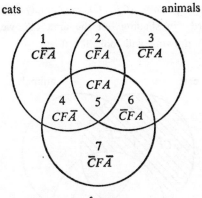

1. $C\overline{F}\overline{A}$. We use this area to assert the existence or nonexistence of cats that are neither furry nor animals.

2. $C\overline{F}A$. Cats that are animals, but not furry.

3. $\overline{C}\overline{F}A$. Non-furry animals other than cats.

4. $CF\overline{A}$. Cats that are furry, but not animals. Bear in mind that we have not yet asserted either that there are, or that there are not, any such creatures. An area which neither contains an X nor is shaded should be regarded as the background for assertions. Sketching such a background commits us to nothing.

5. CFA. This central sector is for cats, if any, that are both furry and animals.

6. $\overline{C}FA$. Furry animals other than cats.

7. $\overline{C}F\overline{A}$. Furry things which are neither cats nor animals.

We shall now use this background to test the Boolean Barbara. Let us take as an example, the argument "All cats are furry, and all furry things are animals; hence, all cats are animals." In Boolean notation, and using an arrow ($\rightarrow$) for "therefore," the argument can be written:

$$(C\overline{F}=O \ \text{ and } \ F\overline{A}=O) \rightarrow C\overline{A}=O$$

In drawing the minor premise $(C\overline{F}=O)$, we simply ignore the "animal" circle. In other words, in shading out the area $C\overline{F}$, we shade out both $C\overline{F}A$ and $C\overline{F}\overline{A}$. Our drawing will look like this:

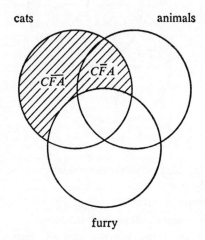

All cats are furry. $(C\overline{F}=O)$

Now we must draw $F\overline{A}=O$. Here we ignore the "cats" circle. That is, we shade out both $CF\overline{A}$ and $\overline{C}F\overline{A}$. The result is:

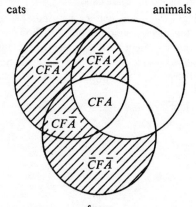

$$\begin{array}{ll}\text{All cats are furry.} & (\overline{F}C = O)\\ \text{All furry things are animals.} & (F\overline{A} = O)\\ \hline \text{All cats are animals.} & (C\overline{A} = O)\end{array}$$

We now look to see whether we have drawn the conclusion $C\overline{A} = O$ in the course of drawing the premises. Lo! We have! The $C\overline{A}$ area consists of the two smaller areas, $CF\overline{A}$ and $C\overline{F}\overline{A}$. The first of these was shaded out in drawing the major premise, while the second was shaded out in drawing the minor premise. There simply isn't any room left in our picture for existing things (X's) which are cats but not animals. We award Barbara a judgment of "valid."

The Venn drawing technique effectively exposes the fallacy of undistributed middle. The argument "All cats are furry, all animals are furry; hence, all cats are animals" happens to have a true conclusion; the inference, of course, is still invalid. In Boolean notation the argument can be written:

$$(C\overline{F} = O \text{ and } A\overline{F} = O) \rightarrow C\overline{A} = O$$

In drawing the minor premise, we shade out $C\overline{F}A$ and $C\overline{F}\overline{A}$. In drawing the major premise, we shade out $\overline{C}\overline{F}A$ and $\overline{CFA}$, with the result:

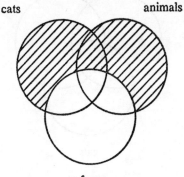

$$\begin{array}{ll}\text{All cats are furry.} & (C\overline{F} = O)\\ \text{All animals are furry.} & (A\overline{F} = O)\\ \hline \text{?All cats are animals?} & ?(C\overline{A} = O)?\end{array}$$

UNDISTRIBUTED MIDDLE

For the conclusion to be true, however, the entire area, $C\overline{A}$, would need to be shaded out. *Part* of this area *is* shaded out, the $CF\overline{A}$ part. But our drawing of the premises has left the area $CF\overline{A}$ entirely untouched. Since it is still possible to insert an X in this area, the syllogism is declared invalid. For all we can tell from the stated premises, there might *be* cats that are not animals.

EXERCISE FOR SECTION 2.2.4

Draw Venn pictures of the first ten syllogisms in the exercise on page 59, and assess as valid or invalid accordingly.

We shall now draw some syllogisms containing **I** and **O** sentences. Since the same class cannot be both empty and not empty, we must be careful not to insert X's in shaded areas or shade areas which have X's in them. We must also be careful not to place an X in a subarea when the premise we are drawing has to do only with a larger area. Suppose, for example, that we set out to draw "Some cats are furry" on the following background:

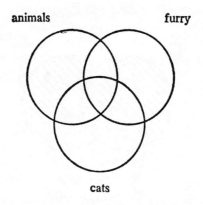

"Some cats are furry" concerns the CF area. To draw the proposition, we must place an X somewhere in this area. When we set out to do this, however, we notice that CF consists of the two subareas, CFA and $CF\overline{A}$. Now our proposition does not tell us to put an X in CFA, nor does it tell us to put one in $CF\overline{A}$. Where, then, shall we put the X in CF? To avoid drawing more than we have been told to draw, we must locate the X *on the line* separating CFA from $CF\overline{A}$, thus:

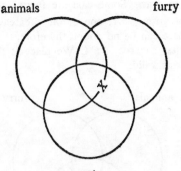

Some cats are furry.
$CF \neq O$

When we inspect a picture at the end, we must, of course, interpret X's on the line accurately. In our last picture, for example, we have not drawn either the proposition "Some animals are furry" *or* the proposition "Some animals are not furry." In general, an X on the line at the end of a picture is the sign of an invalid syllogism.

We can avoid some X's on the line if we make it a practice to draw universal premises before particular ones. Suppose, for example, that we set out to draw the syllogism "Some cats are furry, all cats are animals; hence, some animals are furry." If we draw the universal minor premise first, we have the following:

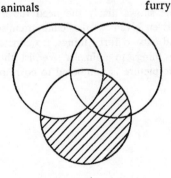

All cats are animals.
$C\bar{A} = O$

Now if we set out to draw "Some cats are furry," the problem of an X on the line does not arise. $CF\overline{A}$, one of the subareas of CF, has already been shaded out. There can be no doubt, therefore, that all X's in CF must be placed in the other subarea, CFA. We place it there, with the result that our syllogism tests valid.

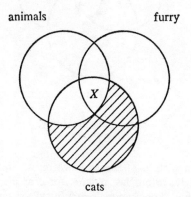

Some cats are furry.
All cats are animals.
———————————————
Some animals are furry.

$$(CF\neq O)$$
$$(C\overline{A}=O)$$
$$\overline{(AF\neq O)}$$

The Venn technique shows nicely the need for a universal premise in deductive inference. Even given *six* particular premises about the relations of cats to animals and cats to furry things, no conclusion is justified as to the relation of furry things to animals. We list the premises below the picture. Each X in the picture is numbered to correspond with the premise it represents.

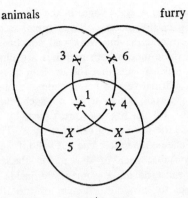

1. Some cats are animals. *(CA≠O)*
2. Some cats are not animals. *(CĀ≠O)*
3. Some animals are not cats. *(C̄A≠O)*
4. Some cats are furry. *(CF≠O)*
5. Some cats are not furry. *(CF̄≠O)*
6. Some furry things are not cats. *(C̄F≠O)*

The array of *X*'s on the line justifies no conclusion whatever as to the emptiness or non-emptiness of *FA*, *F̄A*, or *FĀ*.

We conclude by drawing a case of Barbari, one of the valid classical moods whose Boolean counterpart is invalid.

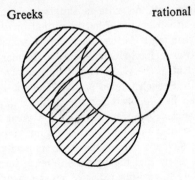

All men are rational.   *(MR̄=O)*
All Greeks are men.   *(GM̄=O)*
_____
Some Greeks are rational.   *(GR≠O)*

The conclusion calls for an X somewhere in the GR area, but, search as we may, we find no X's in the picture of our premises. The same result is reached with all nine moods having weakened conclusions or strengthened premises: in each of these moods both premises are universal and the conclusion is particular, which means that the Boolean counterpart of the conclusion expresses an affirmative existential claim—a claim that there does exist something of a certain kind—while no such claim is contained in the premises. In each case the premises are drawn by shading out certain areas, but in each case the conclusion calls for an X. The Boolean counterparts of these moods can be made to come out valid if we *add* to our original premises the assertion that each of our major classes has at least one member—that there must be an X somewhere inside each of our three circular areas. Indeed, to save our example of the Boolean Barbari, we need only assert that the minor term "Greeks" is not null. The only subarea of G in which there is room for an X is the area GMR, since our original premises have declared the rest of G to be null.

EXERCISE FOR SECTION 2.2.4.

Draw Venn pictures of the last ten syllogisms in the exercise on page 59 and 60, and judge valid or invalid accordingly.

3. The syllogism in everyday thinking

People do sometimes talk or write in simple, standard-form syllogisms, but not usually. If a proposition is either important or debatable, there may be some point in presenting it as the conclusion of a syllogism. In a recent issue of *Foreign Affairs*, Paul-Henri Spaak, a former Secretary-General of NATO and President of the U. N. General Assembly, applied Barbara to an important aspect of French foreign policy. "General de Gaulle's thinking might be summed up in simplified form as follows: 'Every great country must have its own nuclear deterrent. France is a great country. Therefore France must have her own nuclear deterrent.' I am convinced that nothing will persuade him to advance beyond the stark simplicity of this syllogism." This example shows nicely that the central inference form of classical logic can be directly applied to real-life issues of great practical importance.

More often, however, the everyday applications of the syllogism are indirect. In the next few pages we shall consider ways of using the principles of classical logic to analyze arguments which are not actually syllogisms.

We saw in 1.2.3. that many sentences other than **A, E, I,** and **O** sentences can be analyzed as statements of **A, E, I,** or **O** propositions. In the next few pages we shall see that many arguments which do not look much like our arguments about Greeks being rational can nonetheless be analyzed as syllogistic inferences. For convenience we shall simply list a few of the more useful ways of reducing actual arguments to syllogistic form.

3.1. Removing synonyms

Every syllogism involves three and only three terms. Obviously, however, if two terms have exactly the same meaning, there is no harm in replacing one with the other in stating or analyzing an argument. "All *Greeks* are rational because *they* are all *men,* and all *human beings* are rational" is a perfectly good argument. "They" is clearly a stand-in for "Greeks," while in this context "men" and "human beings" are used as synonyms. Be cautious, though, about assuming that different expressions are synonyms. As we stressed in Chapter 1, *one* word or phrase is sometimes used with various meanings in the same argument. "Men," for example, in the argument "All rational animals are men, no men are women; hence, no women are rational animals." Now if the *same* word can have different meanings, it stands to reason that different words are likely to differ in meaning at least slightly in most contexts. No matter what the words are, if only three kinds of things are mentioned in an argument composed of **A, E, I,** or **O** propositions, you can treat the argument as a syllogism. But be sure your count of kinds of things is accurate.

3.2. Removing denials of **A, E, I,** and **O**

Every syllogism is an inference through a middle term. "Immediate" inference is inference without a middle term. We have already considered some forms of immediate inference. The classical square of opposition is a network of immediate inferences, and the "conversion" of **E** and **I** propositions is a technique of immediate inference used in deriving other valid syllogistic moods from Barbara and Celarent in the first figure. In the next few paragraphs we shall show how these and other types of immediate inference can be used to reduce nonsyllogistic arguments to syllogistic form.

The contradictory relationships in the square of opposition allow us to replace the denial of one **A, E, I,** or **O** proposition by the assertion of another. If it is false that *some* men are *not* rational, it must be true that *all* men *are* rational. Accordingly, we can transform the following argument into our old stand-by illustration of Barbara. "All Greeks are men. It is not true that some men are not rational. Hence, all Greeks are rational." By a similar route we can proceed to our spaniels argument from the following. "It is false that some dogs are cats. It is also false that some spaniels are not dogs. Therefore no spaniels are cats." The first premise *denies* "**I** dogs/cats." We can thus replace it by the *assertion* of "**E** dogs/ cats." The second premise denies "**O** spaniels/dogs," and thus can be replaced by the assertion of "**A** spaniels/dogs." These transformations give us our favorite case of Celarent. By the same principle, "not-**A**" can be replaced by **O**, and "not-**E**" can be replaced by **I**.

3.3. Reduction to three terms by obversion and conversion

A family of interesting and sometimes useful immediate inference forms is generated from the relation between a term and its contradictory. As we saw in 1.1.2., a term and its contradictory (such as "voter" and "nonvoter") divide up the world in such a way that one of them belongs to whatever, and only to whatever, the other does not belong to. Everything is either a voter or a nonvoter, for example, and nothing is both. Accordingly, to the extent we are willing to affirm a term of a subject, we must be willing to deny that its contradictory belongs to that subject, and to the extent we deny the term, we must be willing to affirm the contradictory. If we were willing to say that all citizens of the United States are voters, we would be committed to the proposition that no citizens of the United States are nonvoters. If we are only willing to claim that a term applies (affirmatively or negatively) to *part* of a subject, the same principle holds: we are committed to the opposite (negative or affirmative) partial application of the term's contradictory. If some citizens are voters, then they are *not* nonvoters; and if some are *not* voters, it follows that the same some *are* nonvoters.

This form of immediate inference is called *obversion*. The rules for obverting an **A, E, I,** or **O** proposition are quite simple: (1) Change the quality of the *proposition*, from affirmative to negative, or from negative to affirmative; and (2) change the quality of the *predicate*—for a positive term, substitute the negative term which is its contradictory; for a negative term, substitute the contradictory positive term. (This last clause means that the examples given in the last paragraph also work backward: from "**A** citizens/voters" we went to "**E** citizens/nonvoters"; we can also start at the other end, going from "**E** citizens/nonvoters" to "**A** citizens/voters.") Using bars for negative term expressions, as we did in 2.2.4., we can write the formulas for obversion as follows:

$$Aab \leftrightarrow Ea\bar{b}$$
$$Aa\bar{b} \leftrightarrow Eab$$
$$Eab \leftrightarrow Aa\bar{b}$$
$$Ea\bar{b} \leftrightarrow Aab$$
$$Iab \leftrightarrow Oa\bar{b}$$
$$Ia\bar{b} \leftrightarrow Oab$$
$$Oab \leftrightarrow Ia\bar{b}$$
$$Oa\bar{b} \leftrightarrow Iab$$

By appropriate obversions, we can sometimes reduce arguments with more than three terms to standard syllogistic form. For instance, if both premises of the following five-termed argument are obverted, we reach a case of Barbara.

| No men are nonrational. | $\xrightarrow{\text{obv}}$ | All men are rational. |
| No Greeks are non-men. | $\xrightarrow{\text{obv}}$ | All Greeks are men. |

All Greeks are rational.

Some pairs of terms in ordinary language are contradictories with respect to a specific subject matter. If a given argument is itself limited in range, it is valid to obvert from one such term to another. For example, as we ordinarily use them, "true" and "false" are contradictories with respect to statements and propositions: every statement or proposition is either true or false, and no statement or proposition is both. This does not mean that "true" and "false" are contradictories pure and simple, for there are many things in the universe which are neither true nor false (cabbages and kings, for example). Still, if we are concerned only with statements or propositions, we can validly proceed from "X is not true" to "X is false," or from "X is not false" to "X is true." Since the *universe of discourse* of the following four-termed argument is in fact appropriately limited, we can reduce the argument to a syllogism.

| Everything he says is false. | $\longrightarrow$ | Nothing he says is true. |

Everything you've said has been said by him.

Nothing you've said is true.

Terms which are *contraries* but not contradictories, give rise to immediate inferences somewhat like obversion, but slightly weaker. If we know that one of a pair of contrary terms *does* belong to a subject, we can be sure that the other contrary does not belong to it, but we can make no inference in the other direction. If we know, for example, that all the coals on the stove are hot, we can be sure that none of them is cold. Furthermore, if we knew that all the coals were cold, we could infer that none was hot. But from the fact that one contrary does *not* belong to a subject, we cannot infer that another one does. From "**E** coals/hot" we cannot infer "**A** coals/cold" or even "**I** coals/cold." Some or all of the coals in question might be merely warm or cool.

It may be worth noting again here that in everyday life "Some *A*'s are *B*'s" often is meant to suggest that "Some *A*'s are not *B*'s." "Some," in other words, often means the same as "only some." This is not always the case, however, even in everyday life, and **I** and **O** clearly do not have this meaning. Accordingly, we shall not count "Some *A*'s are *B*'s; therefore, some are not" as valid.

EXERCISE FOR SECTION 3.3.

Obvert each of the following.
1. No responsible person is a nonvoter.
2. Some of his listeners were unconvinced by his arguments.
3. A few cherry trees had blossoms by Easter.
4. At least two of us were not present at the meeting.
5. His argument was not valid.
6. You've never had it so good.

In 2.2.1. we "converted" **A** and **E** propositions in deriving other valid syllogistic moods from Barbara and Celarent. If obversion and conversion are combined, additional transformations are possible. Converting and then obverting the first premise of the following argument reduces it to a case of Camenes:

$$\textbf{E } \overline{\text{dogs}}/\text{spaniels} \xrightarrow{\text{conv}} \textbf{E spaniels}/\overline{\text{dogs}} \xrightarrow{\text{obv}} \begin{array}{c} \textbf{A spaniels/dogs} \\ \textbf{E cats/dogs} \\ \hline \textbf{E cats/spaniels} \end{array}$$

Similar tactics may be used to reduce the following *six*-termed argument to a case of Celarent:

$$\cfrac{\textbf{A } \overline{\text{birds}}/\overline{\text{owls}} \xrightarrow{\text{obv}} \textbf{E } \overline{\text{birds}}/\text{owls} \xrightarrow{\text{conv}} \textbf{E owls}/\overline{\text{birds}} \xrightarrow{\text{obv}} \textbf{A owls/birds}}{\textbf{E owls/cows}}$$

with the top:
$$\textbf{A birds}/\overline{\text{cows}} \xrightarrow{\text{obv}} \textbf{E birds/cows}$$

If you are wondering whether A and O propositions convert, the answer is "partly" for A's, and "no" for O's. In classical logic, "All men are mortal" implies "Some mortals are men." In general, A $ab \rightarrow$ I ba. We must note that the Boolean counterpart of this form of inference is invalid. From the fact that there are no men who are nonmortal, it does not follow that there exist any mortals at all, let alone any who are men. From $A\bar{B}=O$, we have no right to infer $BA \neq O$. As for O sentences, they do not convert on any interpretation. From "Some animals are not cows" it does not follow that some or all cows are not animals, or that some or all cows are animals.

MORE EXERCISES FOR SECTION 3.3.

1. Assuming that all nightingales are birds, what follows as to the truth or falsity of each of the propositions listed below? What steps of immediate inference, or moves within the square of opposition, justify your answer?
   a. Some birds are nightingales.
   b. No nightingales are non-birds.
   c. Some non-birds are nightingales.
   d. Some non-nightingales are not non-birds.
   e. All non-birds are non-nightingales.

2. If we assumed that some mice were not rodents, what would follow as to the truth or falsity of the propositions given below? Justify your answers.
   a. Some rodents are mice.
   b. Some non-rodents are not non-mice.
   c. No non-rodent is a mouse.
   d. All non-mice are rodents.
   e. All non-rodents are non-mice.

3.4. Supplying unstated propositions

Shakespeare has Julius Caesar say, "Yon Cassius has a lean and hungry look. Such men are dangerous." What is this supposed to mean? If Mark Antony had been a diligent syllogizer, he would have drawn the unstated conclusion, "Cassius is dangerous." There are many arguments in ordinary life which can be analyzed as syllogisms if we are ready to add a proposition to those actually stated. We often let others "draw their own conclusions," as in the example from Shakespeare. More often, we state a conclusion but give only one premise for it. Caesar could have said, "Cassius is dangerous, for he has a lean and hungry look," or, "Everyone with a lean and hungry look is dangerous; hence, Cassius is dangerous." Our first revised version becomes a syllogism if we add as a premise, "Such men are dangerous," while our second revision of Shakespeare needs "Cassius has a lean and hungry look" to become a syllogism. All told, then, we have three different condensations of the same syllogism. In Shakespeare the conclusion is left unstated. In our first alternative to Shakespeare the major premise is left unstated; the minor premise is left out of our other version. The two *stated* propositions in each case form an *enthymeme*. An enthymeme, in other words, is a pair of propositions intended as either the premises, or as the conclusion and one premise, of a syllogism. As can be seen from our examples, there are three large families of enthymemes:

(Everyone with a lean and hungry look is dangerous.)
Cassius has a lean and hungry look.

Cassius is dangerous.

FIRST-ORDER ENTHYMEME—MAJOR PREMISE UNSTATED

Everyone with a lean and hungry look is dangerous.
(Cassius has a lean and hungry look.)

Cassius is dangerous.

SECOND-ORDER ENTHYMEME—MINOR PREMISE UNSTATED

Everyone with a lean and hungry look is dangerous.
Cassius has a lean and hungry look.

(Cassius is dangerous.)

THIRD-ORDER ENTHYMEME—CONCLUSION UNSTATED

We have frequently advised caution in applying the abstract patterns of formal logic to ordinary discourse. A special caution must be offered in connection with enthymemes. People do not always *mean* for us to add propositions to their arguments. There is a difference between asserting a conclusion and suggesting one, and also a difference between actually using a proposition as a syllogistic premise and presenting an argument which *would* be a syllogism if the proposition were added. When we treat two propositions as an enthymeme, we assume, in effect, that something is *missing* from the statement of an argument. This is not always a safe assumption. When, for example, Descartes said, "I think, therefore I am," *he*, at least, did not think he was omitting anything. One of his contemporaries suggested that the argument should have been stated as: "All who think, exist. I think.

Therefore, I exist." Descartes emphatically rejected this as a translation of what he had meant to say. The added premise is necessary, of course, if we are to have a syllogism. Perhaps, indeed, it is necessary to get a valid inference. Descartes, however, seems to have meant not to propound a syllogism, but to draw a unique immediate inference. Whether the inference is valid is a nice philosophic problem. This problem will be completely overlooked if we make the mistake of rewriting Descartes' stated argument. Adding a premise to the key argument of a great philosopher is thus a dubious undertaking. In some cases it is best to assume that a person has not only meant what he said, but said all that he meant.

But of course we sometimes do *not* say all that we mean. We sometimes do not say what is obviously true and obviously relevant. If someone says, "Of course spaniels aren't cats; they're dogs," it seems fair to assume that "Dogs aren't cats" is somewhere in his mind. This proposition "hardly needs saying," except in a logic book, since everyone knows it. Still, the proposition does complete the argument. Without it, the argument has the form "(All) *S*'s are *D*'s, therefore (no) *S*'s are *C*'s." This is so obviously invalid that it seems only just and proper to add, "No *D*'s are *C*'s," which is true, and relevant to the argument at hand.

Propositions are sometimes omitted for less commendable reasons than that they are obviously true. Some people deliberately leave shaky premises unstated in order not to focus attention on them. This tactic is especially effective if the shaky premise *looks* like another proposition which is true, though irrelevant. Our examples of excluded middle in 2.2.2. might have been even more persuasive if they had been stated as first-order enthymemes. "Knownothing is against flouridation. This shows that he's just too stupid ever to try anything new" might have been effective because of the resemblance between "All who are stupid are against fluoridation" and "All who are against fluoridation are stupid." The latter proposition would make the argument formally valid, the former does not. But the former proposition, at least in our story, happened to be true, while the latter was questionable. If either of these propositions is brought out into the open, Wiseacre's argument against Knownothing is likely to be exposed as a bad one. If we are allowed to focus on "All who are against fluoridation are fools," we are liable to see that the argument, though valid, does not establish the truth of its conclusion, since it has a possibly false premise. If we focus on "All fools are against fluoridation," we are liable to see that the argument is invalid and thus does not establish its conclusion even though both premises happen to be true. The argument is likelier to succeed if neither of these propositions is stated.

Whatever the motive for not stating a proposition, it is useful to be able to transform an enthymeme into a full syllogism. If you are given two **A, E, I,** or **O** propositions, one as a premise and one as a conclusion, it is relatively easy to supply a relevant proposition for the other premise. The two stated propositions must, of course, have a term in common—otherwise, they cannot possibly be parts of the same syllogism. The situation will thus be as follows. The premise will state a relation between the common term and some second term, while the conclusion will state a relation between the common term and a third term. The *missing* premise will involve a relationship between the second and third terms (the terms not related already in the stated propositions). Suppose, for example, that we are given as an enthymeme "**A** Greeks/men, therefore **A** Greeks/rational." The common term of the enthymeme is "Greeks." The premise states a relation between "Greeks" and "men,"; the conclusion states a relation between "Greeks" and "rational." We must now look for a proposition which relates the terms not related in the enthymeme, "men" and "rational." "**A** men/rational" does just this, and hence, adding it to the enthymeme gives us a syllogism.

If we are given two *premises* and left to draw our own conclusions, our problem, once again, is to supply a proposition which relates the two terms not already related in the enthymeme we begin with. "**A** Greeks/men" and "**A** men/rational" lead naturally enough to the conclusion "**A** Greeks/rational." Here we have been given a third-order enthymeme. The "common term" in a third-order enthymeme is the middle term of the corresponding syllogism. The terms not related in the enthymeme are the extremes of the syllogism, and these, of course, are the terms to be related in a syllogistic conclusion.

The search for a missing proposition aims at supplying what someone or other "had in mind" or "meant" when he stated part of a syllogism. Unless you are a mind reader, you will sometimes find it impossible to say which of several possible syllogisms the propounder of an enthymeme did actually have in mind. In some cases, considerations of logical economy have some weight in determining what should be filled in as "the" missing premise or conclusion. Suppose, for example, that someone argues that since all Herefords are cattle, some cattle are brown. If we treat the argument as an enthymeme, we know at once that "the" missing premise must have something to do with "Herefords" and "brown." Now presumably our informant does not think that *no* Herefords are brown, for this proposition is not only false, but it fails to turn the enthymeme into a *valid* syllogism. "**O** Herefords/brown" can be rejected on the same grounds. But it is hard to choose between "**A** Herefords/brown" and "**I** Herefords/brown." Both are true propositions, and both will give us a valid syllogism. Adding the first gives us a case of Darapti; adding the second yields a case of Datisi. On the basis of logical economy, we may be inclined to choose "**I** Herefords/brown," for we do not *need* to claim that all Herefords are brown in order to establish the conclusion that some cattle are brown. The second A premise in Darapti accomplishes no more than the I premise in Datisi.

Similarly, given the premises A*ab* and A*bc,* we can draw either A*ac* or I*ac* as a conclusion. Considerations of logical economy may prompt us to fill in A*ac.* The premises are strong enough to establish a universal conclusion. It would be something of a waste of logical power, therefore, to draw only a particular conclusion.

To sum up, our policy for completing enthymemes should be this. We look for a proposition which (1) is true and (2) turns the enthymeme into a valid syllogism. In choosing a *premise,* we look for the *weakest* proposition that meets both requirements. In supplying a *conclusion,* we prefer the *strongest* proposition that meets both requirements.

An enthymeme should be *rejected* if no one proposition can be found which satisfies both of the requirements stated in the last paragraph. As noted earlier, there are cases in which one imagined proposition meets one of the requirements, while another proposition meets the other requirement. Such enthymemes should be rejected. Our enthymeme about Knownothing is an example of this situation. Here is another example. "He can't possibly have a phone, since he's not listed in the directory." "The" missing premise must be an A proposition relating having a phone to being listed in the directory. The two possibilities which present themselves are "All who are listed have phones" and "All who have phones are listed." Of these possibilities, the first is fairly plausible as a proposition; it tends to meet our first requirement. It does not meet our second requirement, however, for "A listed/have phones, E_s he/listed, therefore E_s he/has phone" commits the fallacy of illicit major. The second possibility, "A have phones/listed," meets our second requirement: it produces a valid syllogism when added to the enthymeme. It is, however, a somewhat shaky premise. Some people have unlisted numbers, after all. Since no *one* proposition meets both of our requirements, we reject the enthymeme.

EXERCISE FOR SECTION 3.4.

Identify each of the following as a first-, second-, or third-order enthymeme, supply the "missing" proposition, and assess the soundness of the resulting argument.

1. It must be a good mink coat. It's expensive, isn't it?
2. We know that all roses are flowers. It follows, therefore, that some flowers are red.
3. All my senses have failed me in the past; it follows, therefore, that they are not to be trusted now.

4. I admit that all bank robbers are scoundrels, but I'll have you know that none of my friends is a bank robber.
5. Many Americans have grown up among automobiles. Surely, therefore, at least a few Americans are able to fix their cars when things go wrong with them.

3.5. Supplying links in syllogistic chains

Toward the end of 2.1., we mentioned, as a *multiple* syllogism, the argument "Socrates is a Greek, all Greeks are men, all men are rational, therefore Socrates is rational." We have here two enthymemes which are related to each other in a very interesting way: the unstated conclusion of one is the unstated premise of the other. If we supply the same proposition twice, we come up with the following pair of valid syllogisms:

> Socrates is a Greek.
> All Greeks are men.
> _____
> (Socrates is a man.)

> (Socrates is a man.)
> All men are rational.
> _____
> Socrates is rational.

A chain argument of this kind is called a *sorites*. Finding the missing links in the following soriteses by the author of *Alice in Wonderland* will be a useful and delightful exercise to conclude our treatment of the syllogism.

EXERCISE FOR SECTION 3.5.

In each of the following examples, taken from Lewis Carroll's *Symbolic Logic,* the premises of a valid sorites are given. What conclusion is finally to be drawn in each case? Obvert and convert when necessary.
1. Babies are illogical. Nobody is despised who can manage a crocodile. Illogical persons are despised.
2. My saucepans are the only things I have that are made of tin. I find all *your* presents very useful. None of my saucepans are of the slightest use.
3. No ducks waltz. No officers ever decline to waltz. All my poultry are ducks.
4. No terriers wander among the signs of the zodiac. Nothing that does not wander among the signs of the zodiac is a comet. Nothing but a terrier has a curly tail.

5. Puppies that will not lie still are always grateful for the loan of a skipping rope. A lame puppy would not say "thank you" if you offered to lend it a skipping rope. None but lame puppies ever care to do worsted work.

6. All my sons are slim. Nobody is healthy who takes no exercise. Gluttons are always fat. No daughter of mine takes any exercise. (Treat "daughter" as "non-son.")

7. Things sold in the street are of no great value. Nothing but rubbish can be had for a song. Eggs of the Great Auk are very valuable. It is only what is sold in the street that is really *rubbish*.

8. Any remedy for bleeding which fails to check it, is a mockery. Tincture of Calendula is not to be despised. When you cut your finger, you will find *any* remedy useful which will check the bleeding. All mockeries are despicable.

9. No birds, except ostriches, are nine feet high. There are no birds in this aviary that belong to anyone but *me*. No ostrich lives on mince pies. I have no birds less than nine feet high.

10. Promise breakers are untrustworthy. Wine drinkers are very communicative. A man who keeps his promises is honest. No teetotalers are pawnbrokers. One can always trust a very communicative person.

11. No kitten that loves fish is unteachable. No kitten without a tail will play with a gorilla. Kittens with whiskers always love fish. No teachable kitten has green eyes. No kittens have tails unless they have whiskers.

12. When I work a logic example without grumbling, you may be sure it is one that I can understand. These sorites are not arranged in regular order, like the examples I am used to. No easy example ever makes my head ache. I can't understand examples that are not arranged in regular order, like those I am used to. I never grumble at an example, unless it gives me a headache.

13. Any idea of mine that cannot be expressed as a syllogism is really ridiculous. None of my ideas about pancakes are worth writing down. No idea that fails to come true can be expressed as a syllogism. I never have any really ridiculous idea that I do not at once refer to my lawyer. My dreams are all about pancakes. I never refer anything to my lawyer unless it is worth writing down.

14. No shark ever doubts that it is well dressed. A fish that cannot dance a minuet is contemptible. No fish is quite certain that it is well dressed unless it has three rows of teeth. All fishes except sharks are kind to children. No heavy fish can dance a minuet. A fish with three rows of teeth is not to be despised.

15. Animals are always mortally offended if I fail to notice them. The only animals that belong to *me* are in that field. No animal can guess a

conundrum unless it has been properly trained in high school. None of the animals in that field are badgers. When an animal is mortally offended, it always rushes about wildly and howls. I never notice any animal unless it belongs to me. No animal that has been properly trained in high school ever rushes about wildly and howls.

16. All the dated letters in this room are written on blue paper. None of them are in black ink, except those that are written in the third person. I have not destroyed any that I can read. None of those on one sheet are undated. All that are not checked are in black ink. All Brown's letters begin with the words "Dear Sir." Those written on blue paper are all destroyed. No letter on more than one sheet is checked. No letter that begins with the words "Dear Sir" is written in the third person.

17. The only animals in this house are cats. Any animal is suitable for a pet if it loves to gaze at the moon. When I detest an animal, I avoid it. No animals are carnivorous unless they prowl at night. No cat fails to kill mice. No animals ever take to me except what are in this house. Kangaroos are not suitable for pets. None but carnivora kill mice. I detest an animal that does not take to me. Animals that prowl at night always love to gaze at the moon.

4. Some problems concerning what logic is about

By now you have done a fair amount of work *in* logic, or more precisely, in one important branch of deductive logic. We would like to use this work now as a basis for raising some problems in the philosophy *of* logic. Our purpose will not be to solve these problems, for that would take us beyond our subject. We are convinced, however, that a clearer and more useful view of the ground we have already covered can be gained if we survey the whole field from a broader philosophical viewpoint. Our aim, then, will be to push right up to the borders of logic without getting quite beyond them. We do not wish to lay down a philosophic position on the place of logic in the nature of things, but we are convinced that a look at some of the positions which *might* be taken will reflect some light on the logical terrain covered earlier in the chapter.

The central question in the philosophy of logic is perhaps this: What is logic about? The best answer we can give to this question without going beyond the borders of logic is probably, "Logic is about terms, propositions, and inferences, and their formal relations." A philosopher might accept this as a description of the proximate or immediate subject matter of logic, but he would be likely to push the original question a step further by asking, "What are terms, propositions, and inferences about? What is the *ultimate* subject matter of logic? What is logic *really* about?" We can bring these questions down to earth by recalling some points and problems from earlier parts of our own work. We said in 1.1.1., for example, that terms both mention things and express ways of looking at things. How, we may ask, do these two aspects of a term fit together? *How* is it that terms mention things, how do they express concepts; what exactly do our terms and ideas have to do with the real things they are about? Or for that matter, *do* the basic units of our discourse always have some bearing on real things? This question was touched on in 2.2.4., when we referred to the controversy among logicians as to the proper interpretation of **A, E, I,** and **O** sentences. The propositions of classical logic all seem to claim some sort of existence for their subjects, while the propositions of Boolean algebra either assert or deny the existence of things of a certain kind. The controversy, then, has to do with the "existential import" of **A, E, I,** and **O** sentences and propositions. Another question we have rubbed against several times is this. To what extent do the fixed meanings and necessary truths of formal logic have application in ordinary language and life? "To no extent at all," some philosophers have said. "You cannot step into the same river twice, for new waters are ever flowing in upon the old." Since we ourselves are also always changing, at least physically, a serious problem is raised here. If logic is about terms, propositions, and inferences which are fixed and unchanging, then, ultimately, it may not be "about" anything real at all. Or so the argument goes.

The philosopher's question thus raises several hard problems. We shall concentrate on two of these, one a traditional problem, the other a relatively modern issue, the issue of *existential import*. Even in a simple statement of it, this issue must be broken down into two questions: Which interpretation of **A, E, I,** and **O** *sentences* should be preferred in various contexts, the Boolean or the classical? And secondly, if we are willing to defend the classical interpretation in some cases, what shall we say about **A, E, I,** and **O** *propositions* concerned with nonexistent subjects? We shall have an easier time with both of these questions if we devote some attention first to the traditional problem of "universals." Simply stated, the problem is this: What is there about things which allows us to talk about them in universal (that is, general) terms? For a single proper name, such as "Greta Garbo," we can find a single individual covered by the name. Accordingly, if we ask, "What is the term 'Greta Garbo' about?" the answer seems simple enough: "The term 'Greta Garbo' refers to Greta Garbo. It's her name." But what about a general term, like "square"? What, if anything, does "square" name? This square: □ ? Perhaps, but certainly not in the same way that "Greta Garbo" names Greta Garbo. For one thing, "square" can be used to designate other squares without any shift in meaning. "Greta Garbo" does shift in meaning if it is used to designate anyone besides *the* Greta Garbo. We shall see that general terms have other peculiarities which keep them from naming things in quite the same way as singular terms. Since most of what we say is said in general terms, it is a matter of practical importance to be aware of these peculiarities. Although we shall not take a stand on the philosophical problem of universals, some of our remarks on the logical functions of general or universal terms will be of practical value. The whole discussion will clear the ground for a logical treatment of existential import. Both the problem of universals and the problem of existential import are special forms of the philosophical question "What is logic (really) about?" For in both cases we are asking about the relation between language and reality. If the immediate subject matter of logic is terms, propositions, and inferences, then a consideration of how these units of discourse are "about" reality will help us to see what logic itself is really about.

4.1. The problem of universals (what general terms are about)

Before we consider the problem of universals, some rather basic points should be made about the use of general terms. To begin with, we can point out that the use of any one general term involves us in a more or less definite web of commitments concerning the use of other terms. Every general term, in other words, is part of a linguistic scheme, or network, or system. When we call something a spaniel, for example, we are committed to calling it a dog; and we are also committed to *not* calling it a collie, a Pekingese, a terrier, or any other breed of dog. To identify a bird as a robin implies a willingness to deny that it is a cuckoo or a chickadee, and a willingness to admit that it normally has feathers, is capable of flying, and so on. What we *mean* by "spaniel" is a certain breed of dog, and what we *mean* by "robin" is a certain kind of bird. As we stressed in the last chapter, most words in ordinary language are inherently vague. On the whole, ordinary language is not a very tight system. For example, a person who says that a piece of ground is covered with "plants" may be committing himself to nothing more than the presence of mushrooms, yet someone else may understand him to have implied that there are leafy, green things in the area. This is to say that the web of commitments surrounding a general term is sometimes a loose one. But still, using even the vaguest of general terms implies *some* commitment to affirming or denying that *some* other terms apply to the subject at hand. If the ground is covered with plants in some sense, it is not a barren waste.

One aspect of the point we have just made deserves further attention: normally, general terms go together in layers and clusters. Some are more general than others, so that we have layers of specificity and generality. "Spaniels," "dog," and "animal" are not merely different general terms, they have different orders of generality: "spaniel" is more specific than "dog," while "animal" is more general. But further, a more general, general term ordinarily has a well- or ill-defined set of specific terms "under" it. "Spaniel," "collie," and "Pekingese" belong to the cluster of specific terms under "dog." "Black Angus," "Hereford," and "Holstein" are part of the set of specific terms under "cattle." "Dog" and "cattle" are together specific in relation to the more general term "animal." We can refer to each of these sets of relatively specific terms as a *generic* cluster, since the more general term which holds the set together is, technically speaking, a logical *genus*. To continue on a technical level, the members of a generic cluster are the logical *species* of the genus involved. For a logician, "spaniel" and "collie" are species of the genus "dog." "Dog" and "cattle" are species of the genus "animal." "Red" and "green" are logical species (not, of course, biological species) of the genus "color."

The points made in the last two paragraphs may sound abstractly technical as we have stated them, yet they are involved in every case of knowledge in everyday life. We could say that a person simply doesn't know what he is talking about unless he is aware of the species-genus relations of the terms he is using. A child who uses "robin" to name an individual red and brown speck in his back yard does not know the meaning of the word, and not knowing the meaning of the word, he does not know as much as, say, his mother, about the speck in their yard.

So far as the problem of universals is concerned, the points we made about general terms can be summed up in this way. As we normally use them, general terms do not merely point to bare and isolated individual things. Rather, they characterize things in their similarities or dissimilarities to other things. A general term can indeed be used to designate an individual, but not purely *as* an individual. When we refer to "that robin over there," we are talking about a distinct, individual thing, but we are designating it *as* a-thing-of-a-certain-kind—which is to say that we are referring to it as similar to some individuals (other robins) and different from other individuals (cuckoos, chickadees, and collie dogs). We can now refine our original statement of the problem of universals. Instead of asking, somewhat vaguely, what there is in things which allows us to talk about them in general terms, we can ask any or all of the following questions. What is there about an individual which allows us to classify it with other individuals? What relation is there between the characteristics an individual has in *common* with other individuals and that which makes it a really existing individual distinct or separate from all other individuals? Or, more simply, what, really, is similarity, and what do we mean by "dissimilarity"? We shall survey the chief competing philosophical answers to these questions when we have made one further point about general terms.

Our immediate aim in the last few paragraphs has been to show that the use of some quite ordinary words involves us in a complicated web of logical relationships. We wish now to make a contrasting point, namely, that no matter how tight and complex a web we weave around a thing by applying a general term to it, there is always room for the use of other general terms to describe the same individual. No one description of anything can possibly be the *only* true description of it. People learn the logic of species-genus relations quite naturally, but the point we wish to make now is either seldom learned or easily forgotten. Everyone assumes at some time or other that if his view of a subject is correct, then any view different from his own must be flatly wrong. We wish to show that this assumption is itself unwarranted.

The basic reason it is wrong to assume that any one description of a subject is the only one possible is that every general term *omits* mentioning many features of the things to which it applies. Being a mother and being a Hereford, for example, are not the same, and yet the same cow may be both. The reason for this is that when one applies the term "mother" to a given cow, he normally leaves completely to one side the question whether that cow is or is not a Hereford. The features whose possession would justify us in describing a cow as a Hereford are irrelevant if we are wondering whether the cow in question is a mother. Accordingly, we ignore those features in affirming or denying "mother" of the cow at hand. "Mother" does not mention them. But—and here is the point—the fact that we do not pay attention to some features in describing a thing does not mean that the thing ceases to have the features. The fact that Bossy is a Hereford is no less a fact because we ignore it in calling her a mother. So far as the truth of "Bossy is a mother" is concerned, the fact that she is a Hereford is, to use a technical term originating with Aristotle, an "accident." But in another context it might be quite essential. If we set out to assort cows by breed, then Bossy's Herefordness would be the essential thing about her. In *that* context, from our generically different standpoint in counting, it is Bossy's motherhood which would be an accident. Thus, calling a cow either a Hereford or a mother leaves unmentioned a host of features which the cow really still possesses, to be taken account of, perhaps, in other descriptions of it. If "She's a Hereford" or "She's a mother" were *all* that could be said of Bossy, we could not even call her a cow or an animal—perhaps we could not properly call her Bossy.

Few of us would go wrong about mother cows. We have little difficulty in seeing that the same cow may be both a Hereford and a mother. Many a woman, however, can justly complain that "mother" or "woman" is applied as an exclusive description to her, when in fact she has features not mentioned by those descriptions but quite important nonetheless. For instance, there is no formal contradiction involved in the idea of a woman being a good logician—even if she happens to be a mother. Yet it is a standard male debating tactic to say, or to think, "You're a woman; you can't think clearly," as if "woman" and "clear thinker" were mutually exclusive species of the same genus.

Let us make the point as strong as possible. A general term *cannot* say everything there is to be said about an individual. For if it did, then it would distinguish that individual from absolutely every possible other individual in the universe, which means that it would no longer be a general term, but would become instead a proper name.

The moral would seem to be, therefore, that we can indeed use general terms to mention things, but should be aware that everything has characteristics not mentioned by any one general term we may apply to it. This moral is a good one to bear in mind in a dispute. People often suppose that when they have given a correct description of a thing, all other descriptions can be rejected as false. Our analysis suggests that this supposition is always false.

We are now in a position to survey briefly the main competing solutions which have been proposed for the philosophical problem of universals. We do not, as logicians, wish to defend or attack any of these solutions, but we remain convinced that the immediate subject matter of logic (terms, propositions, and inferences) will be seen in a clearer light if at least the *problem* of universals receives some attention. As philosophers, of course, we would be delighted to see the problem laid to rest, either by a direct solution or by a demonstration that there was no real problem in the first place. Further, we assume that attention to the logical peculiarities of general terms would be helpful in attacking the philosophical problem. Yet we cannot persuade ourselves that clarity about the immediate subject matter of logic is entirely sufficient for settling questions as to what logic is ultimately about.

Some philosophers, notably Plato, have argued that in describing ordinary individual things we are stating their resemblances to certain nonindividual, nonphysical ideal types. You cannot know something as a square, such philosophers argue, unless you already know what a square is. But no ordinary individual thing is, purely and simply, a square. In experience, we are only confronted with a-square-in-the-center-of-the-rug, or a-square-on-such-and-such-a-page-of-a-logic-book, or black-and-white-squares-on-a-checkerboard. To know *these* things as squares, we must in some sense already know what a square is *apart* from these things. The most we can hope for from an ordinary square is that it will "suggest" to us what a square really is. Actually to know what a square really is requires some acquaintance with the ideal type or form of all squares, a pure and simple squareness unmixed with the other shapes on a book page, or the texture of a rug, or the black and white of a checkerboard. Thus, in the Platonic view, the meaning of a general term is distinct both from the ordinary things to which the term is applied and from the minds of those who apply the term. The real basis for applying a general term is the always imperfect resemblance of an ordinary thing to a certain perfect form. Things of the same kind (various squares, for example) are "similar" to each other only by participation in an ideal reality distinct from, and above, them all.

Other philosophers, notably William of Ockham in the fourteenth century and Berkeley and Hume in the eighteenth, have argued that reality consists entirely of individual things. This view does not rule out all nonphysical things, but it does rule out the kind of nonphysical reality Plato argued for. In this view, the generality of a general term does not stem from the term's association with an ideal archetype; rather, a term is general if it is in fact *used to refer* to many individuals. The question of why a term refers to just those things which it does refer to, and not to others, has no single answer. We must look at the sets of individual things involved in the reference of specific terms. This view is known as *nominalism,* since its distinctive claim is that generality belongs exclusively to names (*nomina*) and not to things. The Platonic view is known as *realism,* as involving the claim that generality is to be found in reality, or in things (*res*).

It is not easy to determine what position Aristotle took on these questions. Some realists, Duns Scotus for example, have cited him as an authority for their views; yet Ockham was convinced that Aristotle was on his side. Other philosophers in the Aristotelian tradition, among them St. Thomas Aquinas, have aimed at a view somewhere between extreme realism and extreme nominalism, while such non-Aristotelians as Kant have also taken a middle view. *Conceptualism* and *moderate realism* are names often applied to such mediating positions. Insofar as a common tenet can be found for philosophers in so diverse a group, it is perhaps the following. Universals have no reality *apart* from individual things and the minds which know them, yet they have a sort of being *in* things which is no less real or objective than the features which make things distinct and separate from one another. For conceptualists or moderate realists, then, a general term refers to a thing as having a specific form really identical with a form to be found in certain other things or, conceptually, in various minds.

The history of the problem of universals is long, fascinating, and as yet unfinished. Perhaps the main lesson we can draw from the debates of realists, nominalists, and conceptualists is that we should be modest in our claims to know what logic and language are ultimately about. No doubt we all want to distinguish in some way between words and facts, and we undoubtedly hope that our words at least sometimes refer to or describe facts accurately. These normal wishes and hopes finally lead us, however, to some out of the ordinary questions. Questions like "What *is* a fact?" and "*How* do terms describe facts?" The debate about universals should teach us that these are not easy questions. We shall find this philosophically negative lesson quite helpful in our attempt to reach a logically adequate answer to the problem of existential import.

4.2. *Existential import and the null class (what propositions are about)*

The idea of existential import was touched on in our presentation of Boolean algebra in 2.2.4. We did not then go into the logical controversies surrounding this idea, but we did note some important formal consequences of the Boolean interpretation of such sentences as "All men are mortal" and "Some men are mortal." We shall now attempt to settle the logical controversies. As a preliminary step, we may recall the formal contrasts mentioned earlier between the classical and Boolean interpretations of **A**, **E**, **I**, and **O** sentences.

In the Boolean interpretation of "All men are mortal," this sentence would appropriately be used to make the claim that the class of nonmortal men is empty, has no members, or is null. "Some men are mortal," Booleanly interpreted, means that the class of mortal men has at least one member, that there exists at least one thing which is both mortal and a man. In earlier parts of the chapter we were careful to explain the classical reading of these sentences in other terms. A universal proposition, we said, is a claim about the whole of a given subject, while a particular proposition is a claim about part of a subject. The Boolean and classical readings of "all" and "some" do not at first seem very different. We noticed in 2.2.4., however, that they are in fact startlingly different in their logical consequences. From the Boolean "All men are mortal" we cannot possibly deduce the Boolean "Some men are mortal," for it does not follow from the fact that things of one kind do not exist that things of another kind do exist: from the nonexistence of nonmortal men, we cannot infer the existence of mortal men; from the emptiness of one class, we cannot infer that another class has members. If, on the other hand, we interpret "all" and "some" in classical, whole-part terms, the inference from "all" to "some" is quite legitimate. Claims about the whole of something are stronger than claims about part of the same thing, and accordingly, a universal proposition may be taken to imply a corresponding particular proposition: **A***ab* implies **I***ab*, and **E***ab* implies **O***ab*.

The initial difference over inferences from "all" to "some" produces other differences. No less than nine of the twenty-four valid moods of the classical syllogism have *in*valid Boolean counterparts. Perhaps the most startling contrasts, however, are between the classical and Boolean accounts of the "All . . . no . . ." and "Some are . . . some are not . . ." relations. The classical **A***ab* and **E***ab* are contraries: they may both be false in a given case, but they cannot both be true. Hence, if it is true that all men are mortal, then, on an **A-E** analysis, it must be false that no men are mortal. On a Boolean analysis, no such consequence follows. If there were no men, the class of nonmortal men would be empty, but so, too, would the class of mortal men be empty. The relationship of subcontrariety between "Some are" and "Some are not" is also broken. "Not-Iab" implies **O**ab, and "not-**O**ab" implies **I**ab. Again, however, if there were no men, it would be false that there existed mortal men, but also false that there existed nonmortal men. To sum up, then: on a Boolean reading, corresponding "all" and "no" sentences may, in some cases, be both true, and in those cases the corresponding "Some are" and "Some are not" sentences will both be false. In a classical reading, one, at least, of a matched pair of "all" and "no" sentences will be false, while at least one of a matched pair of "Some are" and "Some are not" sentences will be true.

So much for the contrasting formal consequences of the two interpretations of **A, E, I,** and **O** sentences. We come now to the *problem* of existential import. We can break the problem down into two questions, the answers to both of which are controversial. One question concerns the "existential import" of the key expressions of classical logic, **A, E, I,** and **O** *propositions*. The propositions of Boolean algebra plainly are existential in import. That is, a Boolean proposition asserts either that there does not exist something of a certain kind $(A=O,\ AB=O,\ A\overline{B}=O$, etc.) or that there does exist something of a certain kind $(A{\neq}O,\ AB{\neq}O,\ A\overline{B}{\neq}O$, etc.). What about **A, E, I,** and **O**? Do any of them assert existence? If so, which of them? Or do they perhaps "presuppose" a really existing subject matter without actually asserting the existence of their subjects? But if **A, E, I,** and **O** assume existence without asserting it, what shall we say of their truth or falsity in cases where the assumption is wrong? Supposing that there were no men, would **"A men/mortal"** be true or false? The last several questions can all be summed up under the general question "What is the existential import of the central propositional forms of classical logic?" This is the first of the two questions we shall attempt to answer in the next few pages.

The other question can be stated more simply, though there is no simple answer to it. The question is, which interpretation of "all," "no," "Some are," and "Some are not" should we adopt? To some extent this is a question of which interpretation fits more closely our ordinary ways of talking. If we do normally intend an "all" statement as a deductively sufficient warrant for a "some" statement, then a logical system in which the corresponding inference form is valid gives a better fit with ordinary reasoning than a system in which the corresponding inference form is invalid. We should not be too hasty to decide the main question on this basis, however. Ordinary reasoning is not the only kind of reasoning. In doing mathematics, or science, or formal logic, conformity to ordinary reasoning is not an end in itself. It may be that a classical usage of "all" and the rest is preferable in some contexts and a Boolean usage better in others.

The answer usually given to our first major question is that **A, E, I,** and **O** do, all of them, assert existence. A three-step argument may be given for this answer. (1) The difference seems so slight between "Some A are B" and "There is something which is both an A and a B" that we can assume that the *particular* propositions of classical logic assert existence. It seems, in other words, as if the Boolean and classical interpretations of "Some" are equivalent. Since $AB \neq O$ asserts existence, Iab is also taken to assert existence. This first step, we think, is wrong. More about it later. (2) Particular and universal propositions must be assigned the same kind of existential import. Otherwise, a great many inferences considered valid in classical logic have to be rejected as invalid. (3) Accordingly, **A** and **E** are assigned positive existential import. They are said to assert the existence of their subjects.

As an additional argument, it sometimes is said that Aristotle, the inventor of **A-E-I-O** logic, was interested only in real things and thus would have had no use for nonexistential propositions.

If this interpretation of **A, E, I,** and **O** propositions is correct—if they all do assert the real existence of their subjects—then the null class proves fatal to classical logic. To see this, let us consider the set of corresponding **A, E, I,** and **O** propositions having "square circle" as subject and "circles" as predicate. If **A, E, I,** and **O** all assert existence, then "**A** square circles/circles," "**E** square circles/circles," "**I** square circles/circles," and "**O** square circles/circles" are *all* false, since there aren't any square circles. Yet according to classical logic, the falsity of any one of these propositions implies the truth of its contradictory opposite. Since they are all false, the contradictory opposite of each one of them should be true. *But each of them is the contradictory opposite of one of the others.* Thus, if they are all false (because there are no square circles), then each must also be true (because it is the contradictory of a false proposition), which is absurd. Now a form of inference is deductively worthless, if *any* case can be found in which it leads us to say that the same proposition is both true and false (on this point see the reduction of Baroco and Bocardo to Barbara in 2.2.1.). Accordingly, if **A, E, I,** and **O** propositions have positive existential import, we must give up the square of opposition, and presumably also the syllogism.

Various efforts have been made to save the inference forms of classical logic without giving up the idea that existence is in some way or other involved in what is asserted by an **A, E, I,** or **O** proposition. It has been suggested, for example, that such propositions *presuppose* existence without actually asserting it. We can say, on this basis, that the question of truth or falsity just doesn't make sense if the presupposition turns out to have been wrong. "All square circles are circles," for example, is *neither true nor false* on this view. "All the books in his room are logic books" can be tested for truth *or* falsity only if there are books of *some* kind in his room.

Only then can we say that "they" either are all, or are not all, logic books.

A better estimate of this last suggestion will be possible if we go on to consider the usual answer to our second main question, "Which interpretation, the classical or the Boolean, should we adopt for our own usage of 'all,' 'no,' etc.?" When we have considered the standard answer to this question we shall state our own views on both main questions.

The usual answer is that we should adopt the Boolean interpretation, at least in contexts in which precision is needed. Two reasons can be given in support of this choice. One is that we sometimes do *not* want to presuppose existence. It is admitted, of course, that we do feel deceived if someone tells us, "All the apples in that barrel are Jonathans," and the barrel turns out to be empty. He didn't, perhaps, *say* there were apples in the barrel, but he gave us every right to assume that there were. Still, there are some quite ordinary situations in which an "all" statement seems clearly meant *not* to refer to anything real. When a man tacks up a sign saying, "All trespassers will be prosecuted," his whole aim is to ensure that there will *not* be any trespassers. And in some scientific contexts, universal claims are made with full knowledge that their subject terms do not refer to anything actually existing. For example, in Newtonian physics it is asserted that every body not acted upon by an external force continues in its present state of motion or rest indefinitely. Now according to another law of the same system of physics, every body in the universe is acted upon, gravitationally, by every other body in the universe. There simply *aren't* any bodies not acted upon by external forces . . . and yet the law concerning the motion of such bodies is of great theoretical importance. One reason for a Boolean use of "all," then, is that it allows us *not* to presuppose existence in cases like those just cited. Another reason given sometimes is that **A, E, I,** and **O** provide no way of asserting or denying existence and nothing but existence. If we read "**A** men/mortal" as *asserting* both the existence and the mortality of men, the classical scheme of inferences would break down if there were no men, and if there are men, we have asserted *more* than this in "**A** men/mortal." If, on the other hand, we read "**A** men/mortal" as *presupposing* existence, then the existential claim is hidden. Now we do sometimes want to say such things as "There are no square circles." Boolean algebra provides us a direct way of saying just this sort of thing; and "Square circles=**O**" says nothing in addition to this. To sum up, the reasons offered for preferring Boolean to classical interpretations of **A, E, I,** and **O** sentences are: (1) that we sometimes want to talk about nonexistent things, such as bodies not acted upon by external forces, square circles, and trespassers; and (2) we sometimes want to say, simply, that things of a certain kind do or do not exist. Boolean algebra satisfies these wants, while classical logic apparently does not.

The preceding may serve as an account of the usual answers to our two questions about existential import. It is now time that we stated and defended our own position. One aim we have in doing this is to give you, for your own thinking through, some *problems* about logic. So far as this aim is concerned, it will not much hurt if what we have to say is somewhat unorthodox. To the first question, then, "What is the existential import of the constants of classical logic?" we venture to answer, "None." As we see it, A, E, I, and O are all completely neutral as to the real existence or non-existence of the things they are about. In answer to the second main question, "Which usage of A, E, I, and O sentences should we adopt, the classical or the Boolean?" we shall argue that the classical interpretation of these expressions is quite adequate in general, though the Boolean interpretation may be preferable in special cases.

We said that A, E, I, and O are neutral as to the *real* existence of the things they are about. In some contexts it may be well to distinguish between real existence and "logical existence," or existence as a topic of discourse. In terms of this distinction we are perfectly willing to admit that the classical propositional forms claim *some* sort of existence (namely, logical existence) for their subjects, but this can be said about any proposition whatsoever, including the propositions of Boolean algebra. We shall return to this point at the end. Right now, however, we would like to defend our claim that A, E, I, and O are neutral in regard to the ordinary, garden-variety, genuine existence of their subjects. The claim is, in other words, that they are neutral in regard to the kind of existence which real persons and physical objects do have and which such things as square circles do not have. So far as this kind of existence is concerned, we hold that the constants of classical logic neither assert nor presuppose any claims at all.

Let us begin with A and E. As we explained these earlier, each is used to make a claim about the whole of a subject. It will be worth our while to ask, then, whether it ever makes sense to claim something about the whole of a nonexistent subject. The cases considered on the last page suggest that the answer is "yes." We do sometimes wish to make claims about all trespassers, all bodies not acted upon by external forces, etc. In these cases, as it happens, we know, or hope, that there will *not* be any existing things for our subject terms to refer to. In other cases (the Jonathans in the barrel, all men being mortal), we know, or normally have reason to expect, that there *are* existing things for our subject terms to refer to. This *variation* in the existential convictions associated with universal claims suggests that making a claim about all of a subject is simply not the same as making a claim about the existence of the subject.

We can add two further points. One is that *analytic* statements are *always* logically indifferent to the existence or nonexistence of their subjects. "All Herefords are cattle" and "No Herefords are Holsteins" are true for all conceivable universes, even for universes empty of cattle (for "analytic," see Chapter 1, 2.1.). The other point is a historical one. Aristotle, quite clearly, was not interested in talking only about real things. To begin with, he spent much of his time refuting the observations and theories of his philosophical predecessors. In this line of work he often found it necessary to discuss things which he, at least, regarded as unreal. He argued, for example, that there are no absolutely indivisible material particles. Yet he discussed the atomic theory of Democritus, using **A, E, I,** and **O** sentences to do so. But furthermore, Aristotle's own physical theory includes something very much like Newton's bodies not acted upon by external forces, namely, "prime matter," matter completely without shape or form. According to the laws of Aristotelian physics, matter cannot actually exist without form, and yet the properties of prime matter are of great theoretical importance.

The points made in the last two paragraphs apply most straightforwardly, perhaps, to universal propositions. There is some basis, however, for extending them to the particulars **I** and **O**. Most **I** and **O** propositions may in fact be concerned with existent subjects, or at least with subjects believed to exist. There are, however, exceptions. We shall consider three. "Some of Shakespeare's heroes met tragic ends" is a true particular proposition about a subject which does not have garden-variety, real (that is, nonfictional) existence. The *evidence* for this proposition is a set of sentences (his plays) which Shakespeare uses in order to *pretend* that Hamlet, etc., have garden-variety existence, but we are not quoting Shakespeare every time we make a statement about his heroes. Or again, the analytic **A** proposition "All triangles are plane figures" seems to yield an equally analytic partial converse, "Some plane figures are triangles." Both propositions are independent of the actual existence, in the ordinary sense, of plane figures and triangles. It is worth recalling here that quite a few competent philosophers have denied that there are any perfect triangles or any perfectly plane figures in physical existence. Whether or not this view is correct, it is still the case that mathematicians do not make physical observations to verify such propositions as "Some plane figures are triangles." For our third example of a nonexistential particular proposition, we return to the man with the sign against trespassers. We can easily imagine a sign which distinguished between different kinds of trespassers. "Trespassers under twelve years of age will be taken home to their parents. Other trespassers will be prosecuted." Or "First-time trespassers will be evicted. Those who trespass again will be prosecuted." The first sign offers an ample warrant for the **I** propositions "Some trespassers will be taken home to their parents" and "Some trespassers will be prosecuted." The second sign implies that some trespassers will be (merely) evicted, others prosecuted. Neither sign implies that there are or will be any trespassers. The examples considered in this paragraph have this much in common. Each involves some claim about *part* of a possibly, probably, or necessarily nonexistent subject.

We conclude, then, that none of the constants of classical logic asserts or presupposes real existence. What shall we say, then, as to the *truth* or *falsity* of propositions with null subjects? In some cases we can say quite a bit, in others nothing. Analytic propositions give little trouble. "All the apples in that barrel are *apples*" is perfectly true, even though the barrel is empty. It would be more natural to say, "Any apples there may happen to be in that barrel are apples." Yet both sentences seem to express the same true **A** proposition. With some contingent propositions we also seem to have some basis for a true-false decision. If the man who puts up the no-trespassing signs is known to have a bark bigger than his bite, we may be inclined to dismiss as false the claims made on his signs. If, on the other hand, he is a resolute defender of all his legal rights, we might say, "He really means it. Trespassers *will* be prosecuted." In other cases, however, we would hardly know what to say. Consider "All the apples in that barrel are Jonathans." If there turn out to be no apples in the barrel, then what? We might ask, "What apples?" If our informant says, "Oh, I thought there were some left. Johnny must have eaten the last one," we seem to be out of trouble. He was talking about apples that *were* in the barrel, and perhaps we can find out whether they were all Jonathans or not. If he repeats his original statement, even after being informed that the barrel is empty, we seem to have two choices. We can assume that he was using an **A** sentence to express the singular proposition normally expressed by the sentence "That barrel has no non-Jonathans in it." Our other choice is to engage in some sort of metaphysical dialogue with him, in the hope of arriving at a sound criterion of truth and falsity for contingent propositions about nonexistent subjects. It does not seem to us that formal logicians are obliged to anticipate the results of such a dialogue.

We come now to the second main question, "How shall we use 'all,' 'no,' and 'some'? In a classical way or in a Boolean way?" Our position here is that the classical interpretation is in general adequate, though in special cases the Boolean interpretation of these expressions may be preferable. We have already shown that one of the supposed inadequacies of classical logic is imaginary. It is commonly assumed that **A, E, I,** and **O** have positive existential import, and this is correctly regarded as a drawback in cases where we want to talk about nonexistent subjects. If the argument of the last few pages is at all sound, however, these constants do *not* have positive existential import. Accordingly, they are just as well suited for talking about nonexistent subjects as they are for talking about existent ones. Thus the first objection to using them to interpret **A, E, I,** and **O** sentences vanishes.

The second reason given for rejecting a classical interpretation was that it gives us no way of simply and directly asserting the existence or nonexistence of a subject, and *only* its existence or nonexistence. This objection is sound as far as it goes. What it overlooks is the fact that classical logic does have a propositional form for asserting or denying existence. Not **A, E, I,** or **O,** but the *indefinite* propositional form "*X* exists." A proposition of this form may be understood as presupposed in most real-life statements of **A, E, I,** and **O** propositions. Such a proposition is not *always* presupposed, however, and it need not remain hidden. In any event it is a logically distinct, though still classical, propositional form.

It can even be argued that in most everyday and scientific contexts the classical interpretation has an advantage over the Boolean reading of "all," "no," etc., for the classical constants interpret as expressions of valid inferences certain sets of sentences which we *intend* as expressions of valid inferences. To make this point clear, let us go back to our examples from the null class. It seems clear that the man who puts up a sign against trespassers intends us to regard as *false* the assertion that *no* trespassers will be prosecuted. And it seems natural to suppose that when Newton made his statement about all bodies not acted upon by an external force, he meant to imply the *falsity* of the **E** proposition, "No bodies not acted upon by an external force will continue in their state of rest or motion indefinitely." As we saw toward the beginning of our discussion, a Boolean reading of "All *A* are *B*" and "No *A* are *B*" makes both these kinds of sentence come out *true* when there exist no *A*'s. The Boolean reading thus helps us very little in talking about nonexistent subjects, for it makes *every* universal claim about such subjects true, and every particular claim about them false.

In certain contexts, however, the constants of classical logic are *less* adequate than those of Boolean algebra. As we noted in 1.2.3., classical logic is quite poor in quantifiers, and also unsuited for dealing with hypothetical and disjunctive propositions. So far as quantity is concerned, it has only four kinds of propositions: singular, indefinite, universal, and particular; and only the latter two types are involved in the system of the syllogism presented by Aristotle. As we shall see in a moment, all the propositions of Boolean algebra fall under just one of the four classical quantitative types. Nonetheless, Boolean algebra is so successful in its exploitation of this single propositional type that it can represent precisely and compactly a vast assortment of quantitative situations. Furthermore, the Boolean interpretation of **A, E, I,** and **O** sentences ties in very nicely with certain formulas of modern propositional logic. On these grounds, we must concede that in some scientific and logical contexts, Boolean algebra has decisive advantages over the logic of Aristotle. This concession will be clearer in the light of our discussion of modern logic in the next chapter.

We said earlier that it is sometimes well to distinguish between "real" existence and "logical" existence. In terms of this distinction, we were quite willing to admit that **A, E, I,** and **O** claim *some* sort of existence for their subjects (namely, logical existence), but this, we said, is true of all propositions whatsoever, including those of Boolean algebra. It is time to explain these remarks, and thus to conclude our account of what logic is about. We must say, first, what sort of existence logical existence is. Then we must explain how **A, E, I,** and **O** make claims about this sort of existence. We shall conclude by pointing out how the propositions of Boolean algebra also involve such claims.

A thing has logical existence if it can be talked about. A moment's reflection will show that the domain of things which can be talked about is far broader than the domain of garden-variety existents. To begin with, we can talk about things whose existence is physically possible, yet not actual. An engineer talks a good deal about the bridges he can build—before they are built. A salesman will tell you about the special products he can have made for you—if only you will place an order. A fisherman will tell you about the fish he might have caught—though in fact it got away. Not all such talk is fruitless, and it is all in some sense meaningful. But beyond the physically possible is the imaginable. Men have talked for thousands of years about perpetual-motion machines, undaunted—in their talk—by the fact that no such machine can possibly be built. "We can dream, can't we?" And what we can dream about, we can talk about. Still more rarefied subjects for discourse are to be found in the region of the *conceivable*. No one can clearly *imagine* a thousand-sided figure, or a space in which a straight line is not the shortest distance between two points, yet mathematicians have no difficulty in discussing either of these subjects, and their discourse about the latter has been of great use to modern physicists. But even chiliagons and non-Euclidean spaces are not an end to the things that can be talked about. No one can even conceive a square circle. Indeed, it is inconceivable that anyone ever should be able to conceive such a thing. Still, in an extremely rarefied sense of "logical existence," square circles do, undoubtedly, logically exist. We can, after all, talk about them. We can say, truly, that "they" are circles. We can say, truly, that they "are" square. It is in fact on the basis of just such statements that we say that they cannot even be conceived to "exist." Now we know perfectly well what we are talking about in all of these statements. Only the person who does know what a square circle is can be quite, quite sure that there are no square circles. In general, then, so long as we can give a meaningful response to the question "What are you talking about?" we can claim to be talking about a logical something—perhaps about a logical impossibility—but still a *logical* something.

But *how* do we claim to be talking about something? Quite simply: by talking about it. The proposition "All men are mortal" neither asserts nor *presupposes* the existence of men. It would be more accurate to say that this proposition *poses* or, more technically, "posits" the existence of its subject.

At a bare minimum, the *logical* existence of its subject is posed by any proposition whatsoever. More often we *sup*pose that what we are talking about is at least conceivable; we do not spend much time trying to arrive at a coherent concept of a square circle. Indeed, most of us spend most of our time talking about things which we have reason to believe are physically or personally real. The only point we wish to make, as logicians, is that the bare act of stating a proposition involves the presentation of something as a logical subject. As we said earlier, we see no need to interpret the propositional forms of classical logic as claiming any sort of existence *other than* that which can be talked about. Still, the difference between a term and a meaningless sound is that a term mentions something. The only way to mention something is to mention it; we claim to be talking about something by talking about it.

The existential significance of the constants of classical logic should now be clear. In stating an **A, E, I,** or **O** proposition, we posit a general subject and make a claim about all or part of that subject. If a second **A, E, I,** or **O** claim is then made, we may have the basis for a valid syllogism. Validity will depend entirely on what term relations are asserted in the premises at hand, and not at all on the existence or nonexistence of anything outside those premises. The *logical* existence of square circles is involved in every proposition or inference about square circles—but, we can still state, and even prove, that square circles do not exist . . . really. **A, E, I,** and **O,** we have argued, do not commit us one way or the other as to the real existence of the subjects to which they are applied.

The only task remaining is to clear up the existential significance of the propositions of Boolean algebra. This task is in a way quite easy. We need only look at the equations and inequations studied in 2.2.4. to see that every proposition of Boolean algebra is a *singular* proposition whose subject is an indicated *class* and whose predicate is either *empty* or *not empty*. Boolean propositions do not posit the existence of things *within* classes, for they are not directly *about* class members; rather, they are one and all about classes. To put the point slightly differently, it does not make sense to say about the *members* of most classes that *they* are empty, but it makes perfectly good logical sense to say of a *class* that *it* is empty. Thus every Boolean proposition posits a singular subject and makes one of two claims about it: either that it has members or that it does not. In either case, Boolean propositions, like **A, E, I,** and **O,** posit the logical existence of their subjects.

We can conclude by recalling a remark we made at the beginning of part 4. We said that when the question "What is logic about?" is pushed far enough, it ceases to be a question *in* logic and branches out instead into philosophical questions *about* logic. In these pages we have tried to push the question as far as possible while still keeping it a question in logic. The result of all our efforts is to reveal questions which we cannot answer. For something like the traditional problem of universals has, of course, cropped up again in the preceding paragraph. The old question as to the basis in reality for general terms has a counterpart in the question "What basis is there in reality for the singular class terms of Boolean algebra?" Neither question is within the scope of formal logic. The logicians' answer to the question "What is logic about?" must remain "Logic is about terms, propositions, and inferences." These are the things studied from a classical viewpoint in this chapter, and these are the things which will be studied from a modern viewpoint in the next chapter.

Chapter 3

Symbolic Logic

1. What symbolic logic is

We might begin our exposition of the recent and advanced portions of formal deductive logic by explaining why they are called "symbolic logic." They are called symbolic logic because they rely so heavily on artificially defined symbols. This heavy reliance on symbols is a consequence of some of the properties of formal logic which we mentioned in the first chapter, especially of the demand for maximum generality and for precision.

We pointed out, in particular, that "Socrates is a man; Socrates is married; therefore Socrates has a wife" would not count as an inference in formal logic, whereas "Socrates is a man; all men are mortal; therefore Socrates is mortal" would be included within formal logic. The difference is that the validity of the first deduction depends directly upon the meaning of "man," "married," and "wife." It does not have a form which could be used to validate inferences on other topics. The inference about Socrates' mortality does have such a form. In other words, the first deduction would not be included within formal logic because the principles which make it valid are not general enough.

The principles of formal logic are very general indeed. This is one of the things which enable logicians to produce lengthy researches in formal logic, all of which are stated using symbols. The symbols, with their rather faceless character, can be used because the logical principles being developed could be used in reasoning on any topic. Indeed the use of symbols brings home that fact. It also is less cumbersome than the use of words would be, especially since the use of words would have to be accompanied by some statement of the fact that the particular nouns used did not matter.

Another reason why symbols are used in advanced formal deductive logic is that formal logic is distinguished by its precision. Artificial languages (such as languages composed of defined symbols) are, as we pointed out, by their nature more precise than natural languages. Words in natural languages tend to have the vagueness that Wittgenstein pointed out in the case of "game." Symbols in artificial languages, on the other hand, are as precise as we care to make them.

There have been two major conceptual developments in modern formal deductive logic that we shall deal with. First, techniques were developed for dealing with logical relationships among propositions by means of examining patterns of component assertions. In Aristotelian logic, of course, logical relationships among propositions (such as implication) are dealt with, but only by means of analysis of relationships among the terms of propositions. Assertions that proposition P implied proposition Q were made only on the basis of analysis of the terms of P and Q. Modern logicians, on the other hand, can examine the relationships among some propositions (which can be regarded as built up out of component assertions) without considering the terms at all.

The second conceptual development that we shall deal with involves thorough exploitation of the notion of quantification. Quantification involves talking about "all x's," or "at least one x," or "no x" when we are talking about x's. Quantification of course did appear in Aristotelian logic. Syllogisms could draw out the consequences of all men being rational, and no fish being rational, etc. But in symbolic logic, quantification is emancipated from the two-term subject-predicate sentence. Consequently more complicated work can be done with quantifiers, and with relations among the classes which are defined by use of quantification symbols.

In this chapter we shall deal extensively with both of these advances. In the first part of the chapter we shall explore the part of symbolic logic in which the ingredients are symbols for propositions and for negation, conjunction, alternation, equivalence, and the "If . . . then" relation. A good deal of this discussion will include work with truth tables, which are a device to solve mechanically a good many of the problems in this part of symbolic logic. Then we shall explore the use of quantifiers, and the logic which results from this. At the end of the chapter we shall say a little about two special topics in advanced symbolic logic.

1.1. Introduction to truth functional logic

The first part of symbolic logic which we shall consider is called *truth functional logic*. All of the formulas considered are *truth functions*. That is, their truth is determinable strictly on the basis of the "truth values" (i.e., truth or falsity) of component propositions. For example, "P is true and Q is true" is a truth function. Its truth depends *entirely* on the truth or falsity of P and of Q. In the same way, the truth of "P is true, or Q is true, but not both" is a function of the truth or falsity of P and of Q.

There are plenty of propositions that are not truth functions of component assertions. For example, the truth of "X happened because Y happened" cannot be analyzed as a function of the truth values of "X happened" and "Y happened." The causal relation, or lack of relation, between Y and X is also a determining factor of the truth of "X happened because Y happened." Even if both "X happened" and "Y happened" were true, this would not show that "X happened because Y happened" was true.

In this part of logic, however, propositions like "X happened because Y happened" are not dealt with. The only propositions that will be dealt with are truth functional.

As we said, the ingredients of truth functional logic are symbols for propositions, negation, conjunction, alternation, equivalence, and the "If . . . then" relation. We shall explain in detail the use of these symbols. When the reader has a basic understanding of the use of the symbols, he is a good way toward understanding the logic which employs them.

1.1.1. Symbols for propositions

The symbols for propositions are simplest to explain. We shall use P, Q, and R to stand for propositions. By propositions of course we mean meaningful assertions, like "It is now eleven," or "Jack is not at home," or "Heavy objects when released tend to fall toward the center of the earth." In a line of reasoning in which the same proposition is referred to more than once, we shall of course use the same letter to symbolize it; where different propositions are referred to, we use different letters.

1.1.2. Negation

The negation symbol is $\sim$. It deserves a longer account. The basic fact about language that brings it into play is that every statement has an opposite. For any statement that anyone makes, we can construct an opposite (i.e., contradictory) statement. One way of doing this is to prefix the statement with "It is not true that . . ." For example, if someone says, "It is now eleven," we can construct the opposite of this by saying, "It is not true that it is now eleven." Similarly, "It is not true that Jack is not at home" is the opposite of "Jack is not at home."

The word for the opposite of a statement is its "negation." The negation of any statement is that statement which is true if and only if statement X is false (and which thus is false if and only if statement X is true). The point deserves elaboration. The "negation" is a technical term: one aspect of its use is that not every statement which involves the denial of a given statement would be classed as its negation. Take, for example, the statement "It is now 50° F." "It is now 70° F." involves the denial of the former statement, but we would not classify it as its negation. That is because it could be false that it is 50° without its being 70°. The statement that we call a negation of another statement is the statement that *must* be true if the other statement is false, and which cannot be true unless the other statement is false. Thus the negation of "It is now 50° F." is "It is not now 50° F." The reader can keep this clearly in mind if he recalls that "negation" means the same as "opposite."

There are many ways of constructing negations of statements. The most mechanical is the one that we explained earlier: one simply tacks on "It is not true that . . ." to the front of the statement. However, instead of saying, "It is not true that it is now eleven," we could say, "It is not now eleven." It comes to the same thing. Instead of saying, "It is not true that Jack is not at home," we could say, "Jack *is* at home."

The latter transformation is made possible by a well-known rule about double negatives. Let us suppose that we want to find the negation of "It is not true that it is now eleven." We could say, "It is not true that it is not true that it is now eleven." But there is a simpler way of saying the same thing. After all, the negation of a negation is an affirmation. "It is not true that it is not true" means "It *is* true." Thus a simpler way of saying, "It is not true that it is not true that it is now eleven" would be to say, "It is now eleven." The rule that this embodies would be stated symbolically as follows: "$\sim \sim P$ is equivalent to P."

In the case of "Jack is not at home," our grammatical sense tells us that "Jack is not at home" means the same thing as "It is not true that Jack is at home." Thus to negate "Jack is not at home" is to negate "It is not true that Jack is at home," which gives us "Jack is at home." Thus the negation of "Jack is not at home" is "Jack is at home."

In pointing this out, we were also illustrating a point made earlier. This is that when formal logic is applied to sentences in natural languages, we need a feel for language (which may sometimes be quite rudimentary) in order not to go wrong. Take, for example, the statement "He was not welcome in our house." It is fairly clear that the negation of "Jack is not at home" is "Jack is at home": if (and only if) one is not true, the other is. But can we say that the negation of "He was not welcome in our house" is "He was welcome in our house"? The way the phrase "not welcome" is normally used, there seems to be a middle ground. Some people who are cordially disliked are "not welcome." People who are liked are "welcome." There may be people whom we do not dislike enough to speak of as "not welcome," but do not like enough to speak of as "welcome." Consequently we cannot

guarantee that "He was welcome in our house" is true if "He was not welcome in our house" is false. Thus neither statement would be classified as
the negation of the other. We can realize this, not by applying any rules of
formal logic, but by our sense for the nuances of language.

1.1.3. Conjunction

The next logical symbol that we wish to discuss is the one for conjunction.
This is simply a dot, i.e., P and Q would be written as $P \cdot Q$. Sometimes also
conjunction is conveyed simply by printing the letters which symbolize
propositions next to each other. Thus one might render the conjunction
of propositions P and Q simply as PQ. PQ is another way of saying $P \cdot Q$.

The nature of the conjunction symbol is very simple. PQ is a way of writing the assertion "P is true and Q is true." In general, the conjunction of any
two symbols or collections of symbols will be treated as the assertion that
what both symbols, or collections of symbols, assert is true.

1.1.4. Alternation

The alternation symbol is **v**. It corresponds loosely to the English word
"or." That is, PvQ might be rendered as "P or Q." However, in ordinary
speech we use the word "or" in a variety of ways, and only one of these
ways corresponds to the alternation symbol as it is used in symbolic logic.
The alternation symbol, **v**, has the following meaning. To assert PvQ is to
assert that P is true or Q is true, *or both are true*. In other words, it is to
assert that at least one of the assertions joined by the alternation symbol is
true, and that possibly both are true.

We can contrast the alternation symbol to the use of "or" in a statement
like "Either the messenger arrives within five minutes or I shall leave without
seeing him." This statement is of the "one or the other" variety. Two possibilities are referred to: the messenger arriving within five minutes, and my
leaving without seeing him. It is asserted that one or the other of these possibilities will be the case. But not both: no room is left for the possibility
that the messenger will arrive within five minutes but that I shall leave without seeing him. That possibility is ruled out. Consequently the statement is
of the form "Either P will be true or Q will be true, but not both."

This statement would *not* be symbolized as PvQ. How it would be symbolized (a more complicated business) will be made apparent later in the
chapter. But the point to bear in mind now is that the statement would not
be symbolized as PvQ because it rules out the possibility of the two things

referred to both counting as true. To say *PvQ*, on the other hand, is to leave open the possibility of *P* and *Q* both being true.

There is another respect in which some ordinary uses of the word "or" differ from the use of the logical symbol **v**. If I say, "We must be energetic or our enterprises will fail," I am asserting a causal connection between the two things joined by "or." I am asserting, among other things, that our not being energetic will cause our enterprises to fail. Thus I am asserting not only something about the truth values of the two halves of the statement (namely, that at least one will be true), but also that the facts referred to are very definitely related.

The use of the logical symbol **v** never has these latter connotations. It always refers *only* to truth values. To say *PvQ* is never to assert any relation between facts that *P* refers to and facts that *Q* refers to. It is only to assert that at least one out of the two is true. The use of **v** can be illustrated by the following example from ordinary language. Let us suppose that a gambler bets that "Either the Yankees will win the American League pennant or the Giants will win the National League pennant." In such a case, normally, no connection is asserted (or denied) between the two events referred to. What the bet amounts to is that the gambler's statement will count as true (that is, he will collect) if the Yankees win and the Giants do not, if the Giants win and the Yankees do not, and also if both teams win.

The logician's use of **v** is like that gambler's use of "or." The symbol **v** of course can, when used with words in natural languages, connect references to facts which are causally related; but the symbol **v** never implies causal relation. The use of the **v** symbol in fact never says more than that at least one (or both) of the assertions connected by the **v** is true.

1.1.5. The "If . . . then" symbol

For the time being the last logical symbol that we wish to explain is the symbol for "If . . . then." This is $\supset$. When the logician writes, $P \supset Q$, this can be understood as "If *P*, then *Q*." But once again we must distinguish between the logical symbol and the variety of ordinary uses of the corresponding English words. The symbol $\supset$, like **v**, is concerned only with truth values. $P \supset Q$ asserts that if *P* is true, then *Q* is true. It does not assert (or deny, for that matter) that there is some causal relation between what *P* refers to and what *Q* refers to. It neither asserts nor denies that we could logically infer *Q* from *P*. All it asserts is that, if *P* is true, *Q* also will be true. The only thing then which could render $P \supset Q$ false would be *P*'s being true and *Q*'s being false.

The reader will see how this distinguishes the meaning of $P \supset Q$ from the most usual use in English of "If P, then Q." Normally when we make remarks like "If it rains, we will not go to the picnic," or "If a number is greater than five, then its square is greater than twenty-five," we are asserting that there is some definite connection between what is referred to in the two halves of the sentence. In the case of the statement about the picnic, the connection is causal. Not merely are we denying that the case will arise of its raining and our going to the picnic, but also there is an implicit assertion that if it rains we will cancel the picnic *because* of the rain. In the other statement, the connection is mathematical. Not only are we denying that there can be a number greater than five whose square is not greater than twenty-five, but we are also implicitly asserting that this is no accident: that, given a number greater than five, one can prove that its square is greater than twenty-five. In the case of both statements, we are conveying more than just something about truth.

In making an expanded precise statement of the meaning of the $\supset$ symbol, we should remind the reader of the meaning of two technical words. In any statement of the form "If P, then Q" we can separate two elements besides the "If . . . then." The element occupying the place of P is spoken of as the *antecedent;* the element occupying the place of Q is spoken of as the *consequent.*

What we have been saying about the $\supset$ symbol is that its use involves an assertion about nothing other than possible combinations of truth and falsity of the antecedent and consequent. It does not make any claim that there is any causal or deductive relation between the truth of the antecedent and the truth of the consequent.

There are four possible combinations of truth and falsity of the antecedent and consequent. They can both be true. They can both be false. The antecedent can be true and the consequent false, and the consequent can be true and the antecedent false. The precise meaning of the $\supset$ symbol is as follows. When we say $P \supset Q$, the assertion stands as true in the case of three out of the four possible combinations. It counts as true if both the antecedent and consequent are true. It counts as true, by default you might say, if the antecedent is false, whether or not the consequent then is true. It counts as false only in the case in which the antecedent is true and the consequent is false.

1.1.6. *Some remarks about logical symbols*

At this point we might anticipate an objection likely to occur to many readers. "What you are doing here seems against common sense," they might urge. "If we have stated, 'If it rains we will stay at home,' and afterward it does not rain and we stay at home anyway, we do not thereby automatically conclude that the statement 'If it rains we will stay at home' was true. We might instead say that it has not been tested. Yet you say that the logician's 'If . . . then' symbol, ⊃, has a meaning such that 'It rains ⊃ we will stay at home' counts as true automatically if it does not rain and we stay at home anyway."

The answer to this complaint is that English is a natural language, whereas the logician speaks an artificial language. Any logical symbol means precisely what logicians decide that it will mean. For the sake of popularizing their operations, logicians will claim that the symbol ⊃ means roughly the same as the English "If . . . then." This is more correct than not, but in a way is misleading. The logicians' symbol does not have a meaning identical with that which "If . . . then" has in most contexts. Nor does it have to have a meaning closely similar to that of the English words. It means what logicians make it mean.

Accordingly, the meaning of the symbol ⊃ can be explained adequately only in terms of combinations of truth values, the way we have done. In a short while we shall explain a mechanism by which such explanations can be conducted with facility.

First, however, we should make two further remarks about the logical symbols whose use we have explained. The first is that they can be used in a variety of combinations. For example, after we have said PvQ we may wish to negate this complex assertion. The conventional way of doing this is to put the assertion that we are negating within parentheses, and to put the negation symbol before the parentheses. Thus the negation of PvQ is $\sim(PvQ)$. In much the same way, if we wish to connect two complex expressions by ·, v, or ⊃, we put a pair of parentheses around each of the two expressions which we wish to connect. An exception to this is if one of the expressions consists of an expression already in parentheses and preceded by a negative. Then a further pair of parentheses is unnecessary. Thus, the alternation of PQ and $Q⊃R$ is $(PQ)v(Q⊃R)$. The conjunction of PvR and $\sim(PvQ)$ is $(PvR)·\sim(PvQ)$. This statement would be read as "It is true that at least one of P and R is true, and also is false that at least one of P and Q is true.

In even more complicated cases we may find an expression preceded by double or triple parentheses. We shall show the reader how one of these expressions can be built up. Let us take first the alternation of P and $\sim Q$. This would be rendered as $Pv\sim Q$. We then take the conjunction of this complex expression with R. This would be $(Pv\sim Q)·R$. Let us now take the alternation of *this* complex assertion with $P⊃R$. In rendering this, we put a pair of parentheses around the expression that we just had, and also around $P⊃R$, and put an alternation symbol in between. This gives us $((Pv\sim Q)·R)v(P⊃R)$.

One of the things for which logicians have developed techniques is to find relatively simple equivalents for such highly tangled expressions as the one that we just produced. These techniques will be discussed later in the chapter, after we explain the workings of truth tables.

The other remark which we wish to make illustrates our continuing theme of the gap between symbolic logic, on one hand, and everyday speech and reasoning, on the other. In everyday speech, assertions of descriptions of facts are connected not only by words like "and," "or," and "If . . . then," but also words such as "but," "since," and "although." There are no symbols even remotely corresponding to "but," "since," and "although" in symbolic logic. The reason for this lies mainly in the difficulty that logicians would have in giving symbols corresponding to "but," "since," and "although" the same neat, extremely systematic treatment that is accorded to $\cdot$, v, and $\supset$. But the resulting fact—that symbolic logic covers only a small area within the logic of our language—is very worth keeping in mind. Symbolic logic is extremely useful, and can in its own way be beautiful; but it falls far short of providing a complete theoretical framework of reasonableness.

1.2.1. Basic truth tables

Not only are symbols corresponding to "but," "since," and "although" missing from logic, but also (as we pointed out) the logicians' use of the v and $\supset$ symbols does not correspond very closely to the most usual ordinary use of "or" and "If . . . then." In fact logicians define the $\sim$, $\cdot$, v, and $\supset$ symbols all very precisely as truth functional symbols. This means that in the case of each one of these symbols the meaning of the symbol can be explained entirely in terms of combinations of truth and falsity ("truth values") of the assertions that it connects or applies to. An account of these truth functional meanings was implicit in our exposition of the use of the symbols. We shall now, however, spell out the truth functions corresponding to the four symbols.

For the sake of convenience, in spelling out these truth functions we shall use a device called the *truth table*. The truth table simply lists the possible combinations of truth and falsity for propositions, and for each possible combination records whether the truth function would be true or false. If we are dealing with only one proposition—call it *P*—there are only two possibilities. If we are dealing with two propositions—call them *P* and *Q*—there are two squared, or four, possibilities. *P* and *Q* may be both true; they may be both false; *P* may be true and *Q* false, and vice versa. If we are dealing with three propositions, there are two cubed, or eight, possible combinations. With four propositions, there are two to the fourth, or sixteen, possible combinations. And so on.

The truth table for the $\sim$ symbol is the following:

P	$\sim P$
T	F
F	T

The first column records possible values for P (there are of course two—true or false), and the second column records the corresponding values for $\sim P$. Thus one reads the table across. One reads that when P is true, $\sim P$ is false; and in the bottom line one reads that when P is false, $\sim P$ is true.

The truth table for PQ involves the four possible combinations of truth and falsity for two propositions. The truth table is as follows:

P	Q	PQ
T	T	T
T	F	F
F	T	F
F	F	F

In the first two columns we have spelled out the four possible combinations of truth values for P and Q. The first line, for example, represents the case that P is true and that Q is true. If we move our eye to the right—to the first line of the third column—we see that in that event PQ counts as true. Reading the second line, we see that in the event that P is true and Q is false, PQ will count as false. The third and fourth lines tell us that PQ will count as false also in the event that P is false and Q true, or in the event that both P and Q are false. Thus PQ counts as true in the event of only one out of the four possible combinations of truth and falsity of P and Q.

The reader should see all this as precisely *defining* the meaning of PQ. PQ, as we explained earlier, has the same meaning as "P is true and Q is true." Such a complex assertion counts as true *only* in the event that both P and Q are true; if either P or Q or both are false, then the assertion counts as false. The truth table above is a precise schematic way of rendering this.

The truth table for PvQ is as follows:

P	Q	PvQ
T	T	T
T	F	T
F	T	T
F	F	F

Once again (as indeed always), the lines simply represent the complete assortment of possible combinations of truth and falsity of the component propositions. There are four possible combinations if one is given two component propositions. The first line represents one of these possibilities—that P and Q both will be true—and the third entry in the line, in the column under PvQ, tells us that in such a case PvQ would count as true. The second line represents the possibility that P will be true and Q false, and the third entry tells us that in such a case PvQ would count as true. The third and fourth lines are to be read similarly. We might remark now that there is no necessity, other than that involved in custom, for stating the possible combinations of truth values in the order which we have adopted. All that matters is that the possible combinations all be stated, and that the truth or falsity of the function in question be worked out for each of the possible combinations.

PvQ counts as true in three of the four possible combinations of truth values of its components. The only thing that would make it false would be for both P and Q to be false. This fits the meaning that we assigned to the v symbol earlier, when we said that PvQ asserted that either P was true or that Q was true or that both were true.

The truth table for $P \supset Q$ is as follows:

P	Q	$P \supset Q$
T	T	T
T	F	F
F	T	T
F	F	T

Thus $P \supset Q$ counts as true in three of the four cases. It is false only if P is true and Q is false. This fits what we had said about the use of the $\supset$ symbol. Again we might point out that the truth table that we have just presented should be interpreted as a definition. It is a precise schematic way of indicating what we mean by the $\supset$ symbol.

1.2.2. Constructing truth tables

We come now to the construction of truth tables for more complicated truth functions. There are various short cuts for doing this, but it seems best that we teach a thorough step-by-step method that makes mistakes unlikely.

Let us take as an example the function $(PvQ) \cdot \sim P$. This is the conjunction of two assertions, PvQ and $\sim P$. We might begin by working out the truth or falsity, for each of the four combinations of truth and falsity for P and Q, of these two assertions.

This gives us:

P	Q	PvQ	~P
T	T	T	F
T	F	T	F
F	T	T	T
F	F	F	T

The reader will note that even though we have added PvQ and ~P to our table, there are still only two propositions, P and Q, upon which our table is built; and that consequently there are still only four possible combinations of truth and falsity to be worked out.

Reading the first line of the table, we see that when P and Q both are true, PvQ counts as true and ~P counts as false. (~P of course counts as false in all those cases in which P is true, and counts as true in all those cases in which P is false.) In the second line we see that when P is true and Q false, PvQ counts as true and ~P counts as false. The third line tells us that in the case in which P is false and Q true, PvQ still counts as true, and ~P counts as true. The fourth line tells us that in the case in which both P and Q are false, PvQ counts as false, and ~P counts as true.

Now let us set up a fifth column which gives the truth or falsity of (PvQ)·~P for each of the four possible combinations of truth values of P and Q. We have seen before that a conjunction of assertions counts as true only in a case in which both of the assertions are true. For example, in the truth table for PQ, there was a T value in the last column only in the case in which both P and Q were true. Consequently the fifth column would be added as follows:

P	Q	PvQ	~P	(PvQ)·~P
T	T	T	F	F
T	F	T	F	F
F	T	T	T	T
F	F	F	T	F

The fifth column represents the conjunction of the assertions represented by the third and fourth columns. Consequently we have a T value in the fifth column only in those cases in which there are T values in both the third and fourth columns. This turns out to be only the third case. Only in the case in which P is false and Q is true will both PvQ and ~P count as true; as a result, only in this case will the conjunction of PvQ and ~P count as true. We can say therefore that the function with which we are dealing is true if and only if P is false and Q is true.

Let us take another example. This is the function (P·~Q)vR. This is the alternation of $P \cdot \sim Q$ and R. We shall construct a truth table for this function again by stages, constructing first truth tables for $P \cdot \sim Q$ and for R.

$P \cdot \sim Q$ is the conjunction of P and $\sim Q$. Thus it counts as true if and only if both P and $\sim Q$ are true: that is to say, if and only if P is true and Q is false. Consequently its truth table is as follows:

P	Q	$P \cdot \sim Q$
T	T	F
T	F	T
F	T	F
F	F	F

If we write out the truth table for $P \cdot \sim Q$ for the eight possible combinations of truth values of P, Q, and R, we get the following:

P	Q	R	$P \cdot \sim Q$
T	T	T	F
T	T	F	F
T	F	T	T
T	F	F	T
F	T	T	F
F	T	F	F
F	F	T	F
F	F	F	F

Since the truth or falsity of R does not affect at all the truth value of $P \cdot \sim Q$, we simply, as before, write T for $P \cdot \sim Q$ in those cases in which P is true and Q false, and otherwise write F. The reader will see that there are T values for only two of the eight cases: these are the two possible cases in which P is true and Q false.

$(P \cdot \sim Q) \lor R$ is true in any case in which either $P \cdot \sim Q$ is true or R is true or both are true, and otherwise counts as false. Thus its truth table would be:

P	Q	R	$P \cdot \sim Q$	$(P \cdot \sim Q) \lor R$
T	T	T	F	T
T	T	F	F	F
T	F	T	T	T
T	F	F	T	T
F	T	T	F	T
F	T	F	F	F
F	F	T	F	T
F	F	F	F	F

The last column has a T in each possible case in which at least one of $P \cdot \sim Q$ and R is true, and an F in the other cases.

To make our example still more complicated, let us suppose that we want to construct a truth table for $((P \cdot \sim Q) \lor R) \supset PR$. This is an "If . . . then" formula, with $(P \cdot \sim Q) \lor R$ (for which we already have a truth table) as the antecedent and PR as the consequent.

The truth table for PR, for the eight possible combinations of truth values for P, Q, and R, is as follows:

P	Q	R	PR
T	T	T	T
T	T	F	F
T	F	T	T
T	F	F	F
F	T	T	F
F	T	F	F
F	F	T	F
F	F	F	F

PR counts as true if and only if both P and R are true, and regardless of whether Q is true or not.

The truth table for $((P \cdot \sim Q) \lor R) \supset PR$ is:

P	Q	R	$(P \cdot \sim Q) \lor R$	PR	$((P \cdot \sim Q) \lor R) \supset PR$
T	T	T	T	T	T
T	T	F	F	F	T
T	F	T	T	T	T
T	F	F	T	F	F
F	T	T	T	F	F
F	T	F	F	F	T
F	F	T	T	F	F
F	F	F	F	F	T

The reader will remember, as part of our explanation of the meaning of the $\supset$ symbol, that any assertion of the form $X \supset Y$ counts as true *unless* the antecedent (the X) is true and the consequent (the Y) is false. Thus the complex assertion we are dealing with counts as true in every possible case except the ones in which its antecedent is true and its consequent false. These turn out to be the cases represented by the fourth, fifth, and seventh lines. If P is true, Q false, and R false, or if P is false, Q true, and R true, or if both P and Q are false and R is true, then our complex assertion will count as false.

We shall deal with two more truth functions, each of which will enable us to relate the meaning of an important technical term to truth tables.

The first of these truth functions is $PQ \supset (PvQ)$. The truth table for PQ is:

P	Q	PQ
T	T	T
T	F	F
F	T	F
F	F	F

The truth table for PvQ is:

P	Q	PvQ
T	T	T
T	F	T
F	T	T
F	F	F

This gives us, as the truth table for $PQ \supset (PvQ)$:

P	Q	PQ	PvQ	$PQ \supset (PvQ)$
T	T	T	T	T
T	F	F	T	T
F	T	F	T	T
F	F	F	F	T

Our complex assertion is true in all cases except those in which the antecedent is true and the consequent false. There turn out to be no cases in which the antecedent is true and the consequent false. Thus the assertion is true in every case.

Truth functions, like the one we just dealt with, which are true for every possible combination of truth values of their component propositions, are called *tautologies*. They have to be true: there is no possible case in which they would be false. Consequently, in making any assertion which has the form of a tautology, one is in a way saying nothing: one is not saying that something is the case rather than something else. Any statement which can be analyzed truth functionally, and given a truth table all the values of which are *T*'s, has this character. Take, for example, "If it is true that Jack has left the house and George has left the house, then it is true that either Jack has left the house or George has left the house or both have left." This has the form $PQ \supset (PvQ)$, which we just examined. It is obviously true, is a tautology, and says nothing.

A statement that is the opposite of tautologous is *inconsistent* or *self-*

contradictory. This is a statement which is false in every possible case. A rudimentary example of such a statement is "It is both true that Jack is at home and that Jack is not at home," if the "Jack" referred to in the two places is the same person. This fits the form, $P \cdot \sim P$. The truth table for $P \cdot \sim P$ is as follows:

P	$\sim P$	$P \cdot \sim P$
T	F	F
F	T	F

A more elaborate example of the same sort of thing is $(P \cdot \sim Q) \cdot (P \supset Q)$. The truth table for $P \cdot \sim Q$ is:

P	Q	$P \cdot \sim Q$
T	T	F
T	F	T
F	T	F
F	F	F

The truth table for $P \supset Q$ is:

P	Q	$P \supset Q$
T	T	T
T	F	F
F	T	T
F	F	T

The truth table for $(P \cdot \sim Q) \cdot (P \supset Q)$ is:

P	Q	$P \cdot \sim Q$	$P \supset Q$	$(P \cdot \sim Q) \cdot (P \supset Q)$
T	T	F	T	F
T	F	T	F	F
F	T	F	T	F
F	F	F	T	F

Thus the function turns out to be false in every possible case. It is inconsistent. Any assertion having this form will involve a self-contradiction.

EXERCISES FOR SECTION 1.2.2.

A. Construct truth tables for the following functions.

 1. $(\sim P \mathbf{v} \sim Q) \mathbf{v} PQ$
 2. $P \supset \sim (P \mathbf{v} \sim Q)$
 3. $(P \supset QR) \supset PQ$
 4. $\sim ((\sim P \mathbf{v} \sim Q) \mathbf{v} (P \cdot \sim Q))$
 5. $(P \supset Q) \mathbf{v} (\sim Q \supset \sim P)$
 6. $(\sim Q \supset \sim P) \mathbf{v} (P \cdot \sim Q)$
 7. $PQ \cdot (\sim P \mathbf{v} \sim Q)$
 8. $(P \mathbf{v} Q) \supset PQ$

B. Which of the foregoing functions is tautologous?

C. Which of the foregoing functions is inconsistent?

1.2.3. *An alternative method of truth functional analysis*

In the next two or three pages we shall offer an alternative method of truth functional analysis to the one that we have been presenting. The alternative method will lead to the same results as the old one: it will lead to determinations of the truth value of an assertion for various combinations of truth values of component assertions. In many cases it is quicker and simpler. The reader thus can use the alternative method, if he pleases, or simply ignore it. If he wishes, he may simply proceed to 1.3., and skip these pages.

As our first example of the workings of the alternative method, let us suppose that we are dealing with the function $(P \mathbf{v} Q \supset ((Q \mathbf{v} \sim P) \supset \sim P)$. The techniques that we have developed so far would allow us to produce a truth table for this function: that is, to determine its truth or falsity for every possible combination of truth values of P and Q. But the procedure is cumbersome. We would have to develop a truth table for $P \mathbf{v} Q$, one for $Q \mathbf{v} \sim P$, another one for $(Q \mathbf{v} \sim P) \supset \sim P$, and then finally one for $(P \mathbf{v} Q) \supset ((Q \mathbf{v} \sim P) \supset \sim P)$.

The alternative method involves substituting T or F (signifying "true statement" or "false statement") for propositions. It also involves applying the following general rules.

(1) The negation of a true statement is false; the negation of a false statement is true. Thus we can replace $\sim T$ by F, and $\sim F$ by T.

(2) The conjunction of two statements is true if and only if both of the statements are true. Thus we can replace TT by T; but on the other hand we replace TF, FT, or FF by F.

(3) The alternation of two statements counts as true if and only if at least one of the statements is true. Thus we can replace *TvT, TvF,* or *FvT* by *T;* but *FvF* is replaced by *F.*

(4) An "If . . . then" function counts as false if and only if the antecedent is true and the consequent is false. Thus we can replace $T \supset T$, $F \supset T$, or $F \supset F$ by *T;* but $T \supset F$ is replaced by *F.*

Let us try this method out on the function we already mentioned, $(PvQ) \supset ((Qv \sim P) \supset \sim P)$. We might first see what the truth of the function would be in the case that *P* is true and *Q* is false. In doing this, we replace *P* by *T* and *Q* by *F*. We get $(TvF) \supset ((Fv \sim T) \supset \sim T)$. We can replace $\sim T$, in the two places in which it occurs, by *F*. This gives us:

$(TvF) \supset ((FvF) \supset F)$

TvF of course is *T*, whereas *FvF* is *F*. Thus we get:

$(T) \supset ((F) \supset F)$

At this stage we can drop some parentheses, which are no longer needed as "punctuation," and write:

$T \supset (F \supset F)$

This says, "If *T*, then it is true that if *F* then *F*." But $F \supset F$ is *T*. Thus we get:

$T \supset T$

This, as Rule 4 tells us, is simply *T*. Thus we arrive at the conclusion that if *P* is taken as true and *Q* as false, then the function that we have been dealing with is true.

Let us examine the same function in the case in which both *P* and *Q* are true. We substitute *T* for both *P* and *Q*. This gives us:

$(TvT) \supset ((Tv \sim T) \supset \sim T)$

We can replace $\sim T$ by *F*. This gives us:

$(TvT) \supset ((TvF) \supset F)$

By Rule 3, we can substitute *T* for both *TvT* and *TvF*, which transforms the formula into:

$T \supset (T \supset F)$

$T \supset F$ by Rule 4 is *F*. We thus can substitute *F* for the $T \supset F$ within parentheses. This gives us:

$T \supset F$

This is *F*.

Thus in the case in which both *P* and *Q* are true, the function turns out to be false.

Using the same techniques, we can show that in the case in which *P* is false and *Q* true, the function is true. It also is true in the case in which *P* and *Q* both are false. The reader might care to work this out for himself.

The results of our analysis of $(PvQ) \supset ((Qv \sim P) \supset \sim P)$ could be expressed as a truth table:

P	Q	$(P \lor Q) \supset ((Q \lor \sim P) \supset \sim P)$
T	T	F
T	F	T
F	T	T
F	F	T

The function is true except in the case in which both P and Q are true.

However, while the results of our analysis could be expressed as a truth table, the method by which we arrived at the results was new. Rather than constructing a series of intermediate truth tables, we worked with substitutions of T's and F's for the component propositions of the truth function. As we said earlier, the two methods ought to give the same results—i.e., the right ones—but the method of substituting T's and F's can be quicker.

Let us deal with a few more examples of this method of analyzing truth functions. First, let us take the function $\sim((\sim P \supset \sim Q) \lor \sim (PQ))$. Let us see whether it would count as true for the case of P being false and Q being true. We substitute F for P and T for Q. This gives us:

$\sim((\sim F \supset \sim T) \lor \sim (FT))$

$\sim F$ is T, and $\sim T$ is F. Thus we get:

$\sim((T \supset F) \lor \sim (FT))$

$T \supset F$ is F, and FT is F. This gives us:

$\sim((F) \lor \sim (F))$

By dropping punctuation which is now unnecessary, we can put the foregoing as:

$\sim(F \lor \sim F)$

$\sim F$ is T. This gives us:

$\sim(F \lor T)$

$F \lor T$ is T. This gives us:

$\sim T$

Finally, $\sim T$ is F.

Thus we see that the function in question counts as false in the case that P is false and Q true.

Let us next take as an example the function $((\sim P \supset Q) \cdot (\sim Q \lor \sim P)) \lor Q$. We shall examine the case in which both P and Q are false. Thus we can replace both P and Q by F. This gives us:

$((\sim F \supset F) \cdot (\sim F \lor \sim F)) \lor F$

$\sim F$ is T. This gives us:

$((T \supset F) \cdot (T \lor T)) \lor F$

$T \supset F$ is F, which leaves us with:

$(F \cdot (T \lor T)) \lor F$

TvT is T. This gives us:

$(F \cdot T)vF$

$F \cdot T$, which could be written FT, is F. Thus we have:

FvF

This is F. Thus we see that the function is false in the case in which both P and Q are false.

Our last example is the function $(Pv{\sim}P) \cdot (PQ \supset {\sim}P)$. We shall examine it for the case in which P is false and Q is true. We replace P by F, and Q by T. This gives us:

$(Fv{\sim}F) \cdot (FT \supset {\sim}F)$

Replacing ${\sim}F$ by T, we get:

$(FvT) \cdot (FT \supset T)$

FvT is T. This gives us:

$T \cdot (FT \supset T)$

FT is F. This gives us:

$T \cdot (F \supset T)$

$F \supset T$ is T. This gives us:

$T \cdot T$

This is T. Thus the function is true in the case that P is false and Q true.

There is one thing about the function we just examined which is worth pointing out. This is, it is true also in the case in which P is false and Q is false. In other words, if P is false the function is true, whether or not Q is true. We could have brought this out by substituting F for P, and not making any substitution at all for Q. This would have given us:

$(Fv{\sim}F) \cdot (FQ \supset {\sim}F)$

Replacing ${\sim}F$ by T, we get:

$(FvT) \cdot (FQ \supset T)$

Replacing FvT by T, we have:

$T \cdot (FQ \supset T)$

Whether or not Q is true, FQ will count as false, since a conjunction one of whose elements is false counts as false. Thus we get:

$T \cdot (F \supset T)$

$F \supset T$ can be replaced by T, leaving us with:

TT

which is T. Thus, if P is false, the function counts as true, whether or not Q is true.

In fact the truth table for this last function is, as the reader can verify:

P	Q	$(Pv{\sim}P) \cdot (PQ \supset {\sim}P)$
T	T	F
T	F	T
F	T	T
F	F	T

EXERCISE FOR SECTION 1.2.3.

Determine the truth value of:
1. $((PQ\mathrm{v}\sim(P\mathrm{v}\sim Q))\supset P)\supset Q$ when both P and Q are false.
2. $(\sim P\cdot\sim Q)\supset Q$ when P is true and Q is false.
3. $(P\cdot\sim Q)\mathrm{v}(\sim P\cdot Q)$ when P is false and Q is true.
4. $P\mathrm{v}(P\supset Q)$ when both P and Q are false.
5. $P\supset(P\supset Q)$ when both P and Q are true.
6. $(P\supset(Q\supset P))\cdot\sim P$ when P is false and Q is true.
7. $(P\supset(Q\supset P))\cdot\sim P$ when P is true and Q is false.
8. $\sim((P\cdot\sim Q)\mathrm{v}PQ)$ when P is true and Q is false.

1.3. Implication and equivalence

We shall now develop the concepts of implication and equivalence, and also develop techniques for determining where relations of implication or equivalence exist among truth functions.

When we speak of assertion X as implying assertion Y, we mean that Y can be deduced from X. Or, to put it another way, we mean that we can show through deductive reasoning that if X is true, Y *has* to be true. When we speak of assertion X as equivalent to assertion Y, we mean that they imply one another: i.e., that we can show through deductive reasoning that if either one is true, the other one has to be true.

We might point out that this meaning of "implication" sharply distinguishes it from the relation we have been using the $\supset$ symbol to represent. As we pointed out earlier, logicians have precisely defined the $\supset$ symbol so that when we say $P\supset Q$ we are *not* asserting anything about the relations between P and Q other than that it does not happen to be the case that P is true and Q false. There is no suggestion that Q can be deduced from P, or even that the truth of P and Q is causally related.

When, on the other hand, we speak of assertion X as implying assertion Y, we are asserting something about X and Y other than that it does not happen to be the case that X is true and Y false. For one thing, we are asserting that it logically could not be the case that X is true and Y false. We are asserting something about, so to speak, the internal relations of the two propositions as well as about their truth values. We are asserting that the meaning of the assertions is such that if X is true Y has to be true.

The relation between the $\supset$ symbol and the logical concept of implication can be summarized as follows. To say that X implies Y implies that it is not the case that X is true and Y false, although it says much more than this. On the other hand, to say $X \supset Y$ involves no judgment, one way or the other as to whether X implies Y. In other words, from the assertion that X implies Y you can deduce $X \supset Y$; but from $X \supset Y$ you can logically derive neither an assertion that X implies Y nor an assertion that X does not imply Y.

In much the same way as $(X$ implies $Y)$ claims much more than $X \supset Y$, to say that X is equivalent to Y involves a greater claim than $(X \supset Y) \cdot (Y \supset X)$. From "$X$ is equivalent to Y," one can deduce the lesser claim $(X \supset Y) \cdot (Y \supset X)$; but from $(X \supset Y) \cdot (Y \supset X)$ one can derive neither the assertion that X and Y are equivalent nor the assertion that they are not equivalent.

The commonly accepted symbol for implication is $\rightarrow$. The reader can interpret $X \rightarrow Y$ as claiming that X implies Y. The commonly accepted symbol for equivalence is $\equiv$. The reader can interpret $X \equiv Y$ as claiming that X and Y are equivalent, and that $(X \rightarrow Y) \cdot (Y \rightarrow X)$.

1.3.1. Using truth tables to demonstrate implication and equivalence

There are two main sorts of techniques for determining whether a truth function implies another, or whether two truth functions are equivalent. One technique involves working with truth tables; the other involves performing transformations directly on the truth functional expressions. We shall explain the method which involves truth tables first, and then explain how one can achieve the same results by practicing transformations on truth functional expressions.

The method involving truth tables relies upon a very simple principle. This is, that if in every possible case in which function X is true, function Y also will be true, then $X \rightarrow Y$. Since equivalence is nothing but mutual implication, we can derive from this the principle that if in every possible case in which X is true, Y will be true, and vice versa, then $X \equiv Y$.

Translated into terms of truth tables, this means that if two truth functions have the same truth table they are equivalent. If Y has a truth table which shows T values in every case in which X has a T value (as well as possibly in other cases), then $X \rightarrow Y$.

Suppose, for example, that we want to see whether $((P \vee Q) \cdot (\sim P \vee \sim Q)) \rightarrow (P \supset \sim Q)$. We can determine this by constructing truth tables for the two functions. In doing this, we shall follow the method developed in 1.2.2. (which is more cumbersome but easier to follow than the method offered in 1.2.3.).

In constructing the truth table for $(P \vee Q) \cdot (\sim P \vee \sim Q)$, we shall begin by

constructing the truth tables for PvQ and $\sim Pv\sim Q$. The truth tables for
PvQ and $\sim Pv\sim Q$ are as follows:

P	Q	PvQ
T	T	T
T	F	T
F	T	T
F	F	F

P	Q	$\sim Pv\sim Q$
T	T	F
T	F	T
F	T	T
F	F	T

The third column has a T value in those cases, and only those cases, in
which there is at least one F value in the first two columns.

We can now construct the truth table for $(PvQ)\cdot(\sim Pv\sim Q)$:

P	Q	PvQ	$\sim Pv\sim Q$	$(PvQ)\cdot(\sim Pv\sim Q)$
T	T	T	F	F
T	F	T	T	T
F	T	T	T	T
F	F	F	T	F

The fifth column, representing the conjunction of the third and fourth,
as a T value if and only if both the third and fourth have T values. In the
case in which both P and Q are true, the function $\sim Pv\sim Q$ is false; therefore we have an F in the fifth column. In the case in which both P and Q are
false, the function PvQ is false; therefore we have an F in the fifth column.
In the other two possible cases, in which P is true and Q false, or P false and
Q true, there are T's in both the third and fourth columns, and consequently
in these cases the function $(PvQ)\cdot(\sim Pv\sim Q)$ counts as true.

The truth table for $P\supset\sim Q$ can be got by easy stages as follows. First
we write out the table for $\sim Q$. This is, of course, the opposite of the table
for Q.

P	Q	$\sim Q$
T	T	F
T	F	T
F	T	F
F	F	T

The truth table for $P \supset \sim Q$ is as follows:

P	Q	$\sim Q$	$P \supset \sim Q$
T	T	F	F
T	F	T	T
F	T	F	T
F	F	T	T

In understanding this, the reader will remember that the meaning of the $\supset$ symbol is such that a function $X \supset Y$ counts as true except in the case in which X is true and Y false. Thus the function $P \supset \sim Q$ counts as true except in the case in which P is true and $\sim Q$ false. Thus, in the truth table above, $P \supset \sim Q$ has a T value except in those cases in which P (the first column) has a T value and $\sim Q$ (the third column) has an F value. This happens only in the first line; therefore only in this line does $P \supset \sim Q$ have an F value.

We can now put the truth table results of $(P \vee Q) \cdot (\sim P \vee \sim Q)$ and for $P \supset \sim Q$ alongside each other. We have:

P	Q	$(P \vee Q) \cdot (\sim P \vee \sim Q)$	$P \supset \sim Q$
T	T	F	F
T	F	T	T
F	T	T	T
F	F	F	T

We see that for the possible cases represented by the second and third lines, both functions are true. For the case of both P and Q being true, both functions are false. For the case of both P and Q being false, $(P \vee Q) \cdot (\sim P \vee \sim Q)$ counts as false, and $P \supset \sim Q$ counts as true.

We are now in a position to say that $(P \vee Q) \cdot (\sim P \vee \sim Q)$ implies $P \supset \sim Q$. $P \supset \sim Q$ is true in every case in which $(P \vee Q) \cdot (\sim P \vee \sim Q)$ is true (as well as in one additional case). To put the matter less technically: we see that it is impossible for $(P \vee Q) \cdot (\sim P \vee \sim Q)$ to be true and $P \supset \sim Q$ not to be true. There is no case possible in which $(P \vee Q) \cdot (\sim P \vee \sim Q)$ would be true and $P \supset \sim Q$ would be not true. Thus the former implies the latter.

Let us take a few more examples. First, let us examine whether $(P \cdot (\sim P \vee \sim Q)) \rightarrow (\sim (\sim Q \supset \sim P))$.

The truth table for $\sim P \vee \sim Q$ is as follows:

P	Q	$\sim P \vee \sim Q$
T	T	F
T	F	T
F	T	T
F	F	T

The truth table for $P \cdot (\sim P \vee \sim Q)$ is as follows:

P	Q	$\sim P \vee \sim Q$	$P \cdot (\sim P \vee \sim Q)$
T	T	F	F
T	F	T	T
F	T	T	F
F	F	T	F

Since the final column represents the conjunction of the first column (P) and the third column $(\sim P \vee \sim Q)$, it has a T value only in a case in which both the first and third columns have T values. This turns out only to be the second case, the case in which P is true and Q false.

The truth table for $\sim Q \supset \sim P$ is as follows:

P	Q	$\sim Q$	$\sim P$	$\sim Q \supset \sim P$
T	T	F	F	T
T	F	T	F	F
F	T	F	T	T
F	F	T	T	T

The reader again ought to be clear that the first two columns simply set up the four possible combinations of truth and falsity of P and Q. The third column simply is the reverse of the second, and the fourth is simply the reverse of the first. Because of the meaning of the $\supset$ symbol, the last column has a T value in any case except one in which there is a T in the third column and an F in the fourth column. Thus it is true in the first, second, and fourth cases.

To get the truth table for $\sim (\sim Q \supset \sim P)$ of course we simply reverse the last column above.

P	Q	$\sim Q \supset \sim P$	$\sim (\sim Q \supset \sim P)$
T	T	T	F
T	F	F	T
F	T	T	F
F	F	T	F

$\sim (\sim Q \supset \sim P)$ turns out to be true only in the case in which P is true and Q false.

We can now answer the question of whether $P \cdot (\sim P \vee \sim Q)$ implies $\sim (\sim Q \supset \sim P)$. The answer is "yes." But also, $\sim (\sim Q \supset \sim P)$ implies $P \cdot (\sim P \vee \sim Q)$. In the only possible case in which either of them is true, the other is true. If either one of them is true, the other *has* to be true. Thus they are equivalent.

Let us take another example, and examine whether $((P \supset Q) \cdot (Q \supset P)) \rightarrow P$. The truth table for $P \supset Q$ is as follows:

P	Q	$P \supset Q$
T	T	T
T	F	F
F	T	T
F	F	T

The truth table for $Q \supset P$ is:

P	Q	$Q \supset P$
T	T	T
T	F	T
F	T	F
F	F	T

The last column has an F value only in the case in which Q is true and P false.

Combining the two truth tables, we get the truth table for $(P \supset Q) \cdot (Q \supset P)$:

P	Q	$P \supset Q$	$Q \supset P$	$(P \supset Q) \cdot (Q \supset P)$
T	T	T	T	T
T	F	F	T	F
F	T	T	F	F
F	F	T	T	T

Thus we see that $(P \supset Q) \cdot (Q \supset P)$ counts as true in the first and fourth of our possible cases: i.e., when P and Q are both true, and when P and Q are both false. On the other hand, P counts as true in the first and second cases: i.e., when P is true and Q true, and when P is true and Q false. We see that there is a case in which $(P \supset Q) \cdot (Q \supset P)$ would be true and P false: namely, the case in which both P and Q are false. Thus $(P \supset Q) \cdot (Q \supset P)$ does not imply P. Also we can see that there is a case in which P is true and $(P \supset Q) \cdot (Q \supset P)$ would be false: namely, the case in which P is true and Q false. Thus it also is false that P implies $(P \supset Q) \cdot (Q \supset P)$. Neither of the two implies the other.

The next example that we shall produce will illustrate an extreme case.

Suppose that we ask whether $((P \supset {\sim}Q) \cdot PQ) \rightarrow (P \vee Q)$. The truth table for $P \supset {\sim}Q$ is as follows:

P	Q	P⊃~Q
T	T	F
T	F	T
F	T	T
F	F	T

The function is true in every possible case except the one in which both P and Q are true: i.e., in which P is true and ${\sim}Q$ false.

The truth table for PQ is:

P	Q	PQ
T	T	T
T	F	F
F	T	F
F	F	F

This gives us the following truth table for $(P \supset {\sim}Q) \cdot PQ$:

P	Q	P⊃~Q	PQ	(P⊃~Q)·PQ
T	T	F	T	F
T	F	T	F	F
F	T	T	F	F
F	F	T	F	F

The truth table for $P \vee Q$ is:

P	Q	PvQ
T	T	T
T	F	T
F	T	T
F	F	F

We can see that $(P \supset {\sim}Q) \cdot PQ$ implies $P \vee Q$. Our requirement of a truth function X implying a truth function Y was, as the reader will remember, that in every possible case in which X will be true Y will be true also. In fact $(P \supset {\sim}Q) \cdot PQ$ is true in no possible case. It is what we earlier called *inconsistent*. Thus it is trivially true—true by default, you might say—that in any possible case in which $(P \supset {\sim}Q) \cdot PQ$ is true, $P \vee Q$ will be true.

The alert reader might ask, "Then would not $(P \supset {\sim}Q) \cdot PQ$ imply any truth function whatsoever? It seems that any truth function that you could produce would fulfill the requirement of being true in any case in which $(P \supset \sim Q) \cdot PQ$ was true."

This is so. In fact we can state a general rule, which extends to all assertions, not merely to truth functional ones. This is, that an inconsistent assertion implies any other assertion. If you are given two assertions, and the first one is inconsistent, then you can conclude that the first implies the second.

This may strike the reader as rather peculiar. The rule is so sweeping that it forces us to treat an inconsistent assertion as implying even assertions which use completely different symbols. But the point to keep in mind here is that the rule just stated is a technical rule in a precisely defined, artificial system. The rule is correct by definition, precisely because it is part of the "grammar" of the artificial language used by symbolic logicians.

Many logicians misrepresent the rule that we have just presented by treating it as if it were a rule of the ordinary use of English language. It is true that in ordinary, nontechnical English, when someone makes an inconsistent statement, someone else is likely to remark, "If you say that, you can say anything." But, on the other hand, if someone says, "The face of the moon is completely green now and is not completely green now," we are not likely to accuse him of implying that Boston is the capital of Russia. In general, the way the word "implies" is used in ordinary English, we do not say that people who make inconsistent statements thereby imply all sorts of things on completely different topics.

In other words, symbolic logicians do give the word "implies" a special technical meaning. The logicians' use of the word is different from, and only slightly related to, the use of the word in ordinary nontechnical English. The rule which we have just presented stands as part of an account of what symbolic logicians mean by "implies." Learning the rule is in effect part of learning the language of logicians.

There is a complementary rule concerning tautologous assertions which we can illustrate by another example. Let us suppose that we inquire as to whether $(P \supset Q) \rightarrow (PQ \vee (\sim P \vee \sim Q))$.

The truth table for $P \supset Q$ is the following:

P	Q	$P \supset Q$
T	T	T
T	F	F
F	T	T
F	F	T

The truth table for *PQ* is:

P	Q	PQ
T	T	T
T	F	F
F	T	F
F	F	F

The truth table for ~*P*v~*Q* is:

P	Q	~Pv~Q
T	T	F
T	F	T
F	T	T
F	F	T

This gives us, as the truth table for *PQ*v(~*P*v~*Q)* the following:

P	Q	PQ	~Pv~Q	PQv(~Pv~Q)
T	T	T	F	T
T	F	F	T	T
F	T	F	T	T
F	F	F	T	T

The final column will have a *T* in every line in which there is at least one *T* in the third and fourth columns. In each line there is at least one *T* in these columns, as it turns out. Thus the final column consists entirely of *T*'s. That is, *PQ*v(~*P*v~*Q)* is true in every possible case. It is tautologous.

The reader will see that *P*⊃*Q* implies *PQ*v(~*P*v~*Q)*. In every possible case in which *P*⊃*Q* is true, *PQ*v(~*P*v~*Q)* will be true also. If *P*⊃*Q* is true, *PQ*v(~*P*v~*Q)* will have to be true. The reader will see also that any function whatsoever would have this relation to *PQ*v(~*P*v~*Q)*. We can generalize, and say that any tautology is implied by any statement whatsoever.

We might point out, as we did in the case of the rule concerning inconsistent assertions, that what we have here provides part of the special meaning that logicians give to the word "implies." Let us illustrate the point. An example of a tautology in English would be the statement, "Either there exists a King of France or there does not exist a King of France." This is a tautology; but we would not feel justified in saying to someone who had just made a remark about the weather, "What you say implies that either there exists a King of France or there does not exist a King of France."

What we are reminding the reader of is that the rule just stated has to be understood within the context of the formal system of symbolic logic. Within this system it is true, as a facet of the meaning of the logician's term "implies," that a tautology is implied by any statement whatsoever.

EXERCISES FOR SECTION 1.3.1.

A. 1. Does $PQv(P\cdot\sim Q)$ imply $\sim Q\supset P$?
    2. Does $\sim(P\supset\sim Q)$ imply $\sim QvP$?
    3. Does $\sim QvP$ imply $\sim(P\supset\sim Q)$?
    4. Does $(\sim P\cdot Q)vP$ imply $\sim(\sim Q\cdot\sim P)$?
    5. Does $\sim(\sim Q\cdot\sim P)$ imply $(\sim P\cdot Q)$?
    6. Does $Pv(QvR)$ imply $(PvQ)vR$?
    7. Does $P\supset(Q\supset R)$ imply $(P\supset Q)\supset R$?
    8. Does $P\supset(Q\supset P)$ imply PvQ?
    9. Does PQ imply $\sim(P\supset(Q\supset P))$?
    10. Does $\sim(P\supset(Q\supset P))$ imply $\sim((PvQ)v(\sim Pv\sim Q))$?
B. Which of the following is equivalent to $(P\supset Q)\cdot(\sim P\supset Q)$?
    PQ
    $\sim Pv\sim Q$
    $Pv\sim P$
    Q
    $(Q\supset P)\cdot(Q\supset\sim P)$
    $P\cdot\sim Q$
C. Which of the following is equivalent to $\sim(Pv\sim Q)$?
    $\sim PvQ$
    $\sim P\supset Q$
    $\sim P\cdot Q$
    $\sim(Q\supset P)$
    $\sim(P\supset\sim Q)$

1.3.2. Demonstrating equivalence without use of truth tables

In this and 1.3.3., we shall consider ways of determining implication and equivalence among truth functions without relying on truth tables. As we stated before, the techniques that we shall now consider ought to provide the same results as techniques which involve truth tables. But once one is familiar with their use, they are less cumbersome. In case of doubt, any result achieved by means of the techniques which we are now presenting can be checked by means of truth tables.

First, we shall consider relations of equivalence. We shall begin by presenting twenty-six basic formulas of equivalence. These formulas are "basic" in that they represent the twenty-six handiest tools to start with. They do not represent anything even approaching an axiomatic treatment of the subject. That is, we are not attempting to reduce logic for the reader to a very neat system; instead, we are giving the reader tools with which he can familiarize himself with techniques of symbolic logic.

Here are the twenty-six formulas:

1. $\sim(PQ)\equiv\sim P v\sim Q$
2. $\sim(PvQ)\equiv\sim P\cdot\sim Q$
3. $\sim\sim P\equiv P$
4. $P\supset Q\equiv\sim PvQ$
5. $PP\equiv P$
6. $PvP\equiv P$
7. $P\cdot QP\equiv QP$
8. $PvQP\equiv P$
9. $Pv(QvP)\equiv PvQ$
10. $P\cdot(QvP)\equiv P$
11. $P\cdot(Qv\sim P)\equiv PQ$
12. $Pv(Q\cdot\sim P)\equiv PvQ$
13. $P\cdot(Q\cdot\sim P)\equiv P\cdot\sim P$ (which is inconsistent)
14. $Pv(Qv\sim P)\equiv Pv\sim P$ (which is tautologous)
15. $P\cdot(Q\cdot\sim Q)\equiv Q\cdot\sim Q$ (which is inconsistent)
16. $P\cdot(Qv\sim Q)\equiv P$
17. $Pv(Q\cdot\sim Q)\equiv P$
18. $Pv(Qv\sim Q)\equiv Qv\sim Q$ (which is tautologous)
19. $PQ\equiv QP$
20. $PvQ\equiv QvP$
21. $P\cdot(QR)\equiv(PQ)\cdot R\equiv PQR$
22. $Pv(QvR)\equiv(PvQ)vR\equiv PvQvR$
23. $P\cdot(QvR)\equiv PQvPR$
24. If $X\equiv Y$, then $\sim X\equiv\sim Y$
25. If $X\equiv Y$, then $Y\equiv X$
26. If $X\equiv Y$ and $Y\equiv Z$, then $X\equiv Z$

The reader might do well to copy these formulas on cards. Just the act of copying the formulas will help him in familiarizing himself with them; and later on, the reader will find it handier to refer to cards than to previous pages in this book.

All of the twenty-six formulas should strike the reader as intuitively "right." For example, the first formula simply states that to negate the conjunction of two assertions is to say that at least one of the two must be false. The second formula, similarly, states that to deny that at least one of two assertions is true is to say that both are false.

The reader may care to verify the first twenty-three formulas by means of truth tables. The last three formulas represent not so much particular relations of equivalence as generalizations built into the meaning of "equivalent."

There are two things that we should point out about the twenty-six formulas. They are both things that the reader has to know if he is to find the formulas useful.

One is that P, Q, R, X, Y, and Z, in our statement of the formulas, should be taken as dummies which can stand for anything. In other words, any expression can be substituted for P, Q, R, X, Y, or Z, and the resulting assertion will be true. Let us take for example the first formula. It is $\sim(PQ)\equiv\sim P\mathbf{v}\sim Q$. We can substitute, say, $R\supset\sim S$ for Q. We would get $\sim(P\cdot(R\supset\sim S))\equiv\sim P\mathbf{v}\sim(R\supset\sim S)$. This is indeed a correct statement. In general, we can substitute any expressions whatsoever for P, Q, R, X, Y, and Z in any of our twenty-six formulas, and come out with a correct statement.

We can even substitute $\sim Q$, say, for Q. In the first formula this would give us $\sim(P\cdot\sim Q)\equiv\sim P\mathbf{v}\sim\sim Q$. Thus the first formula can be used not only to give us an equivalent for $\sim(PQ)$, but also for $\sim(P\cdot\sim Q)$—and for that matter for $\sim(\sim P\cdot Q)$ and $\sim(\sim P\cdot\sim Q)$.

The second point is this. If two truth functions are equivalent, either one can be substituted for the other within the context of a larger expression. This is very much like what we would do if, every time the number 4 occurred within an expression, we substituted "The number which equals 2 plus 2," or vice versa. Such a substitution would have no effect on the truth of what was being asserted. By substituting a truth function for an equivalent truth function in this way, we can transform an assertion into something that reads differently but is equivalent. After a number of such transformations, we may emerge with an expression which looks very different from our original one but still is equivalent.

The most obvious use of our formulas is to reduce complicated truth functional expressions to equivalent simple ones. We shall give some examples of how this is done. Formula 26 will be involved in all our operations, since it states the principle that if an expression X is equivalent to an expression which is equivalent to the expression with which we start out, then expression X is equivalent to the expression with which we start out. As an example of its application: suppose that we have a chain of six expressions each one of which is equivalent to the previous one. Since the third is equivalent to the second, which is equivalent to the first, then the third is equivalent to the first. But since the fourth is equivalent to the third, which is equivalent to the first, the fourth is equivalent to the first. The fifth, being equivalent to the fourth, is equivalent to the first; and the sixth, being equivalent to the fifth, is equivalent to the first. In general, every member of a chain of equivalences is equivalent to the first member of the chain. We shall take this for granted, and not invoke formula 26 during each argument.

Suppose first that we want to find a simple expression that is equivalent to $\sim((PvQ)\cdot(P\supset(Q\cdot\sim P)))$.

We might begin by using formula 4. That reads $P\supset Q\equiv\sim PvQ$. If we let $Q\cdot\sim P$ stand in for Q in that formula, we get $P\supset(Q\cdot\sim P)\equiv\sim Pv(Q\cdot\sim P)$. We can replace the left-hand side of this, $P\supset(Q\cdot\sim P)$, by the right-hand side, $\sim Pv(Q\cdot\sim P)$, in the expression that we are working with. This gives us $\sim((PvQ)\cdot(\sim Pv(Q\cdot\sim P)))$.

We can now use formula 1. This reads $\sim(PQ)\equiv\sim Pv\sim Q$. $\sim((PvQ)\cdot(\sim Pv(Q\cdot\sim P)))$, like $\sim(PQ)$, is the negation of a conjunction. We let PvQ stand in for P in formula 1, and $\sim Pv(Q\cdot\sim P)$ stand in for Q. This gives us $\sim((PvQ)\cdot(\sim Pv(Q\cdot\sim P)))\equiv\sim(PvQ)v\sim(\sim Pv(Q\cdot\sim P))$.

In reducing $\sim(PvQ)v\sim(\sim Pv(Q\cdot\sim P))$, we can apply formula 8 to the $\sim Pv(Q\cdot\sim P)$ component. Formula 8 reads $PvQP\equiv P$. If we let $\sim P$ stand in for P, and Q for Q, we get $\sim Pv(Q\cdot\sim P)\equiv\sim P$. Replacing $\sim Pv(Q\cdot\sim P)$ by $\sim P$, we have:

$\sim(PvQ)v\sim(\sim P)$

We can drop the last parentheses, which are no longer needed as punctuation, and write:

$\sim(PvQ)v\sim\sim P$

Formula 3 applied to $\sim\sim P$ gives us P. Thus we have:

$\sim(PvQ)vP$

Formula 2 allows us to replace $\sim(PvQ)$ by $\sim P\cdot\sim Q$. This gives us:

$(\sim P\cdot\sim Q)vP$

We can now use formula 20, letting $\sim P\cdot\sim Q$ stand in for P, and P stand in for Q. This allows us to write:

$Pv(\sim P\cdot\sim Q)$

Formula 19 allows us to write $\sim P\cdot\sim Q$ as $\sim Q\cdot\sim P$. This gives us:

$Pv(\sim Q\cdot\sim P)$

We can now apply formula 12, letting P stand in for P, and $\sim Q$ for Q. This gives us finally:

$Pv\sim Q$

$Pv\sim Q$ thus is equivalent to $\sim((PvQ)\cdot(P\supset(Q\cdot\sim P)))$. The reader may care to check this by means of truth tables.

As another example, we shall reduce $(Pv(\sim P\cdot\sim Q))\supset PQ$ to a simpler expression.

First we shall apply formula 19 to the $\sim P\cdot\sim Q$ component. Formula 19 reads $PQ\equiv QP$. If we let $\sim P$ stand in for P, and $\sim Q$ stand in for Q, we get

$\sim P \cdot \sim Q \equiv \sim Q \cdot \sim P$. Thus we can substitute $\sim Q \cdot \sim P$ for $\sim P \cdot \sim Q$. This gives us:

$(Pv(\sim Q \cdot \sim P)) \supset PQ$

We can now use formula 12, letting P stand in for P, and $\sim Q$ for Q. This then tells us that $Pv(\sim Q \cdot \sim P) \equiv Pv \sim Q$. Replacing $Pv(\sim Q \cdot \sim P)$ by $Pv \sim Q$, we get:

$(Pv \sim Q) \supset PQ$

We can apply formula 4 to this. Formula 4 reads $P \supset Q \equiv \sim PvQ$. We let $Pv \sim Q$ stand in for P, and PQ for Q. This tells us that $(Pv \sim Q) \supset PQ$ is equivalent to:

$\sim(Pv \sim Q)vPQ$

We apply formula 2 to the $\sim(Pv \sim Q)$ component of this. We let P stand in for P, and $\sim Q$ for Q. This gives us $\sim(Pv \sim Q) \equiv \sim P \cdot \sim \sim Q$. We replace $\sim(Pv \sim Q)$ by $\sim P \cdot \sim \sim Q$ and get:

$(\sim P \cdot \sim \sim Q)vPQ$

Formula 3 tells us that $\sim \sim Q$ is Q. Thus we write:

$(\sim P \cdot Q)vPQ$

Formula 19 allows us to write $\sim P \cdot Q$ as $Q \cdot \sim P$, and PQ as QP. Thus we have:

$(Q \cdot \sim P)vQP$

Formula 20 allows us to write this as:

$QPv(Q \cdot \sim P)$

We now can apply formula 23. This reads $P \cdot (QvR) \equiv PQvPR$. Looking at the right-hand side of this, we let Q stand in for P, P stand in for Q, and $\sim P$ for R. This allows us to put $QPv(Q \cdot \sim P)$ on the right-hand side of an equivalence sign. On the left-hand side would go:

$Q \cdot (Pv \sim P)$

We now apply formula 16, letting Q stand in for P, and P stand in for Q. This shows us that our expression is equivalent to:

Q

Thus $(Pv(\sim P \cdot \sim Q)) \supset PQ$ is equivalent to Q.

We shall give one more example of how the techniques that we are demonstrating can be used in reducing complicated truth functional expressions to less complicated ones, and then we shall move on to give a couple of examples of how they can be used also to establish relations of equivalence of pairs of uncomplicated truth functional expressions. But first we might remark that the techniques that we are demonstrating are not so difficult and slow as they might seem at first. We of course have been spelling out our operations in great detail. The student will find that after practice he will be able to perform many of the operations mentally in a few seconds.

The last complicated truth function that we shall reduce to a simpler form is $(\sim Pv \sim Q) \supset (Q \cdot (Pv \sim Q))$. We can begin by applying formula 11 to the

$Q \cdot (P v \sim Q)$ component. Formula 11 reads $P \cdot (Q v \sim P) \equiv PQ$. If we let Q stand in for P, and P for Q, we get $Q \cdot (P v \sim Q) \equiv QP$. If we replace $Q \cdot (P v \sim Q)$ by QP, we have:

$(\sim P v \sim Q) \supset QP$

We can apply formula 4 to this, letting $\sim P v \sim Q$ stand in for P, and QP stand in for Q. This gives us:

$\sim (\sim P v \sim Q) v QP$

We can apply formula 2 to the $\sim (\sim P v \sim Q)$ component of this, letting $\sim P$ stand in for P, and $\sim Q$ stand in for Q. This gives us $\sim (\sim P v \sim Q) \equiv \sim \sim P \cdot \sim \sim Q$. This allows us to write our expression as:

$(\sim \sim P \cdot \sim \sim Q) v QP$

Formula 3 enables us to replace $\sim \sim P$ by P, and $\sim \sim Q$ by Q, which leaves us with:

$PQ v QP$

Formula 19 allows us to write the QP as PQ. This gives us:

$PQ v PQ$

We now apply formula 6, letting PQ stand in for P. This simplifies our expression further to:

PQ

Thus $(\sim P v \sim Q) \supset (Q \cdot (P v \sim Q))$ is equivalent to PQ.

Our two demonstrations of the equivalence of a pair of uncomplicated truth functional expressions both will involve $P \supset Q$. We shall show that $P \supset Q$ is equivalent to $\sim Q \supset \sim P$, and then we shall show that $P \supset Q$ is also equivalent to $\sim (P \cdot \sim Q)$.

In showing that $P \supset Q$ is equivalent to $\sim Q \supset \sim P$, we shall subject $P \supset Q$ to a series of transformations. Each member in the series of transformations, being equivalent to the previous one, will be equivalent to $P \supset Q$. We can begin by using formula 4, which tells us that $P \supset Q$ is equivalent to:

$\sim P v Q$

Formula 20 allows us to write the foregoing expression as:

$Q v \sim P$

We can now apply formula 3, letting Q stand in for P. This tells us that $\sim \sim Q \equiv Q$. We use this by substituting $\sim \sim Q$ for Q in our expression. This gives us:

$\sim \sim Q v \sim P$

We now can use formula 4 again. We let $\sim Q$ stand in for P, and $\sim P$ stand in for Q. With these substitutions, formula 4 will read $\sim Q \supset \sim P \equiv \sim \sim Q v \sim P$.

Thus we arrive at $\sim Q \supset \sim P$.

The transition from $P \supset Q$ to $\sim (P \cdot \sim Q)$ is shorter.

We begin again by using formula 4, which gives us:

$\sim P v Q$

We now use formula 3, which allows us to replace Q by $\sim\sim Q$. This gives us:

$\sim Pv\sim\sim Q$

If we let P stand in for P in formula 1, and $\sim Q$ for Q, we have $\sim(P\cdot\sim Q)\equiv\sim Pv\sim\sim Q$.

Thus we arrive at $\sim(P\cdot\sim Q)$.

EXERCISES FOR SECTION 1.3.2.

A. 1. Find a relatively uncomplicated expression which is equivalent to $(PvQ)\supset(\sim Qv(P\supset Q))$.

2. Find a relatively uncomplicated expression which is equivalent to $\sim((PvQ)\supset\sim P)\cdot(P\supset Q)$.

3. Find a relatively uncomplicated expression which is equivalent to $(Q\supset(\sim Pv\sim Q))\supset(\sim P\cdot\sim Q)$.

4. Find a relatively uncomplicated expression which is equivalent to $(Pv\sim P)\supset(P\cdot\sim Q)$.

5. Find a relatively uncomplicated expression which is equivalent to $(Pv(QvP))\cdot(\sim P\supset Q)$.

6. Find a relatively uncomplicated expression which is equivalent to $\sim((PvQ)\supset\sim P)$.

B. 1. Show that PvQ is equivalent to $\sim P\supset Q$.

2. Show that PQ is equivalent to $\sim(P\supset\sim Q)$.

1.3.3. *Demonstrating implication without use of truth tables*

We turn now to implication. In one respect, we have been considering implication for some time, since equivalence is simply mutual implication. But in applying our formulas for equivalence, in 1.3.2., we were just finding a number of ways of saying the same thing. If two expressions are equivalent, then they are making the same claim, although they may be making it in different ways. On the other hand, if a formula X implies a formula Y, X may well say more than Y. Thus, in these pages we shall on the whole *not* be producing a number of ways to say the same thing.

The difference between equivalence and implication might be put as follows. To say that X is equivalent to Y is to say that X and Y are saying the same thing. To say that X implies Y is to assert that X says what Y says, but also leaves open the possibility that X says more than what Y says: i.e., that X says what Y says, but also says more. In other words, "X implies Y" can be read as "X says what Y says (and maybe more)." Of course if X implies Y and Y implies X, then, putting together the assertion that X says at least as much as Y and the assertion that Y says at least as much as X, we conclude that X and Y say the same thing. This is equivalence. The reader may find this helpful in understanding the definition of equivalence as being mutual implication.

The best analogy outside of logic to what we have been explaining is the "greater than or equal to" relation in mathematics. If X is greater than or equal to Y, and Y is greater than or equal to X, then we can conclude that X and Y are equal. This is a precise analogue to the fact that when X implies Y and Y implies X we conclude that they say the same thing and are equivalent.

The twenty-six formulas that we gave in 1.3.2. can be regarded as formulas of implication, although they have the special feature that either side of the formula implies the other. They are, that is, formulas of mutual implication. We shall give some more formulas of implication now which will *not* be formulas of mutual implication. That is, we shall produce some basic formulas in which the left-hand side implies the right-hand side, but the right-hand side does not imply the left-hand side.

They are as follows:

I.1 $PQ \rightarrow P$
I.2 $P \rightarrow (P \lor Q)$
I.3 $((P \supset Q) \cdot (Q \supset R)) \rightarrow (P \supset R)$
I.4 $(P \cdot \sim P) \rightarrow R$
I.5 $R \rightarrow (P \lor \sim P)$
I.6 If $X \rightarrow Y$, and $Y \rightarrow Z$, then $X \rightarrow Z$

The reader might again wish to write these formulas down on cards.

All six formulas deserve comment. The first makes the intuitively agreeable claim that if someone asserts two things in conjunction, he has said at least as much as if he had asserted either of them by itself. By asserting both, he has committed himself to either. The second formula also makes a claim that accords well with ordinary language. If someone has asserted something, then he has committed himself to agreeing that at least one of the pair formed by that thing and another thing is true. If I assert that Albany is the capital of New York, then I have committed myself to agreeing that at least one of the statements "Albany is the capital of New York" and "We will get to the moon by 1975" is true.

The third of these formulas also accords fairly well with ordinary language. If, for example, we say that "If X happens, Y will happen; and if Y happens, Z will happen," we ordinarily then feel committed to agreeing that "If X happens, Z will happen."

The fourth formula represents something that was already discussed. Earlier we said that logicians use the word "implies" in such a way that an inconsistent statement is said to imply any statement whatsoever. This convention of the language of logicians is expressed in the fourth formula. We also had reported that logicians use the word "implies" in such a way that any tautologous statement is said to be implied by any statement whatsoever. This is expressed by the fifth formula.

The sixth formula represents something which is intuitively agreeable, but also is required even for very simple logical arguments. It states that if one assertion implies a second assertion, and the second assertion implies a third, then the first assertion implies the third. Thus, for example, we can apply it immediately to the first and second formulas. The first asserts that $PQ \rightarrow P$; the second that $P \rightarrow (P \lor Q)$. Putting the two together, and applying the principle stated in the sixth formula, we can conclude that $PQ \rightarrow (P \lor Q)$.

Another obvious application of the sixth formula concerns equivalence, which is of course mutual implication. Applying the sixth formula, we can conclude that if $X \equiv Y$, and if $Y \rightarrow Z$, then $X \rightarrow Z$. We also can conclude that if $Y \equiv Z$, and $X \rightarrow Y$, then $X \rightarrow Z$. Also, by the same reasoning that we used in 1.3.2. in connection with formula 26, we can conclude that if we have a chain of assertions, each one of which is implied by or mutually implies the preceding one, then any member of the chain is implied by the first assertion in the chain.

The P, Q, R, X, Y, and Z used in stating these six formulas are just dummies, and anything whatsoever can be substituted for them. For example, in formula I.1, we can substitute $\sim(P \lor Q)$ for P, and $\sim P$ for Q, and get the assertion that $(\sim(P \lor Q) \cdot \sim P) \rightarrow \sim(P \lor Q)$. We could simply substitute $\sim P$ for P, and $\sim Q$ for Q, and get $(\sim P \cdot \sim Q) \rightarrow \sim P$. We could even replace both P and Q by P, and get $PP \rightarrow P$.

Let us see now how these six formulas, plus the twenty-six formulas of equivalence that we presented earlier, can be used in determining relations of implication. In annotating steps of arguments, we shall refer to the six formulas by prefixing their numbers with "I." Thus if a step is marked as justified by formula I.5, this means that the step is justified by the fifth of the formulas of implication that we have just presented. If a step is marked as justified by a formula whose number is not prefixed with an "I," that means that the formula in question is one of the twenty-six formulas of equivalence; e.g., if a step is marked as justified by formula 5, this means that it is justified by the fifth of the twenty-six formulas.

Suppose that we wish to determine whether $((P \supset (\sim Q \lor \sim P)) \cdot \sim Q) \rightarrow (\sim Q \lor P)$. We can show that it does by the following method. First we reduce $(P \supset (\sim Q \lor \sim P)) \cdot \sim Q$ to a simple expression which is equivalent to it. Then we show that this simple expression implies $\sim Q \lor P$. By formula I.6, if $(P \supset (\sim Q \lor \sim P)) \cdot \sim Q$ mutually implies (i.e., is equivalent to) the simple expression, and if the simple expression implies $\sim Q \lor P$, then $(P \supset (\sim Q \lor P)) \cdot \sim Q$ implies $\sim Q \lor P$.

In transforming $(P \supset (\sim Qv \sim P)) \cdot \sim Q$, first we apply formula 4 to the $P \supset (\sim Qv \sim P)$ component. We let P stand in for P, and $\sim Qv \sim P$ for Q. This gives us $P \supset (\sim Qv \sim P) \equiv \sim Pv(\sim Qv \sim P)$. We substitute $\sim Pv(\sim Qv \sim P)$ for $P \supset (\sim Qv \sim P)$ in our larger expression. This gives us:

$(\sim Pv(\sim Qv \sim P)) \cdot \sim Q$

We can apply formula 9 to the $\sim Pv(\sim Qv \sim P)$ component, letting $\sim P$ stand in for P, and $\sim Q$ stand in for Q. This allows us to replace $\sim Pv$ $(\sim Qv \sim P)$ by $\sim Pv \sim Q$. This leaves us with:

$(\sim Pv \sim Q) \cdot \sim Q$

Formula 19 allows us to write this as:

$\sim Q \cdot (\sim Pv \sim Q)$

If we now apply formula 10, letting $\sim Q$ stand in for P, and $\sim P$ stand in for Q, we get:

$\sim Q$

The reader should be clear that this latest expression, $\sim Q$, is equivalent to $(P \supset (\sim Qv \sim P)) \cdot \sim Q$. We can now apply formula I.2, letting $\sim Q$ stand in for P, and P stand in for Q. This tells us that $\sim Q$ implies $\sim QvP$. By formula 16, if $(P \supset (\sim Qv \sim P)) \cdot \sim Q$ mutually implies $\sim Q$, and $\sim Q$ implies $\sim QvP$, then we can conclude that $((P \supset (\sim Qv \sim P)) \cdot \sim Q) \rightarrow (\sim QvP)$.

As another example, we shall show that $PQ \rightarrow ((PvQ) \supset (\sim P \supset \sim Q))$. We shall do this by reducing $(PvQ) \supset (\sim P \supset \sim Q)$ to a less complicated expression, and by showing that PQ implies this expression. Then, by formula I.6, we shall be able to conclude that PQ implies $(PvQ) \supset (\sim P \supset \sim Q)$.

In reducing $(PvQ) \supset (\sim P \supset \sim Q)$, we can first apply formula 4 to the $\sim P \supset \sim Q$ component. We let $\sim P$ stand in for P, and $\sim Q$ stand in for Q. This allows us to replace $\sim P \supset \sim Q$ by $\sim \sim Pv \sim Q$. This gives us:

$(PvQ) \supset (\sim \sim Pv \sim Q)$

Formula 3 allows us to replace $\sim \sim P$ by P, leaving us with:

$(PvQ) \supset (Pv \sim Q)$

We now apply formula 4 again, letting PvQ stand in for P, and $Pv \sim Q$ stand in for Q. This gives us:

$\sim (PvQ)v(Pv \sim Q)$

Formula 2 enables us to replace $\sim (PvQ)$ by $\sim P \cdot \sim Q$, giving us:

$(\sim P \cdot \sim Q)v(Pv \sim Q)$

We now apply formula 21, letting $\sim P \cdot \sim Q$ stand in for P, P stand in for Q, and $\sim Q$ stand in for R. This tells us that $(\sim P \cdot \sim Q)v(Pv \sim Q)$ is equivalent to:

$((\sim P \cdot \sim Q)vP)v \sim Q$

Formula 20 allows us to rewrite the above as $\sim Qv((\sim P \cdot \sim Q)vP)$, and then as $\sim Qv(Pv(\sim P \cdot \sim Q))$. Formula 19 allows us to rewrite the $\sim P \cdot \sim Q$ component as $\sim Q \cdot \sim P$, which leaves us with:

$\sim Qv(Pv(\sim Q \cdot \sim P))$

We can apply formula 12 to the $Pv(\sim Q \cdot \sim P)$ component. We let P stand in for P, and Q stand in for Q. This allows us to replace $Pv(\sim Q \cdot \sim P)$ by $Pv\sim Q$ leaving us with:

$\sim Qv(Pv\sim Q)$

We apply formula 9 to this, letting $\sim Q$ stand in for P, and P stand in for Q. This gives us:

$\sim QvP$

which formula 20 allows us to write as:

$Pv\sim Q$

Formula I.1 tells us that PQ implies P. If we use formula I.2, letting P stand in for P, and $\sim Q$ for Q, this asserts that P in its turn implies $Pv\sim Q$. By formula I.6, we can conclude that PQ implies $Pv\sim Q$. Since $Pv\sim Q$ mutually implies $(PvQ)\supset(\sim P\supset\sim Q)$, we can conclude finally that:

$PQ\rightarrow((PvQ)\supset(\sim P\supset\sim Q))$.

The last example we shall give will involve demonstrating that $(P\cdot(P\supset Q))\rightarrow Q$. The assertion that this implication holds, by the way, is traditionally known as *modus ponens*.

We can begin by using formula 4 to transform $P\cdot(P\supset Q)$. If we replace the $P\supset Q$ component in $P\cdot(P\supset Q)$ by $\sim PvQ$, we have:

$P\cdot(\sim PvQ)$

Formula 20 allows us to rewrite the $\sim PvQ$ component as $Qv\sim P$, which gives us:

$P\cdot(Qv\sim P)$

According to formula 11, this is equivalent to:

PQ

Formula 19 permits us to write this as:

QP

We can apply formula I.1 to this, letting Q stand in for P, and P stand in for Q. This gives us $QP\rightarrow Q$. Since QP is equivalent to $P\cdot(P\supset Q)$, we can conclude that $(P\cdot(P\supset Q))\rightarrow Q$.

EXERCISES FOR SECTION 1.3.3.

1. Show that $(P\cdot(\sim Q\supset\sim P))\rightarrow(Qv\sim P)$.
2. Show that $(\sim(\sim(PvQ)vQ))\rightarrow P$.
3. Show that $(P\cdot(\sim Q\supset\sim P)\cdot(\sim R\supset\sim Q))\rightarrow R$.
4. Show that $(P\cdot(Q\supset P)\rightarrow(\sim Q\supset P)$.

2. An introduction to quantificational symbols

The part of symbolic logic that we shall now consider gets its start when we add some more symbols to the symbolic apparatus. The most important new symbols are *(x)* and *(∃ x)*. They are called *quantificational* symbols because they say something about "how many" *X*'s we are talking about. We shall begin by explaining the meaning of these symbols and of the other symbols that we shall add to our apparatus. Then we shall explore some of the logical operations made possible by the use of these symbols.

2.1.1. The symbol (x)

The symbol *(x)* corresponds very closely to the English phrases "for all *x*'s" or "for any *x*." Of course *x* is a variable: that is, it stands for a range of things within a class. When we use the symbol *(x)* we are speaking of a class of things, not of any given (or even unspecified) individual thing. For example, if we say, "*(x)* (if *x* is a man, *x* is mortal)," we are saying that anything, if it is a man, is mortal. We are saying something about all things that are men. This says something by implication about individuals such as Jones and Smith; but what we are referring to directly is not an individual, or individuals, but the class of men.

Using the *(x)* symbol, we can make general claims about any class of things that we wish. All we have to say is "*(x)* (if *x* belongs to such-and-such class, then *x* is so-and-so)." By a statement of this form, we are saying that all members of such-and-such class are so-and-so. "*(x)* (if *x* is a *Y*, then *x* is *Z*)" is just another way of saying, "All *Y*'s are *Z*."

How then would we symbolize the assertion that all men are mortal? Of course we have already written, "*(x)* (if *x* is a man, *x* is mortal)," but we can replace the English word "if" by further symbolization. The correct symbolization is as follows:

"*(x)* (*x* is a man ⊃ *x* is mortal)"

We should explain why this is the correct symbolization, and *not* "*(x)* (*x* is a man·*x* is mortal)" or "*(x)* (*x* is a man→*x* is mortal)."

"*(x)* (*x* is a man *x* is mortal)" is wrong for an obvious reason. We are asserting that all men are mortal. We are not asserting that all things are men (and mortal). But "*(x)* (*x* is a man·*x* is mortal)" says (translated into English) that for all *x*'s, *x* is a man and *x* is mortal. In other words, it says that all things are men and are mortal. This asserts far more than that all men are mortal.

The difficulty with "*(x)* (*x* is a man→*x* is mortal)" is more subtle. This symbolism would be a correct representation of a claim that if something is a man, it thereby has to be mortal. But it appears that "All men are mortal" does not make such a claim. When we say, "All men are mortal," we are saying that all men who happen to exist are mortal. We are saying nothing to deny that one could conceive of creatures like Swift's Struldbrugs, whom we would call men but who are immortal. Thus "All men are mortal" makes no implicit claim that in order to be what we would call a man, a thing *has* to be mortal. But there is an implicit claim in "All men are mortal" that Struldbrugs in fact do not exist, that all men *are* mortal.

There is a point relevant to the preceding discussion which ought to be brought out. Earlier, in explaining logicians' use of the symbol *(x)*, we rendered it as "for all *x*'s." A more accurate general translation of *(x)* would be "for all existing *x*'s." Thus "*(x)* (*x* is a man $\supset$ *x* is mortal)" should be read as asserting that all men that exist are mortal. "*(x)* (*x* is a goldfish $\supset$ *x* has fins)" asserts that all existing goldfish have fins.

This rendering of *(x)* as "for all existing *x*'s" leads to certain peculiarities that we should discuss. Suppose that, for example, we are talking about unicorns. Unicorns, as the reader knows, have a single horn. But unicorns are now generally considered not to exist. It is then true that "*(x)* (*x* is a unicorn $\supset$ *x* has a single horn)"?

The answer is "yes." It is true, so to speak, by default. "*(x)* (*x* is a unicorn $\supset$ *x* has a single horn)" asserts that all unicorns (which exist) have single horns. Or, to put it another way, it asserts that there are no existent unicorns which do not have single horns. And this is obviously true, because there are no unicorns at all. If there are no existent unicorns, there also are no existent unicorns which do not have single horns.

The reader will see, then, that for the very same reason that "*(x)* (*x* is a unicorn $\supset$ *x* has a single horn)" is true, "*(x)* (*x* is a unicorn $\supset$ *x* has ten horns)" would also be counted as true. "*(x)* (*x* is a unicorn $\supset$ *x* has ten horns)" asserts that all existent unicorns have ten horns. In other words, it asserts that there is no existent unicorn which does not have ten horns. Since there are no existent unicorns, there are no existent unicorns which do not have ten horns.

Indeed any sweeping assertion that one cares to make about existent unicorns will be counted by logicians as true. Any statement of the form "*(x)* (*x* is a unicorn $\supset$ *x* is a such-and-such)" will count as true, for the reasons we have given.

Thus the reader should realize two central facts about the use of the symbol *(x)*. One is that it makes a claim about all things. If we wish to make a claim about all things in a certain class—say the claim that all such-and-such's are so-and-so—we write, "*(x)* (*x* is a such-and-such $\supset$ *x* is a so-and-so)." The other is that the range which the variable *x* covers is a range of things that exist. Any general claim that we care to make about a class of things that turns out to be empty—i.e., to have no existent thing within it—

will count as true. Any claim about all *x*'s of a certain type counts as true if in fact there are no *x*'s of that type.

Before discussing the *(∃ x)* symbol, we should present some of the symbolic paraphernalia often used in connection with the *(x)* and *(∃ x)* symbols. This includes the symbols *Fx*, *Gx*, and *Hx*. There are two important differences between the way *F*, *G*, and *H* are used and the way *x* is used. The primary difference is that, whereas *x* is used as a variable whose range consists of existent things, *F*, *G*, and *H* are used to stand for having qualities or membership in a certain class. For example, we might wish to symbolize the fact that Jones is mortal by saying "*G* Jones," and that Jones is a man by "*H* Jones." "If Jones is a man, then Jones is mortal" thus becomes "*H* Jones ⊃ *G* Jones." The second difference is that logicians generally do not quantify *F*, *G*, and *H*, but do quantify *x* (or *y*, and *z*, which are used in the same way as *x*). That is, logicians will speak of "all *x*'s," etc., but in general will not speak of "all *F*'s" or "all *G*'s."

The important thing to keep in mind for the present, though, is that *x*, *y*, and *z* cover a range of things (like Jones, Smith, desks, and tables), whereas *F*, *G*, and *H* will stand for qualities or membership in a class (like being mortal or being a man). A typical example of the way in which the two sorts of symbols are used together is the following. Suppose we wish to symbolize "All men are mortal." Previously we wrote:

"*(x)* (*x* is a man ⊃ *x* is mortal)"

But now we can go further, and write:

(x)(Fx ⊃ Gx)

In this we let *F* stand for being a man, and *G* stand for being mortal.

To take a more complicated example, suppose we wish to symbolize the following argument:

Pigmies are men.

All men are mortal.

Therefore pigmies are mortal.

We can let *Fx* stand for "*x* is a pigmy," *Gx* stand for "*x* is a man," and *Hx* stand for "*x* is mortal." This gives us:

(x)(Fx ⊃ Gx)

(x)(Gx ⊃ Hx)

Therefore *(x)(Fx ⊃ Hx)*

In a short while we shall develop techniques for showing that the above argument is valid.

One further remark should be made about the use of *x*, *y*, *z*, *F*, *G*, and *H* symbols. It is as follows. These symbols are all, so to speak, dummies. If we render symbolically "All men are mortal," it does not matter whether we write *(x)(Fx ⊃ Gx)*, or *(x)(Hx ⊃ Gx)*, or *(y)(Hy ⊃ Gy)*. Any one of these expressions, as well as many others, can adequately symbolize "All men are mortal." Whether we choose *F*, *G*, or *H* to stand for being mortal is an arbitrary matter. But, in constructing a logical argument in symbolic form, there is one basic rule that we must observe. This is that the pattern of symbols must mirror the pattern of words. In any two positions in which the same word occurs (or two words meaning the same thing), we must substitute the same symbol; and in any two positions in which different words occur, we must substitute different symbols.

Take, for example, the argument that we symbolized a short while ago, that all pigmies are mortal. In symbolizing this argument, it is essentially indifferent whether we use (as we did) F to stand for being a pigmy and G for being a man, or G for being a pigmy and F for being a man. The argument can be symbolized equally well in either case. But, once we substitute F for "is a pigmy" in one place, we must substitute F for "is a pigmy" in any other place. If we render, as we did, "Pigmies are men" as $(x)(Fx \supset Gx)$, then in rendering the conclusion that pigmies are mortal, we must once again use F to stand for being a pigmy. Also, once we have used F to stand for being a pigmy, we cannot use it to stand also for being human, or for being mortal. Within the context of a single argument, the same symbol cannot be used to stand for different things.

2.1.2. The symbol $(\exists x)$

We are now ready to discuss our second major new piece of symbolism, $(\exists x)$. The symbol $(\exists x)$ corresponds very closely to the English "There exists at least one x such that." If we want to assert, for example, that there exists at least one carnivorous cat, we could write "$(\exists x)$ (x is a cat $\cdot$ x is carnivorous)." Replacing "is a cat" by F, and "is carnivorous" by G, we can write $(\exists x)(Fx \cdot Gx)$. If we want to symbolize "There exists at least one thing which, if it is a dragon, is fire-breathing," we can write "$(\exists x)$ (if x is a dragon, then x is fire-breathing)." Letting F stand for "is a dragon," and G stand for "is fire-breathing," we could further symbolize this as $(\exists x)$ $(Fx \supset Gx)$.

There are two things which we ought to stress in explicating the $\exists$ symbol. One is that when we write $(\exists x)(Fx)$, we are committing ourselves only to the assertion that there is at least one thing to which F applies. If it turns out that there is only one thing in the universe of which we can say Fx, $(\exists x)(Fx)$ still counts as true. If it turns out that there are a number of things in the universe to which F applies, $(\exists x)(Fx)$ counts as true. The only eventuality in which $(\exists x)(Fx)$ does not count as true is the eventuality that nothing whatsoever exists to which F applies. In this respect it is like the **I** in classical logic.

This point is particularly important because some writers of logic books unwittingly encourage an opposite impression. They speak of the $(\exists x)$ symbol as if it very closely paralleled the phrase "for some x" in English, and as if "$(\exists x)(Fx)$" said very much the same thing as "Some x's are F."

In fact, in most contexts the English word "some" carries with it strong connotations of "at least a few." If you say, "Some people are fishing near the bridge," we shall be surprised if we go down to the bridge and see only one person fishing. The symbol $(\exists x)$, on the other hand, is neutral between interpretations as "one x" or "more than one x." That is, it leaves open both possibilities. When we write $(\exists x)(Fx)$, our assertion would count as true if there was only one thing that was F, and also if there was more than one thing that was F. Thus the meaning of $(\exists x)$ is different from the meaning of "for some x."

The second thing to stress is that the $\exists$ symbol is used by logicians to imply existence. That is, when a logician writes, say, $(\exists x)(Fx \cdot Gx)$, he is asserting that there actually does exist at least one thing in the world which has both the properties F and G. For example, "$(\exists x)$ (x is a cat $\cdot x$ is a carnivorous)" asserts that at least one carnivorous cat does exist.

This feature of the $\exists$ symbol in the logician's artificial language also serves to distinguish it from the use in some contexts of the English word "some." We normally feel that we can truthfully say that "Some sirens sang to Ulysses." Of course what makes the statement true is a fictional episode: what we really are asserting is that in Homer's *Odyssey* there is an episode in which sirens sing to Ulysses. The statement stands as true even though sirens (of the sort that we are talking about) do not in fact exist. On the other hand, if a logician dealt with "$(\exists x)$ (x is a siren $\cdot x$ sang to Ulysses)," he would count it as false when he is informed that no sirens have ever been found in the world. This is because, as we said, the $\exists$ symbol implies actual existence.

The reader can see that the conventions surrounding the $\exists$ symbol run parallel to the conventions surrounding the use of "some" in Boolean algebra. (See 2.2.4. of Chapter 2.) In Boole's artificial variant of English, "some," like the $\exists$ symbol, implies existence.

Because of this feature of the $\exists$ symbol, any statements which are prefixed by it, and which are about a class of nonexistent objects, will count as false. For example, "$(\exists x)$ (x is a unicorn $\cdot x$ has a horn)" counts as false, and so does "$(\exists x)$ (x is a unicorn $\cdot x$ does not have a horn)."

There is one further facet of our use of the $\exists$ symbol that we should explain. We have made clear how the $\exists$ symbol is used in the context of $(\exists x)(Fx)$ ("There exists at least one thing which is an F"), $(\exists x)(Fx \cdot Gx)$ ("There exists at least one thing which is both F and G"), and $(\exists x)(Fx \supset Gx)$ ("There exists at least one thing which, if it is F, also is G"). The reader easily can carry on the use of $\exists$ in other contexts. However, there is one special use of the symbol that we wish to remark upon. This is the use involved when we simply write $\exists x$ without parentheses. When the $\exists x$

symbol occurs in this form, it should be interpreted as asserting simply that there exists at least one thing in the universe. This assertion can be conjoined with assertions about what things in the universe are like. For example, we could write $\exists x \cdot (y)(Fy \supset Gy)$. This conjunction asserts that there exists at least one thing in the universe, and that all things that have the property F also have the property G.

The bare assertion $\exists x$ ("There exists at least one thing in the universe") plays an important part in many logical arguments. This is because logic, as we explained earlier, is concerned with quality of inferences, not with discovery of facts. In doing work in formal logic, logicians prefer not to assume systematically facts about the world. In particular, logicians do not automatically include in all arguments the assumption that there is anything at all in the universe. That is, they do not automatically exclude the possibility that the universe is "empty." If logicians do assume at all, in some given argument, that the universe is not empty, this is stated as a special explicit assumption, and counts as part of the premises of the argument. When this assumption is made, it will be stated as $\exists x$.

2.1.3. Translating from English into quantificational symbols

As we have remarked before, most of formal logic is carried on in an artificial language, the meanings within which are controlled by logicians. Learning logic involves learning to reason within this language (which offers parallels to English, and therefore helps ordinary reasoning). Learning logic also, however, involves simply learning how to *use* the language. The most elementary part of learning logic is learning to judge which logical symbols it is appropriate to use in a given context. Consequently, before we proceed to discuss logical operations which use the symbolism that we have introduced, we should spend a little more time in showing how the symbolism corresponds to English words.

We shall present a number of examples of English sentences and show how these sentences could be translated into logical symbols. Often, of course, there is no very close correspondence between the English words and the logical symbols; and in these cases, part of our explanation will consist in pointing out what is lost in translation.

As our first example, let us take "All whales swim in the sea, and no snark swims in the sea." We shall let F stand for being a whale, G stand for being a snark, and H stand for being something that swims in the sea. The "All whales swim in the sea" component becomes $(x)(Fx \supset Hx)$. We can take the "No snark swims in the sea" component as equivalent to "If something is a snark, it does not swim in the sea." Thus we can render it as

$(x)(Gx \supset \sim Hx)$. The complete expression then would be $(x)(Fx \supset Hx) \cdot (x)$ $(Gx \supset \sim Hx)$.

Let us translate now "Some men are mortal, although there are some men who live to be a hundred." We shall do this by stages, explaining the difficulties as we go along.

First we shall render the part of the sentence which reads "Some men are mortal." Let F stand for being a man, and G stand for being mortal. To say that some men are mortal is to assert that there are beings which are both men and mortal. Thus "Some men are mortal" can be rendered, very roughly, as $(\exists x)(Fx \cdot Gx)$. $(\exists x)(Fx \cdot Gx)$ counts as only a very rough translation of "Some men are mortal," because (as we pointed out earlier) the word "some" carries connotations of "at least a few," whereas the use of the $\exists$ symbol leaves open the possibility of there being only one man who is mortal. Also, while "Some men are mortal" has the flavor of being about existing things, it does not flatly say that mortal men exist.

In rendering "Some men live to be a hundred," we shall, of course, continue to use F for being a man. Let us use H for being a being who lives to be a hundred. In the statement that we are rendering symbolically, there is no implication that the men who are mortal are the men who live to be a hundred. All that is said is that there are some men who are mortal, and some men (who might, for all that is said, be other men) who live to be a hundred. Since this is so, and since we have used x in connection with the existent men who are mortal, we shall use another variable, y, for the men who live to be a hundred. Thus "Some men live to be a hundred" comes out as $(\exists y)(Fy \cdot Hy)$. Once again, of course, this is only a rough translation, since the $\exists$ symbol lacks some of the connotations of "some," and vice versa.

We are now in a position to render symbolically the complete sentence "Some men are mortal, although some men live to be a hundred." What do we do with the word "although"? "Although" has the force of "and." Our sentence asserts, in part, that some men are mortal *and* that some men live to be a hundred. But "although" also has connotations that "and" does not have. It expresses something related to surprise or qualification: when we say *"X, although Y,"* we leave the impression that saying Y diminishes some of the impact of saying X. Being told that some men live to be a hundred takes away a little of the impact of being told that some men are mortal.

These added connotations of "although" cannot be rendered symbolically. There is no symbol in symbolic logic for "although." In translating our sentence into symbolic terms, we have to treat "although" as if it were "and," and confess that a good deal is lost in translation.

Thus in translating "Some men are mortal, although some men live to be a hundred," we get $(\exists x)(Fx \cdot Gx) \cdot (\exists y)(Fy \cdot Hy)$.

Before we go on to examine some further examples, we might state a rule which is helpful in dealing with variables. The rule is this. The symbols *(∃ x)*, *(∃ y)*, *∼(x)*, and *∼(y)* assert existence. The symbols *(x)*, *(y)*, *∼(∃ x)*, and *∼(∃ y)* do not. If the reader keeps this in mind, he can avoid many common errors. For example, students frequently confuse expressions of the form *(x)∼(Fx)* with expressions of the form *∼(x)(Fx)*. They look similar; but the first states that any *x* will lack the property *F*, whereas the second denies that all *x*'s have the property *F,* and thus asserts that there exists at least one *x* which lacks the property of *F*. The first could be true even if in fact no *x*'s exist; the second to be true requires that at least one *x* exists, but could be true even if there are some *x*'s that are *F* as well as some *x*'s that are not *F*.

In symbolizing a statement that calls for symbolization with no more than one symbol asserting existence, one can continue to use the same variable throughout. For example, "All snarks are found on land, and there are kangaroos in Australia" could be symbolized as *"(x) (x* is a snark⊃*x* is found on land) ·*(∃ x) (x* is a kangaroo·*x* is in Australia)." "Everyone who was there was agog; everyone who lives in Florida knows how to swim; and there exist happy sailors" could be symbolized as *"(x) (x* was a person there⊃*x* was agog) ·*(x) (x* is a person living in Florida⊃*x* knows how to swim) ·*(∃ x) (x* is a sailor·*x* is happy)." On the other hand, if two or more symbols asserting existence are called for, and it is not stated that the beings whose existence is being asserted in all cases are the same, then a separate variable should be used with each occurrence of a symbol asserting existence. In one of these occurrences—it does not matter which—the same variable can be used as is used in symbolizing accompanying assertions about "all things" or "no existing thing." E.g., "All kangaroos hop; there are birds in Australia; there are fish in the Pacific Ocean; and the Eiffel Tower exists" could be rendered as *"(x) (x* is a kangaroo⊃*x* hops) ·*(∃ x) (x* is a bird·*x* is in Australia) ·*(∃ y) (y* is a fish·*y* is in the Pacific Ocean) ·*(∃ z) (z* is the Eiffel Tower)."

With the help of this rule, we shall translate three more sample English sentences into symbolic form.

The first is "All kangaroos hop; some kangaroos live in zoos; and some zebras live in zoos." We shall let *F* stand for being a kangaroo, *G* stand for being a zebra, *H* stand for being a thing that hops, and *K* stand for being a thing that lives in a zoo.

The "All kangaroos hop" part of the sentences can be translated quite nicely as *(x)(Fx⊃Hx)*. But what of "Some kangaroos live in zoos"? "Some kangaroos live in zoos" has some of the flavor of being an assertion about existing things: perhaps not so much of this flavor as "Some men are mortal," but much more of the flavor than "Some sirens sang to Ulysses." We might therefore treat it as if it said, "Some kangaroos exist in zoos," and treat "Some zebras are in zoos" as if it said, "Some zebras exist in zoos." In doing this, we are, of course, reading something into our sentence, and also making the symbolic translation that we shall emerge with at best a rough one.

If we treat "Some kangaroos live in zoos" as if it makes a claim about existing kangaroos, we can render it symbolically as $(\exists x)(Fx \cdot Kx)$. This is a rough translation, not only because we have read an assertion of existence into our sentence, but also because the word "Some" in "Some kangaroos live in zoos" has suggestions of "At least a few," which are not conveyed by the symbol $\exists$.

With similar reservations, we might render "Some zebras live in zoos" as $(\exists y)(Gy \cdot Ky)$. Our complete sentence thus emerges, roughly translated, as $(x)(Fx \supset Hx) \cdot (\exists x)(Fx \cdot Kx) \cdot (\exists y)(Gy \cdot Ky)$.

Our next example is "If all zebras have stripes, then all horses feel deprived." We can let F stand for being a zebra, G stand for being something which has stripes, H stand for being a horse, and K stand for being something that feels deprived.

"All zebras have stripes" then would be $(x)(Fx \supset Gx)$. "All horses feel deprived" is $(x)(Hx \supset Kx)$. The "If . . . then" relation between these two expressions is best conveyed by the $\supset$ symbol. The $\supset$ symbol does not enable us to give a perfect translation, since it loses the flavor of the English sentence, in which there is at least a suggestion that the horses feel deprived *because* the zebras have stripes. But the $\supset$ symbol is the best that we can do symbolically. Consequently the sentence would be rendered as $(x)(Fx \supset Gx) \supset (x)(Hx \supset Kx)$.

Our last example is "All dogs can swim, or at least try to swim." We can let F stand for being a dog, and G stand for being able to swim. We cannot use the same letter, G, for being a thing that tries to swim that we use for being able to swim; and indeed there is no way symbolically in which we can capture the semantic connection between being able to swim and merely trying to swim. Thus we shall have to use a new letter, H, for being a thing that tries to swim. The semantic connection between being able to swim and trying to swim will be lost in translation. The best translation that we can muster is $(x)(Fx \supset (Gx \lor Hx))$.

EXERCISE FOR SECTION 2.1.3.

Translate the following into symbols:
1. "All fish are green, and all parrots are green."
2. "All fish are green, and all whales are some color other than green."
3. "If at least one of these plums is ripe, then there is something to eat."

4. "There are huge forests in California, or there are huge forests in Nevada."

5. "There are people who can read Hittite, although everyone in the room was unable to do so."

2.1.4. The relation between the (∃ x) and (x) symbols

Before we begin to develop logical arguments using the (x) and (∃ x) symbols, we should say a little more about their basic function. A good way of exploring this is to discuss at length their relation with one another.

The first point to make is that one can arrive at a statement beginning with (x) by negating a statement beginning with (∃ x), and that one can arrive at a statement beginning with (∃ x) by negating a statement beginning with "(x)". For example, the negation of (∃ x)(Fx) is (x)(∼Fx). The negation of (∃ x)(Fx·Gx) is (x)∼(Fx·Gx). The negation, on the other hand, of (x)(Fx) is (∃ x)(∼Fx). The negation of (x)(Fx⊃Gx) is (∃ x)∼(Fx⊃Gx). We shall illustrate all of these claims so that the reader develops an intuitive feel for the relations between the two symbols.

First we claimed that the negation of (∃ x)(Fx) is (x)(∼Fx). The reader can understand this if he keeps in mind that (∃ x)(Fx) asserts that there exists at least one thing which has the property symbolized by F. To negate that is to deny that there exists at least one thing which has property F: in other words, to assert that there exists no thing which has property F. But to say that there exists no thing which has property F is equivalent to saying that all things which do exist do not have property F. This is symbolized by (x)(∼Fx).

If the universe turns out to be empty—i.e., if no things at all exist—then (x)(∼Fx) will count as true (as indeed will any assertion whatsoever which is prexed by (x) and does not contain any ∃ symbol). If the universe contains existing things, then if at least one of them has property F (∃ x)(Fx) will count as true, and (x)(∼Fx) will count as false. If none of them has the property, then (x)(∼Fx) will count as true, and (∃ x)(Fx) will count as false. The reader can see from all this that (x)(∼Fx) is true in all cases, and only cases, in which (∃ x)(Fx) is false, and vice versa. Thus they can be seen to be negations of one another.

In much the same way, the reader can see how (x)∼(Fx·Gx) would count as the negation of (∃ x)(Fx·Gx). (Indeed this can be viewed as just a special case of (x)(∼Fx) being a negation of (∃ x)(Fx), if we let F and G stand for a combination of properties named earlier by the single letter F.) If we negate the assertion that there exists at least one thing which has properties F and G, then we are in effect saying that there is no thing which has both of these properties, which is to say that all things lack one or both of these properties.

In much the same way, it should be obvious that the negation of $(x)(Fx)$ is $(\exists x)(\sim Fx)$. If we deny that all things have the property F, we are asserting that there exists at least one thing which does not have the property F. Similarly, if we deny that all things that have property F also have property G, we are asserting that there exists at least one thing which has property F but does not have property G. The negation, that is, of $(x)(Fx \supset Gx)$ is $(\exists x)\sim(Fx \supset Gx)$, which of course is equivalent to $(\exists x)(Fx \cdot \sim Gx)$. (The reader can see that $(\exists x)\sim(Fx \supset Gx)$ is equivalent to $(\exists x)(Fx \cdot \sim Gx)$ by reflecting that $\sim(P \supset Q) \equiv P \cdot \sim Q$, and by substituting Fx for P and Gx for Q.)

We can generalize what we have been pointing out. Let us take R to stand for any function or combination of functions, such as (for example) Fx, $Fx \cdot Gx$, $\sim FxvGx$, $Fx \supset \sim Gx$, etc. We can state the following two general formulas of equivalence:

$(\exists x)(R) \equiv \sim(x)(\sim R)$

and $(x)(R) \equiv \sim(\exists x)(\sim R)$

Thus far we have shown that any positive existential statement (i.e., statement prefixed by the unnegated $\exists$ symbol) is equivalent to the negation of a positive universal statement (i.e., statement prefixed by the unnegated (x) symbol), and vice versa. The reader might wonder now: can we derive a positive existential statement from a positive universal statement, or vice versa? For example, if we are given as a premise that all men are mortal, can we draw any conclusion that asserts that men (of some type or other) exist?

A large part of the answer can be stated in the form of a general rule. In a logical argument, we cannot arrive at a positive existential conclusion (i.e., one prefixed by an unnegated $\exists$ symbol), unless we have had at least one positive existential (or negative universal, which comes to the same thing) premise. In other words: unless at some stage we assume that something exists, we shall not be able to arrive at a conclusion which asserts in effect that something exists.

In explaining this rule, we might take the example of an argument which has as a premise "(x) (x is a man $\supset x$ is mortal)" (which is to say, "All men are mortal"), and in which we wish to arrive at the conclusion "$(\exists x)$ (x is a man $\cdot x$ is mortal)" (i.e., that there exists at least one mortal man). It follows from our rule that we cannot derive "$(\exists x)$ (x is a man $\cdot x$ is mortal)" from "(x) (x is a man $\supset x$ is mortal)" alone.

The reason for this is that we have said nothing to exclude the possiblility of no men existing, or even to exclude the possibility of the universe being empty. After all, as we explained in introducing the (x) symbol, "(x) (x is a man $\supset x$ is mortal)" would count as true, by default as it were, even if no man existed, or even if nothing whatsoever existed. Thus, in asserting "(x) (x is a man$\supset x$ is mortal)," we are leaving open the possibility that there is no mortal man. We have not given ourselves a basis for asserting that anything at all exists, let alone that a mortal man exists.

We can fill this logical gap between "All men are mortal" and "A mortal man exists" only with an additional premise which asserts existence. We shall examine two obvious candidates for this role, and show why one of them does not work and the other does.

One obvious candidate is the simple assertion $\exists x$. This asserts that there exists at least one thing in the universe.

From "$(\exists x)$ (x is a man$\supset x$ is mortal)" and $\exists x$ we can indeed derive a positive existential conclusion. This is "(x) (x is a man$\supset x$ is mortal)." Or, to put it in intuitive terms, if we are given the premises that all men are mortal, and that at least one thing exists in the universe, we can conclude that there exists at least one thing in the universe which, *if* it is a man, is mortal. However notice the italicized "if." "$(\exists x)$ (x is a man$\supset x$ is mortal)" leaves open the possibility that the universe has exactly one existing thing, and that that thing is a dinosaur. We might say of this dinosaur that *if* it were a man it would be mortal, and this certainly would be true (by default). In other words, our positive existential conclusion, "$(\exists x)$ (x is a man$\supset x$ is mortal)," does assert that at least one thing exists, and does assert that *if* that thing is a man it is mortal; but it does not assert, or imply, that any men exist. We cannot derive the conclusion that a mortal man exists from the premises thus far supplied.

In order to arrive at "$(\exists x)$ (x is a man$\cdot x$ is mortal)" from "(x) (x is a man$\supset x$ is mortal)," we shall have to add the specific premise that at least one man exists. This could be stated as "$(\exists x)$ (x is a man)." Given the premise that all men are mortal, and the premise that at least one man exists, we can conclude that at least one thing exists which both is a man and is mortal.

If we symbolize being a man as F, and being mortal as G, we can extract two principles of inference from the foregoing discussion. They are as follows:

$(x)(Fx \supset Gx) \cdot \exists x$ implies $(\exists x)(Fx \supset Gx)$

$(x)(Fx \supset Gx) \cdot (\exists x)(Fx)$ implies $(\exists x)(Fx \cdot Gx)$

At this point we have shown under what conditions we can derive positive existential statements from positive universal statements. The reader might now wonder whether the reverse procedure is possible. Can we derive positive universal statements from positive existential statements?

The answer is not simple. First, it is quite obvious that we can get from a positive existential premise to a positive universal conclusion if we add a suitable universal premise. For example, if we are given the premise that there exists at least one mortal man, we can get to the conclusion that all men are mortal *if* we add a premise that, say, no man lives beyond a hundred and twenty.

There are conceivable ways of getting positive universal conclusions from positive existential premises which savor less of cheating. For example, if we assume that there exists at least one mortal man, and add the premise that in fact only one thing exists in the universe, we can conclude that all men are mortal.

This inference might be stated as follows:

    Premise: "$(\exists x)$ (x is a man·x is mortal)"

    Premise: "(y) $(\exists y \supset (y$ is identical with $x))$"

  (in other words: for all things, if a thing exists it is identical with x)

    Conclusion: "(x) (x is a man$\supset x$ is mortal)

We shall not, however, develop within this book the logical apparatus needed to prove this.

In much the same way, if we assume that the universe contains, say, only eight things, and then assume that of the eight things five are not men and three are mortal men, we could conclude that all men are mortal. But arguments of this kind play a small role in logic, and we shall not be concerned with them. None of the arguments that we shall deal with will involve enumerating, or limiting the number of, things in the universe.

2.2.1. Determining equivalence

At this point, having, we hope, strengthened the reader's intuitive feel for the new symbolism, we are ready to introduce some of the apparatus needed to establish relations of equivalence and implication. These pages will be just an introduction to this part of logic, and at their end the reader will be referred to other books for further work in quantificational logic.

First, we shall state five basic formulas of equivalence to be added to the twenty-six stated previously. Two of the five new formulas are ones which we have already discussed.

  27. $(x)(R)\equiv\sim(\exists x)(\sim R)$

  28. $(\exists x)(R)\equiv\sim(x)(\sim R)$

  29. $(x)(P)\cdot(x)(Q)\equiv(x)(PQ)$

  30. If $P\equiv Q$, then $(x)(P)\equiv(x)(Q)$

  31. If $P\equiv Q$, then $(\exists x)(P)\equiv(\exists x)(Q)$

In the statement of these formulas, P, Q, and R are just dummies which can stand for anything whatsoever. For example, if we let P stand for Fx, and Q stand for $Gx\text{v}\sim Fx$, then formula 29 will give us $(x)(Fx)\cdot(x)$ $(Gx\text{v}\sim Fx)\equiv(x)(Fx\cdot(Gx\text{v}\sim Fx))$. If we let P stand for $\sim(Fx\cdot Gx)$, and

Q stand for $\sim Fxv\sim Gx$ (which formula 1 tells us is equivalent to $\sim(Fx \cdot Gx)$), then formula 31 tells us that "If $\sim(Fx \cdot Gx) \equiv \sim Fxv\sim Gx$, then $(\exists x)(\sim(Fx \cdot Gx)) \equiv (\exists x)(\sim Fxv\sim Gx)$."

We shall say a little more about formulas 29 through 31.

The purpose of formula 29 is to allow us to rewrite the conjunction of positive universal statements as the universalization of a conjunction. It allows us to rewrite, for example, the conjunction of $(x)(Fx)$ and $(x)(Gx)$ as $(x)(Fx \cdot Gx)$. Thus the conjunction of "All men are mortal" and "All men are rational" becomes "All men are both mortal and rational." For that matter, formula 29 allows us to rewrite $(x)(Fx \supset Gx) \cdot (x)(Hx \supset Jx)$ as $(x)((Fx \supset Gx) \cdot (Hx \supset Jx))$. Thus "All glass is transparent and all metal conducts heat" becomes "Everything, if it is glass is transparent, and also if it is metal conducts heat."

The purpose of formulas 30 and 31 is to enable us to apply the first twenty-six formulas to our present material. For example, formula 4 asserted that $P \supset Q \equiv \sim PvQ$. Letting Fx stand in for P, and Gx stand in for Q, we get:

$Fx \supset Gx \equiv \sim FxvGx$

Formula 30 allows us to say on the basis of this that:

$(x)(Fx \supset Gx) \equiv (x)(\sim FxvGx)$

Formula 31 allows us to say:

$(\exists x)(Fx \supset Gx) \equiv (\exists x)(\sim FxvGx)$

The reader will notice that our present apparatus would allow us also to conclude that $\sim(x)(Fx \supset Gx) \equiv \sim(x)(\sim FxvGx)$. This can be shown simply by use of formula 24. Formula 24 states that "If $X \equiv Y$, then $\sim X \equiv \sim Y$." We can let $(x)(Fx \supset Gx)$ stand in for X here, and $(x)(\sim FxvGx)$ stand in for Y. This would give us the claim that if $(x)(Fx \supset Gx) \equiv (x)(\sim FxvGx)$, then $\sim(x)(Fx \supset Gx) \equiv \sim(x)(\sim FxvGx)$. In a similar way, we can show that $\sim(\exists x)(Fx \supset Gx) \equiv \sim(\exists x)(\sim FxvGx)$.

We shall give a few more examples of how our new apparatus works. First we shall show that $\sim(\exists x)(\sim(Fx \cdot Gx))$ is equivalent to $(x)(Fx) \cdot (x)(Gx)$. We can begin by applying formula 27, letting $Fx \cdot Gx$ stand in for R. This allows us to rewrite $\sim(\exists x)(\sim(Fx \cdot Gx))$ as:

$(x)(Fx \cdot Gx)$.

We can now use formula 29, letting Fx stand in for P, and Gx stand in for Q. This gives us $(x)(Fx) \cdot (x)(Gx) \equiv (x)(Fx \cdot Gx)$. Formula 26 enables us to conclude that $(x)(Fx) \cdot (x)(Gx)$ is equivalent to $\sim(\exists x)(\sim(Fx \cdot Gx))$.

Our next example involves showing that $(x)(Fx) \cdot (x)(\sim FxvGx)$ is equivalent to $(x)(Fx \cdot Gx)$.

First we can apply formula 29. This allows us to rewrite $(x)(Fx) \cdot (x)(\sim FxvGx)$ as:

$(x)(Fx \cdot (\sim FxvGx))$

We now can apply formula 20, which enables us to rewrite the $\sim Fx \vee Gx$ component as $Gx \vee \sim Fx$. This gives us:

$(x)(Fx \cdot (Gx \vee \sim Fx)$

We now use formula 11, letting Fx stand in for P, and Gx stand in for Q. This tells us that $Fx \cdot (Gx \vee \sim Fx) \equiv Fx \cdot Gx$. Formula 30 allows us to say on the basis of this that $(x)(Fx \ (Gx \vee \sim Fx))$ is equivalent to:

$(x)(Fx \cdot Gx)$

Since $(x)(Fx \cdot (Gx \vee \sim Fx))$ is equivalent to $(x)(Fx) \cdot (x)(\sim Fx \vee Gx)$, formula 26 allows us to conclude that $(x)(Fx \cdot Gx)$ is equivalent to $(x)(Fx) \cdot (x)(\sim Fx \vee Gx)$.

For our last example we shall show that $(\exists x)(Fx \supset \sim Gx)$ is equivalent to $\sim(x)(Fx \cdot Gx)$. We can first use formula 28, which tells us that $(\exists x)(Fx \supset \sim Gx)$ is equivalent to $\sim(x) \sim (Fx \supset \sim Gx)$. Formula 4 allows us to replace $Fx \supset \sim Gx$ by $\sim Fx \vee \sim Gx$, which enables us to write:

$\sim(x) \sim (\sim Fx \vee \sim Gx)$

Formula 2 enables us to replace $\sim(\sim Fx \vee \sim Gx)$ by $\sim \sim Fx \cdot \sim \sim Gx$, and formula 3 allows us to write this as $Fx \cdot Gx$. This leaves us with:

$\sim(x)(Fx \cdot Gx)$

which by formula 26 is equivalent to $(\exists x)(Fx \supset \sim Gx)$.

EXERCISES FOR SECTION 2.2.1.

1. Show that $(x) \sim (Fx \supset Gx)$ is equivalent to $(x)(Fx) \cdot (x)(\sim Gx)$.
2. Show that $\sim(x)(Fx \supset Gx)$ is equivalent to $(\exists x)(Fx \cdot \sim Gx)$.
3. Show that $(\exists x)(Fx \vee Gx)$ is equivalent to $\sim(x)(\sim Fx \cdot \sim Gx)$.
4. Show that $(x) \sim (\sim Fx \cdot \sim Gx)$ is equivalent to $\sim(\exists x)(\sim Fx \cdot \sim Gx)$.

2.2.2. Determining implication

We turn now to implication. We shall add five basic formulas of implication to the six that we stated earlier.
These are:

I.7 $((x)(R) \cdot \exists x) \rightarrow ((\exists x)(R))$

I.8 $((x)(P \supset Q) \cdot (\exists x)(P)) \rightarrow ((\exists x)(PQ))$

I.9 $((x)(P) \vee (x)(Q)) \rightarrow ((x)(P \vee Q))$

I.10 If $Q \rightarrow R$, then $((x)(Q)) \rightarrow ((x)(R))$

I.11 If $Q \rightarrow R$, then $((\exists x)(Q)) \rightarrow ((\exists x)(R))$

Once again P, Q, and R are just dummies which could stand for anything. For example, we could replace Q in formula I.11 by $Fx \cdot Gx$, and R by Fx: this would give us the assertion that if $(Fx \cdot Gx) \rightarrow Fx$ (which according to formula I.1 is correct), then $((\exists x)(Fx \cdot Gx)) \rightarrow ((\exists x)(Fx))$.

The first of the new formulas, I.7, represents a more general form of something that we pointed out earlier. We had shown that from the premises that all men are mortal and that at least one thing exists in the universe, we could infer that at least one thing exists in the universe which, *if* it is a man, is mortal. We express the principle underlying this as $(x)(Fx \supset Gx)$ $\cdot \exists x$ implies $(Fx \supset Gx)$. This is a particular case of the more general principle stated in I.7. If we let $Fx \supset Gx$ stand in for R in I.7, we get $((x)$ $(Fx \supset Gx) . \exists x) \rightarrow ((\exists x)(Fx \supset Gx))$. But equally well we could let Fx stand in for R in I.7, and get $((x)(Fx) \cdot \exists x) \rightarrow ((\exists x)(Fx))$. The latter is the form of inferences such as "If all things are green, and at least one thing exists in the universe, then at least one thing exists which is green." Or we could let $\sim(Fx \cdot Gx)$ stand in for R, which gives us $((x)(\sim(Fx \cdot Gx)) \cdot \exists x) \rightarrow ((\exists x)$ $(\sim(Fx \cdot Gx)))$. This would be the form of inferences such as "If all things are such that they are not both orange and purple, and at least one thing exists in the universe, then at least one thing exists which is not both orange and purple.

Formula I.8 also is related to something that we pointed out earlier. We had shown that, from the premises that all men are mortal and that at least one man exists, we could infer that at least one thing exists which is both a man and mortal. We express the principle underlying this as "(x) $(Fx \cdot Gx) \cdot (\exists x)(Fx)$ implies $(\exists x)(Fx \cdot Gx)$." We can get this same principle from I.8, simply by letting Fx stand in for P and Gx stand in for Q.

I.9 should seem intuitively agreeable. It allows us to assert, for example, that if either all things in the world are black or all things in the world are white, then it must at least be the case that everything in the world is black or white.

The purpose of formulas I.10 and I.11 is to enable us to apply formulas I.1 through I.6 to our present material. For example, formula I.2 asserted that P implies PvQ. Letting Fx stand in for P, and Gx stand in for Q, we get:

Fx implies $FxvGx$.

Formula I.11 allows us to say on the basis of this that:

$(\exists x)(Fx)$ implies $(\exists x)(FxvGx)$.

We shall give a few more examples of how our new apparatus works. We shall show, first, that $(x)(Fx \supset Gx) \cdot (x)(Gx \supset Hx)$ implies $(x)(Fx \supset Hx)$. We can begin by applying formula 29, letting $Fx \supset Gx$ stand in for P, and $Gx \supset Hx$ stand in for Q. This allows us to write $(x)(Fx \supset Gx) \cdot (x)(Gx \supset Hx)$ as:

$(x)((Fx \supset Gx) \cdot (Gx \supset Hx))$

We now use formula I.3, letting Fx stand in for P, Gx stand in for Q, and Hx stand in for R. This tells us that $(Fx \supset Gx) \cdot (Gx \supset Hx)$ implies $Fx \supset Hx$. Formula I.10 enables us to say, on the basis of that, that (x) $((Fx \supset Gx) \cdot (Gx \supset Hx))$ implies $(x)(Fx \supset Hx)$. Since $(x)(Fx \supset Gx) \cdot (x)(Gx \supset$

Hx) mutually implies $(x)((Fx \supset Gx) \cdot (Gx \supset Hx))$, formula I.6 enables us to conclude that $(x)(Fx \supset Gx) \cdot (x)(Gx \supset Hx)$ implies $(x)(Fx \supset Hx)$.

What we have just demonstrated by means of techniques of symbolic logic is, by the way, of considerable importance, especially historically. $((x)(Fx \supset Gx) \cdot (x)(Gx \supset Hx)) \mapsto ((x)(Fx \supset Hx))$ represents the principle that allows us to conclude, syllogistically, that:

If all F's are G's

and all G's are H's

then all F's are H's.

This is just one example of how symbolic logic can cover ground covered by Aristotelian logic.

We shall give a couple of further examples of the use of our new apparatus. One example involves the derivation of a mild claim about existing things from a positive universal premise plus the premise that at least one thing exists. We shall show that $(x)(Fx \cdot \sim Gx) \cdot \exists x$ implies $(\exists x)$ $(\sim Fx \supset \sim Gx)$. The conclusion is not especially remarkable, but demonstrating it will show further the use of our apparatus.

We can begin by using formula I.7, letting $Fx \cdot \sim Gx$ stand in for R. This shows us that $((x)(Fx \cdot \sim Gx) \cdot \exists x) \mapsto ((\exists x)(Fx \cdot \sim Gx))$. If we apply formula I.1, letting Fx stand in for P, and $\sim Gx$ stand in for Q, we see that $(Fx \cdot \sim Gx) \mapsto Fx$. Similarly, formula I.2 enables us to see that $Fx \mapsto (Fx$ $v \sim Gx)$. Thus, by I.6, we can conclude that $(Fx \cdot \sim Gx) \mapsto (Fx v \sim Gx)$. I.11 allows us to say, on the basis of this, that $((\exists x)(Fx \cdot \sim Gx)) \mapsto ((\exists x)(Fx$ $v \sim Gx))$.

The last part of our demonstration consists simply in rewriting $(\exists x)$ $(Fx v \sim Gx)$. Formula 3 enables us to rewrite it as $(\exists x)(\sim \sim Fx v \sim Gx)$. We can now apply formula 4, letting $\sim Fx$ stand in for P, and $\sim Gx$ stand in for Q. This tells us that $\sim \sim Fx v \sim Gx$ is equivalent to $\sim Fx \supset \sim Gx$. Formula 31 allows us to assert, on the basis of this, that $(\exists x)(\sim \sim Fx v \sim Gx)$ is equivalent to $(\exists x)(\sim Fx \supset \sim Gx)$.

Thus $(\exists x)(\sim Fx \supset \sim Gx)$ is mutually implied by an expression which itself is implied by $(x)(Fx \cdot \sim Gx) \cdot \exists x$. I.6 enables us to conclude that $(x)(Fx \cdot \sim Gx) \cdot \exists x$ implies $(\exists x)(\sim Fx \supset \sim Gx)$.

Our last example will involve showing that $(x)(Fx \cdot Gx) v (x)(Fx \cdot \sim Gx)$ implies $(x)(Fx v \sim Gx)$. We shall begin by using formula I.9, letting $Fx \cdot Gx$ stand in for P, and $Fx \cdot \sim Gx$ stand in for Q. This shows us that $((x)(Fx \cdot Gx) v (x)(Fx \cdot \sim Gx)) \mapsto ((x)((Fx \cdot Gx) v (Fx \cdot \sim Gx)))$.

We can apply formula 23 to the $(Fx \cdot Gx) v (Fx \cdot \sim Gx)$ component of this. We let Fx stand in for P, Gx stand for Q, and $\sim Gx$ stand in for R. This gives us $Fx \cdot (Gx v \sim Gx) \equiv (Fx \cdot Gx) v (Fx \cdot \sim Gx)$. Formula 30 allows us to say that $(x)((Fx \cdot Gx) v (Fx \cdot \sim Gx))$ is equivalent to:

$(x)(Fx \cdot (Gx v \sim Gx))$

But formula 16, if we let Fx stand in for P, and Gx for Q, shows us that

$Fx \cdot (Gxv \sim Gx)$ is equivalent to Fx. Thus, again according to formula 30, we can rewrite $(x)(Fx \cdot (Gxv \sim Gx))$ as:

   $(x)(Fx)$

If we let Fx stand in for P, and $\sim Gx$ stand in for Q, then formula I.2 tells us that $Fx \rightarrow (Fxv \sim Gx)$. Formula I.10 allows us to say, on the basis of this, that $((x)(Fx)) \rightarrow ((x)(Fxv \sim Gx))$. Applying I.6 to this chain of implication relations, we can conclude that $((x)(Fx \cdot Gx)v(x)(Fx \cdot \sim Gx)) \rightarrow ((x)$ $(Fxv \sim Gx))$.

This concludes our discussion of techniques of argument in modern symbolic logic. We have given the reader enough material to provide a thorough grounding in truth functional logic, and an introduction to the logic which uses quantificational symbols. If the reader wishes to proceed further in the latter area, he is advised to refer to a text in symbolic logic: for example, W. V. Quine's *Methods of Logic*, (New York, Henry Holt & Co., 1952) or I. Copi's *Symbolic Logic* (New York, The Macmillan Company, 1954).

For the remainder of this chapter we shall discuss briefly two special developments in modern symbolic logic: the theory of types (developed by Bertrand Russell), and Lukasiewicz's use of a modern symbolic apparatus in approaching the problems of Aristotelian logic.

EXERCISES FOR SECTION 2.2.2.

1. Show that $(x)(FxvGx) \cdot (\exists x)(\sim Fx)$ implies $(\exists x)(Gx)$.
2. Show that $\sim (x)(Fxv \sim Gx)$ implies $(\exists x)(\sim Fx)$.
3. Show that $(x)(Fx) \cdot (x)(Gx)$ implies $(x)(Fx \supset Gx)$.
4. Show that $(x) \sim (\sim Fx \supset Gx) \cdot \exists x$ implies $\sim (x)(\sim Fx \supset Gx)$.

3. The theory of types

The theory of types was developed by Bertrand Russell in order to deal with certain paradoxes. Since this book has not gone far enough into symbolic logic to be able to present these paradoxes in symbolic form, we shall attempt to present the gist of the difficulties in ordinary English.

One important paradox occurs when we have developed a symbolic apparatus to the point at which we can symbolize properties of properties. The furthest point that we reached in this book involved our symbolizing properties of things. For example, in Fx, F stands for a property (such as being mortal, or being a member of the class of men), and x is a variable whose range is things.

In ordinary discourse, of course, we can make not only claims like "Jones is mortal," but also claims like "Being mortal is inevitable for a man," or "Being mortal is better than being a Struldbrug." In other words, besides ascribing properties (like being mortal) to things, we can ascribe properties to properties. The property of being mortal, for example, has the properties of being inevitable for a man, and of being better than being a Struldbrug.

Once we see that properties themselves can have properties, we might ask ourselves: "Since properties have properties, and since properties *are* properties, is there any property that has itself as a property?" This sounds like an extremely playful question, but it leads to some deep difficulties.

Obviously, in the example that we were using, that is not the case. Being mortal may have the properties of being inevitable for a man, and being better than a Struldbrug; but we would not say that being mortal is itself mortal. Indeed that sounds like nonsense. However, we can think of some properties which seem as if they have themselves. Being boring is a boring property to have (*so* many things are boring that it's boring to be boring), and being abstract seems abstract.

We can also point right now to at least one property which seems to have the opposite of itself as a property. We remarked just now that being abstract seems abstract. What we had in mind was this. A number of things and properties that we might talk about have the convenient property that we can point to them and measure them. If we can point to them and measure them, we normally would speak of them as concrete. For example, lakes and mountains are concrete things. Being heavy, being green, or being a resident in a certain town all are concrete properties. On the other hand, the general idea of virtue is what we would call abstract. So is being identical with oneself, and so indeed is any property that one can logically analyze but which does not correspond to particular physical observations.

On this basis we can see that the property of being abstract is itself abstract. But so is the property of being concrete. If we say that being green involves reflecting a different frequency of light from what being red involves, then we are saying something concrete and physically determinable about being green. But if we say that the property of being green is concrete, we are making a logical, and abstract, point.

Faced with the fact that being concrete is not concrete, we might name a new property. It is the property of not having itself as a property. Let us call it heterogeneity. We have shown that the property of being abstract does not have the property of heterogeneity, since being abstract is abstract. But the property of being concrete *does* have the property of heterogeneity, since being concrete is not concrete.

We have come now to the crucial question. Does the property of heterogeneity have itself as a property? The reason why the question is crucial is as follows. If we say "yes," that heterogeneity has itself as a property, then we are saying that heterogeneity is heterogeneous. But when we recall what "heterogeneous" *means*, we see that if heterogeneity is heterogeneous it does not have itself as a property. Thus a "yes" answer implies an answer of "no." But if we simply answer "no," that heterogeneity does not have itself as a property, then we are saying that heterogeneity is not heterogeneous. But if we recall the meaning of "heterogeneous," we see that to say that heterogeneity is not heterogeneous is to say that it does have itself as a property. Thus an answer of "no" implies an answer of "yes."

Since an answer of "no" to the question "Is heterogeneity heterogeneous?" implies an answer of "yes," and since an answer of "yes" implies an answer of "no," there seems no obvious way of contradiction and muddle. What we have is a paradox, which seems to demand drastic remedial measures.

Before we present a widely accepted remedy, the theory of types, we might refer to another of the paradoxes which provoked its development. This is a simpler paradox than one involving heterogeneity. Let us suppose that we ask a man to speak, and he says simply, "I am lying." What are we to make of this? If we assume that he is telling the truth, this implies that he was doing what he said he was: i.e., lying. If we assume that he was lying, then he must not have been lying, but rather telling the truth. Thus we find ourselves on the same sort of logical treadmill that we were on in connection with heterogeneity. An answer of "yes" to the question of "Was he lying?" implies an answer of "no," and vice versa.

The theory of types was developed to meet difficulties like these. We shall refer only to its most general features, and speak of these in nontechnical language.

The basic idea underlying the theory of types is that we can avoid paradoxes, like the ones that we presented, by establishing a hierarchy of statements and of properties. We can make the crucial proviso that if a property of type X has properties, these properties are of type $X+1$. If a statement of order X is mentioned, or referred to, by another statement, then the other statement is of order $X+1$.

The reader will realize that we are just presenting the bare bones (and not all the bones, for that matter) of a rich intellectual achievement. But what we have said is already sufficient for us to explain how the theory of types deals with paradoxes like the ones that we have presented.

Take, for example, the paradox of heterogeneity. We can say that properties of things are of type 1. The redness of an apple, the heaviness of a piece of furniture, the simplicity of a design, and the abstractness of a mathematics book all are of type 1. According to the theory of types, any properties of these properties are of type 2. We may speak of simplicity and abstractness as properties that are abstract; but the fact that we use "abstract" with regard both to the mathematics book and to simplicity and abstractness conceals, according to the theory of types, a difference. It is as if we were punning: using the same word with different, but related, meanings. The abstractness of the mathematics book is abstractness of type 1; the abstractness of the properties of simplicity and abstractness is a different property, namely abstractness of type 2. The abstractness of this abstractness will of course be a still different property, abstractness of type 3.

It follows from this quite automatically that any property, even abstractness of type 1, is heterogeneous. No property can be predicated of itself, because no property can have any property whatsoever which is of its own type predicated of itself. But note that the word "heterogeneous" can itself conceal a pun. Abstractness of type 1 is heterogeneous of type 2; abstractness of type 2 is heterogeneous of type 3; and so on. Heterogeneity type 1 is heterogeneous type 2, which is heterogeneous type 3, which is heterogeneous type 4, etc.

The upshot of this is that we can say that heterogeneity (type 1) is heterogeneous (type 2), without implying that heterogeneity (type 1) has *itself* as a property. Thus in saying that heterogeneity (type 1) is heterogeneous (type 2), we are not implying that heterogeneity (type 1) is not heterogeneous.

In much the same way, we can eliminate the paradox of "I am lying." To say "I am lying" is to say, in effect, "This statement is false." But if the statement in question is of, say, order 1, then any statement which refers to it will be of order 2. If the statement could refer to itself it would be both of order 1 and of order 2, which is impossible: a statement can only have a single order number. From this we can infer the consequence that while it is possible to say that a statement is false, it is not possible for that statement itself to say that it is false. More generally, we derive the consequence that a statement cannot refer to itself and cannot refer to any other statement of the same order as itself.

This completes our sketch of how the theory of types eliminates paradoxes. However, since the theory of types is still a live issue, we shall feel free to mention one or two criticisms of the theory of types. There have been attacks made on the theory of types, relating to the difficulties that it creates in proving certain mathematical truths. The points that we shall make against the theory of types, however, will be of a nontechnical nature.

Our major criticism of the theory of types concerns self-referring assertions, which are outlawed by the hierarchy of orders in the theory of types. Our point is that while this is a way of eliminating some paradoxes, it also seems to eliminate some meaningful statements which do not involve paradoxes.

"I am lying" obviously is nonsense. *Prima facie* it seems, though, that there can be self-referring assertions which make sense and are true. Let us take, for example, the following:

"This statement occurs in a logic book."

That certainly seems true. There is, admittedly, something a little peculiar about the statement. When one starts to read it, one assumes that it, like all normal satements, is going to make a claim about something beyond itself, and then one realizes that it is talking about nothing but itself. One normally would wonder why anyone would bother to make the italicized statement. It seems odd.

But even though the italicized statement is peculiar, and even though it would pull most people up short, it seems true. The statement does occur in a logic book. It makes sense, and is correct, when it says that it does.

According to the theory of types, however, the italicized statement is illegitimate. It has two orders at once. If we adopt the theory of types, we are in effect agreeing to eliminate such statements from the language.

The reaction of the reader to this might well be, "Well, that's no great loss." We can get along quite well without ever making self-referring statements like the one italicized.

However, the issue is not a practical one but a theoretical one. If the theory of types brands as illegitimate some statements which in fact seem to make sense, this is an important point against the theory of types. It is not a decisive point. Logic does not have to mirror ordinary language; and, in instances that we have pointed out, logic in fact does not mirror ordinary language. But the theory of types has a peculiar role, as compared to other parts of logic. It was designed to deal with paradoxes, some of which (like "I am lying") were paradoxes in ordinary language. It thus is vulnerable if it claims to solve paradoxes of ordinary language by using rules which do not mirror the rules of ordinary language.

This is as far as we wish to carry our discussion of the theory of types. Both the full case for the theory of types and the full case against the theory of types would take too long to present. But we have indicated some of the difficulties that the theory of types incurs with regard to our ordinary language. On the basis of the difficulties that we have pointed out, we might frame a general complaint against the theory of types. It is this. The theory of types originated with the desire for a very general solution of the problems involved in various paradoxes. But perhaps any very general solution of these problems would involve throwing out some legitimate statements along with the paradoxes. Perhaps, indeed, the only solution that would be faithful to our normal sense of what is a legitimate utterance, and what is not, would be a piecemeal solution. That would be a solution which recognized that certain statements, or types of statements, are nonsensical, and did not try to arrive at a completely general formula for eliminating nonsensical statements.

3.1. The categorical syllogism from a modern point of view

In the next few pages we want to give you a taste of *systematic* symbolic logic. We shall start with a brief account of what a logical system is. We shall then actually present the beginnings of such a system. The system we have chosen was developed by the Polish logician Jan Lukasiewicz. It is presented in full in Lukasiewicz's book *Aristotle's Syllogistic—From the Standpoint of Modern Formal Logic.* In laying out the beginnings of Lukasiewicz's system, we shall be completing our treatment of deductive logic in a fitting way. Classical logic is essentially a logic of terms, while modern logic is essentially a logic of propositions. In Lukasiewicz's system, the rigor of modern propositional logic is used in the derivation of the formulas of classical term logic.

The most outstanding characteristic of a logical system is that it is completely explicit about its starting points and about its method of proceeding from those starting points. (1) Every constant used is either completely defined in terms of other constants in the system or else is left completely undefined. The undefined constants are known as *primitives*. Although the primitives of a logical system may sometimes be thought of as having the same meaning as expressions in other systems or words from a natural language, such interpretations fall *outside* the system. The only explanation of its primitives within the system is the use it makes of them. (2) Assertions within a logical system are made either *axiomatically* or on the basis of the axioms; in other words, it is clearly indicated what is laid down without proof (as axiomatic) and what is maintained on the basis of proof. Points (1) and (2) have to do with being explicit about starting points. A logical system is also explicit as to the permissible ways of proceeding from its starting points. (3) Substitution rules are laid down for any variables used, and (4) all *rules of inference* used in the system are clearly stated. The aim here is to make every deduction within the system completely *rigorous*. That is, every step taken in deriving an assertion from the axioms must be completely justified by clearly stated rules of substitution and inference.

The points mentioned in the last paragraph will be illustrated in the portion of a logical system presented below. There are other important features which logicians aim at in constructing their systems. We shall mention some of these features briefly here, though they will not be illustrated below. *Consistency of axioms* is a "must." If the basic assertions of a system are themselves contradictory, then all sorts of contradictory theorems can be deduced from them. Indeed, so far as modern logic is concerned, any proposition whatsoever can be deduced from a pair of contradictory premises. If, on the other hand, consistency of axioms can be shown, and if suitable rules of substitution and inference are used, one can be sure that all (usually an infinite number) of the theorems deducible from those axioms are consistent with one another. Accordingly, modern logicians always aim at showing the consistency of their axioms. *Independence of axioms* is desirable, though not essential. If one "axiom" can be derived from the others, it is at least "inelegant" to include it in your list of underived starting points. The ideal logical system is one in which a great many different sorts of theorems can be derived from a very small number of axioms. *Deductive completeness* is a highly prized feature of certain logical systems. A system is deductively complete if every assertion possible in the language of the system can be judged true or false on the basis of the axioms and rules of the system. For example, ordinary English would be a deductively complete logical system if we could correctly decide the truth or falsity of every possible statement in English purely on the basis of logical rules and a limited number of basic propositions assumed as axioms. Of course we can't. The number of axioms required for deciding the truth or falsity of all such statements as "It's raining outside" and "Some cows are brown" would be infinite. One can never actually have in hand an infinite set of axioms, and thus our ordinary language, to the extent that it is a logical system at all, is a deductively incomplete one. To decide the truth or falsity of "It's raining outside" we do not ordinarily appeal to axioms and logical rules. We look out the window to see. This sort of extra-linguistic checkup is unnecessary in the case of certain systems constructed by modern logicians. Certain logical systems are and can be *proved to be* deductively complete. If *P* is an assertion in the language of such a system, one can start from the axioms of the system and *show*, in a finite number of steps—each one fully warranted by the stated rules of the system—either that *P* is analytically true or that *P* is self-contradictorily false.

We shall now present the beginnings of the logical system mentioned earlier. *Aristotle's Syllogistic—From the Standpoint of Modern Formal Logic* was published first in 1951 and then, in an enlarged edition, in 1957. As we indicated in the last paragraph, we shall not be concerned with the deductive completeness of the system, or with the consistency and independence of its axioms. These points are covered, however, by Lukasiewicz himself. He shows both the consistency and the independence of his axioms, and he shows that the system is deductively complete if two axioms and three rules are added to those stated below.

We shall use only symbols already introduced in this book. Lukasiewicz's notation looks very different, but this difference in way of writing makes no difference logically. It should be noted, however, that the assertions proved below do differ logically in one respect from the implications studied in our chapter on Aristotelian logic. As we presented the syllogism, the conjunction of the premises of a valid syllogism implies ($\rightarrow$) the conclusion. Lukasiewicz demonstrates that if the conjunction of the premises is true, then the conclusion is true. These two relations between premises and conclusion can be symbolized as follows:

$$(\text{Premise} \cdot \text{Premise}) \rightarrow \text{Conclusion}$$

and

$$(\text{Premise} \cdot \text{Premise}) \supset \text{Conclusion}$$

As the reader is aware, the ideas represented by the symbols → and ⊃ differ sharply where actual propositions are involved. To say that "He's married" *implies* "He has a wife" is to claim that the former proposition is a sufficient basis for *deducing* the latter. For such a claim to be true, the two propositions must normally have something to do with one another. On the other hand, "(The moon is made of green cheese) ⊃ (The earth is flat)" makes a much weaker claim. This weaker claim can be perfectly translated as "∼(The moon is made of green cheese) v (The earth is flat)." In this there is no implication that the facts described or the words used in one of the component propositions have any connection with the experience or language involved in the other component proposition. It should be clear then that when one is dealing with actual propositions, it is a gross mistake to confuse the ⊃ and → relations. If we are dealing with *formulas,* however, the difference is not always so sharp. Consider, for example, the formula I*ab* ⊃ I*ba*. The meaning of this formula involves the claim that no matter what general terms are substituted for *a* and *b,* the result will be a true "If . . . then . . ." proposition. Now this assertion would, of course, be true if it *just happened* to be the case that if an I*ab* proposition is true, the corresponding I*ba* proposition is true. But to *know* that this was *always* the case would require us to inspect every possible substitution instance of the formula—if it is merely a matter of fact that all the substitution instances verify the formula. Needless to say, an inspection of all possible cases of I*ab* and I*ba* is beyond the competence of mortal man. It is also outside the scope of formal logic. Yet the logicians do assert "If . . . then . . ." formulas. How? On what basis? On the basis of *formal* relations between the expressions they connect by the ⊃ sign. In other words, the only basis a formal logician, *qua* formal logician, has for connecting two expressions with a ⊃ is an analytic, rather than a contingent, relationship between the two expressions. This means, in turn, that the component propositions of any substitution instance of such a formula will also be analytically related —which is to say that if I*ab* ⊃ I*ba* is a true formula, then any substitution for I*ab* will *imply* the corresponding substitution for I*ba*. The difference between the formulas about to be demonstrated and the implications already studied is thus, in practice, not very great at all. While in most treatments of symbolic logic they would not be regarded as identical, in practice symbolic logicians do establish ⊃ relations only by establishing → relations.

Thus Lukasiewicz's logic is not so different from the logic that you have studied as it might seem.

And now we proceed to Lukasiewicz's system.

SYMBOLS

Variables: *a, b, c,* etc., for general terms.

P, Q, R, S, etc., for propositions.

Constants: **A, E, I,** and **O.** (as explained in Chapter 2)

$\supset$, $\cdot$, and $\sim$. (as explained in this chapter)

Definitional rules: **A** and **I** are primitives. **O** and **E** are defined as their negations. Accordingly:

Rule RE: "$\sim$**I**" may be everywhere replaced by **E** and conversely.

Rule RO: "$\sim$**A**" may be everywhere replaced by **O** and conversely.

AXIOMS

1. **A**aa
2. **I**aa
3. (**A**bc·**A**ab)$\supset$**A**ac (*Barbara*)
4. (**A**bc·**I**ba)$\supset$**I**ac (*Datisi*)

The first two axioms are laws of identity. Outside the system, they would naturally be interpreted as "All *a* are *a*" and "Some *a* are *a*," where any general term may be substituted for *a*. Besides these laws, only the two syllogistic moods, *Barbara* and *Datisi,* need to be laid down as axioms in order to derive the entire Aristotelian syllogistic.

AUXILIARY THEORY

The following are taken over from the truth functional logic studied in the first part of this chapter. We list only those truth functions actually used in the following proofs. Each may be verified by truth-table analysis.

I. $(Q\supset R)\supset[(P\supset Q)\supset(P\supset R)]$

II. $[P\supset(Q\supset R)]\supset[Q\supset(P\supset R)]$

III. $(P\supset Q)\supset(\sim Q\supset\sim P)$

IV. $[(P\cdot Q)\supset R]\supset[P\supset(Q\supset R)]$

V. $[(P\cdot Q)\supset R]\supset\{(S\supset Q)\supset[(P\cdot S)\supset R]\}$

VI. $(R\supset S)\supset\{[(P\cdot Q)\supset R]\supset[(Q\cdot P)\supset S]\}$

VII. $[(P\cdot Q)\supset R]\supset[(P\cdot\sim R)\supset\sim Q]$

VIII. $[(P\cdot Q)\supset R]\supset[(\sim R\cdot Q)\supset\sim P]$

RULES OF INFERENCE

(a) *Rule of Substitution:* If α is an asserted expression of the system (either an axiom or a previously proved theorem), then any expression produced from α by a valid substitution is also an asserted expression. The only valid substitution is to put for term variables (*a, b, c*) other term variables (e.g., *b* for *a*). (And, of course, any assertions whatsoever may be substituted for the propositional variables *P, Q, R,* and *S*.)

(b) *Rule of Detachment:* If α and $(\alpha \supset \beta)$ are asserted expressions of the system, then β is an asserted expression of the system.

PROOFS (The theorem to be proved is listed first. Arabic numerals in the proofs refer to the four axioms and to previously demonstrated theorems. Roman numerals refer to the eight truth functions listed above.):

A. DEDUCTION OF THE LAWS OF CONVERSION

5. Abc $\supset$ (Iba $\supset$ Iac)

In IV, substitute Abc for *P*, Iba for *Q*, and Iac for *R*, giving:

[(Abc · Iba) $\supset$ Iac] $\supset$ [Abc $\supset$ (Iba $\supset$ Iac)]

The antecedent of this conditional is axiom 4. Hence, by the rule of detachment, the consequent is demonstrated.

6. Iab $\supset$ Iba (*Law of conversion for* I *propositions*)

In 5, substitute *a* for *b*, *a* for *c*, and *b* for *a*, giving:

Aaa $\supset$ (Iab $\supset$ Iba). The antecedent is axiom 1. Hence, the consequent is demonstrated. (Note that the substitution of *a* for both *b* and *c* is quite legitimate. In substituting for variables, the rule is that the same expression must be substituted for each occurrence of the same variable. There is nothing in this to prevent us from substituting the same expression for more than one variable. Thus, although "I cows/ brown," is not a proper substitution for "Iaa," "I cows/cows" *is* a legitimate substitution for "Iab." Similarly, "Aaa $\supset$ (Iab $\supset$ (Iba)" is a proper substitution for "Abc $\supset$ (Iba $\supset$ Iac)," though the latter formula may not be substituted for the former.)

7. Iba $\supset$ (Abc $\supset$ Iac)

In II, substitute Abc for *P*, Iba for *Q*, and Iac for *R*, giving:

[Abc $\supset$ (Iba $\supset$ Iac)] $\supset$ [Iba $\supset$ (Abc $\supset$ Iac)]

The antecedent is 5 (the first theorem demonstrated above).

8. Aab $\supset$ Iab (*Subalternation for affirmative propositions*)

In 7, substitute *a* for *b*, and *b* for *c*, giving:

Iaa $\supset$ (Aab $\supset$ Iab) The antecedent is axiom 2.

9. (P $\supset$ Iab) $\supset$ (P $\supset$ Iba)

In I, substitute Iab for *Q*, and Iba for *R*, giving:

(Iab $\supset$ Iba) $\supset$ [(P $\supset$ Iab) $\supset$ (P $\supset$ Iba)]

Since the antecedent is 6 (the second theorem demonstrated above), the consequent is demonstrated.

10. Aab $\supset$ Iba (*Conversion per accidens of* A *propositions*)

In 9, substiute Aab for *P*, giving:

(Aab $\supset$ Iab) $\supset$ (Aab $\supset$ Iba)

The antecedent is 8.

From now on, in order to condense the proofs somewhat, we shall adopt the following conventions. Instead of writing, "In 9, substitute A*ab* for *P*, giving:" we shall write, "9: A*ab* for *P*:"; this will enable us to write the result of a substitution on the same line as the instructions for the substitution. Then, instead of writing out in full that the antecedent is such-and-such an axiom or earlier theorem, we shall simply write the number of that axiom or theorem, connecting it by a horseshoe to the number of the theorem being proved (the consequent of the conditional). The *proof* of 10 would be written as follows, in accordance with these conventions:

9: A*ab* for *P*: (A*ab* ⊃ I*ab*) ⊃ (A*ab* ⊃ I*ba*): 8 ⊃ 10

11. I*ba* ⊃ I*ab*

  6: *b* for *a*, and *a* for *b*: 11 (Here the rule of substitution is sufficient.)

12. ∼I*ab* ⊃ ∼I*ba*

  III: I*ba* for *P*, I*ab* for *Q*: (I*ba* ⊃ I*ab*) ⊃ (∼I*ab* ⊃ ∼I*ba*): 11 ⊃ 12

13. E*ab* ⊃ E*ba* (*Conversion of* E *propositions*)

  12: Apply *rule RE*: 13

14. ∼I*ab* ⊃ ∼A*ab*

  III: A*ab* for *P*, I*ab* for *Q*: (A*ab* ⊃ I*ab*) ⊃ (∼I*ab* ⊃ ∼A*ab*): 8 ⊃ 14

15. E*ab* ⊃ O*ab* (*Subalternation for negative propositions*)

  14: Apply *Rules RE* and *RO*: 15

B. *DEDUCTION OF THE AFFIRMATIVE MOODS*

16. (*S* ⊃ I*ba*) ⊃ [(A*bc* · *S*) ⊃ I*ac*]

  V: A*bc* for *P*, I*ba* for *Q*, I*ac* for *R*:

  [(A*bc* · I*ba*) ⊃ I*ac*] ⊃ {(*S* ⊃ I*ba*) ⊃ [(A*bc* · *S*) ⊃ I*ac*]}: 4 ⊃ 16

17. (A*bc* · I*ab*) ⊃ I*ac* (*DARII*)

  16: I*ab* for *S*: (I*ab* ⊃ I*ba*) ⊃ [(A*bc* · I*ab*) ⊃ I*ac*]: 6 ⊃ 17

18. (A*bc* · A*ab*) ⊃ I*ac* (*BARBARI*)

  16: A*ab* for *S*: (A*ab* · I*ba*) ⊃ [(A*bc* · A*ab*) ⊃ I*ac*]: 10 ⊃ 18

19. A*ba* ⊃ I*ba*

  8: *b* for *a*, *a* for *b*: 19

20. (A*bc* · A*ba*) ⊃ I*ac* (*DARAPTI*)

  16: A*ba* for *S*: (A*ba* ⊃ I*ba*) ⊃ [(A*bc* · A*ba*) ⊃ I*ac*]: 19 ⊃ 20

21. [(*P* · *Q*) ⊃ I*ba*] ⊃ [(*Q* · *P*) ⊃ I*ab*]

  VI: I*ba* for *R*, I*ab* for *S*: (I*ba* ⊃ I*ab*) ⊃ {[(*P* · *Q*) ⊃ I*ba*] ⊃ [(*Q* · *P*) ⊃ I*ab*]}:
  11 ⊃ 21

22. (A*ba* · I*bc*) ⊃ I*ca*

  4: *a* for *c*, *c* for *a*: 22

23. (I*bc* · A*ba*) ⊃ I*ac* (*DISAMIS*)

  21: A*ba* for *P*, I*bc* for *Q*, *c* for *b*: [(A*ba* · I*bc*) ⊃ I*ca*] ⊃ [(I*bc* · A*ba*) ⊃ I*ac*]:
  22 ⊃ 23

24. (A*ba* · I*cb*) ⊃ I*ca*

  17: *a* for *c*, *c* for *a*: 24

25. $(Icb \cdot Aba) \supset Iac$ *(DIMARIS)*

    21: Aba for P, Ibc for Q, c for b: $[(Aba \cdot Icb) \supset Ica] \supset [(Icb \cdot Aba) \supset Iac]$: $24 \supset 25$

26. $(Aba \cdot Acb) \supset Ica$

    18: a for c, c for a: 26

27. $(Acb \cdot Aba) \supset Iac$ *(BRAMANTIP)*

    21: Aba for P, Acb for Q, c for b: $[(Aba \cdot Acb) \supset Ica] \supset [(Acb \cdot Aba) \supset Iac]$: $26 \supset 27$

We omit the deductions of most of the negative moods. In view of the difficulties posed by Baroco and Bocardo in classical reduction to the first figure, it will be of some interest to the reader if we present Lukasiewicz's demonstrations of these two in a modern framework. We can note that axiom 3, Barbara, has not been used in any of the earlier proofs. All the other affirmative moods, except Barbara herself, and all the negative moods, except Baroco and Bocardo, can be deduced from Datisi and the two laws of identity, Aaa and Iaa.

53. $(Abc \cdot \sim Aac) \supset \sim Aab$

    VII: Abc for P, Aab for Q, Aac for R:

    $[(Abc \cdot Aab) \supset Aac] \supset [(Abc \cdot \sim Aac) \supset \sim Aab]$: $3 \supset 53$

54. $(Abc \cdot Oac) \supset Oab$

    53: O for $\sim A$ *(Rule RO)*: 54

55. $(Acb \cdot Oab) \supset Oac$ *(BAROCO)*

    54: c for b, b for c: 55

56. $(\sim Aac \cdot Aab) \supset \sim Abc$

    VIII: Abc for P, Aab for Q, Aac for R:

    $[(Abc \cdot Aab) \supset Aac] \supset [(\sim Aac \cdot Aab) \supset \sim Abc]$: $3 \supset 56$

57. $(Oac \cdot Aab) \supset Obc$

    56: O for $\sim A$ *(Rule RO)*: 57

58. $(Obc \cdot Aba) \supset Oac$ *(BOCARDO)*

    57: b for a, a for b: 58

This completes the rigorous and thoroughly formal deduction of the twenty-four syllogistic moods recognized as valid in classical logic. Lukasiewicz goes on to two additional problems, the formal rejection of all the *in*valid moods and the expansion of the axioms and rules of the system so as to make it a deductively complete formal system. Aristotle's method for showing invalidity was to propose a set of concrete terms which gave a substitution instance with true premises and a false conclusion. Holding that such terms as "man" and "animal" should not be introduced into formal logic, Lukasiewicz rejects two invalid moods axiomatically and derives the necessity for rejecting the remaining 230 invalid moods from this basis. The deduction of the laws of conversion and the valid moods, and the rejection of a sample of the invalid moods, takes up, in all, four pages in Lukasiewicz's book. Thirty-two pages are devoted to "The Problem of Decision." It turns out that there is an infinite number of expressions possible in the language of the system which can be neither demonstrated nor rejected on the basis of the axioms and rules already put forth. The quest for a "decision procedure," a means for deciding, in a finite number of steps, the truth or falsity of every expression possible in the system, is a long and difficult one. It is in the end a successful quest. The Aristotelian syllogistic, as completed by Lukasiewicz, is a deductively complete formal system.

Chapter 4

Induction

Given the propositions that Socrates was a married man and that all married men have wives, we can infer with certainty that Socrates had a wife. If we add to this that most married men have children, we can reasonably infer, though not with certainty, that he had children. These two inferences illustrate the essential difference between deduction and induction as these types of inference were defined in Chapter 1. Taking another look at this difference now will give us a clearer view of the problems before us in the present chapter.

The premises of a valid deductive argument provide a completely sufficient basis for asserting the conclusion. No additional evidence could make the conclusion more certain (except psychologically), and no additional evidence could make it logically less certain—so long as the original premises are allowed to stand. The logical situation is quite different in induction. Although the inference forms to be studied in the present chapter may help us in assembling reasonably sufficient evidence for our estimates about reality, the premises of even the best inductive argument do not provide complete evidence for the conclusion: it is always possible to think of additional propositions whose truth, if we knew it, would make us more certain of an inductive conclusion; and one can also think of propositions in every case which do not contradict the original premises but which nonetheless render the original conclusion less certain. If we were seriously interested in Socrates' parental status, for example, we might not stop with the inference in the last paragraph, reasonable as it is. We might look around for records mentioning that he did indeed have children. If we found such records, we would have a better basis than before for concluding, "Socrates had children." If we found frequent denials, and no assertions, that he had children, we would probably abandon our original conclusion. In either case, our logical basis for accepting or rejecting the proposition "Socrates had children" would have been improved by the search for additional evidence, but in neither case would we have a basis for complete certainty about this proposition, even after our search.

The problem of the present chapter is thus to determine what types of inference lead us to "reasonable," albeit not completely certain, conclusions if we start from true premises. Although we seem to learn quite early in life that there *are* such ways of thinking—that reasoning well does not always involve being certain—it may be well to analyze the whole notion of inductive reasonableness in some detail before proceeding to particular forms of valid induction. If we can get clear what inductive validity is in general, we shall have an easier time appreciating how some valid inductions may leave us with less rational uncertainty than others.

1. Inductive validity in general

The example of Socrates and his probable children suggests that an inductive inference form should be counted valid if it leads us from true premises to a true conclusion in *most* of the cases to which it is applied. In our opinion this is not an adequate account of inductive validity. It is, however, a natural view, and it will be worth our while to explore it further in order to reach a better one.

1.1. The success theory of inductive validity

There can be no doubt that we do expect valid inductive techniques to "pay off" over the long run. As we remarked in our introductory chapter, the major human need which inductive logic attempts to fill is our need to predict, or make estimates about, reality which we have not experienced. Although no inference technique can be guaranteed to meet this need perfectly, it would seem as if any valid form of inference should yield accurate estimates of unexperienced reality at least *most* of the time. The old saying "You can't argue with success" suggests a label for this view of inductive validity. We shall call it the *success theory*. The proposal of the success theory is that inductive validity should be *defined* in terms of successful prediction of unexperienced reality.

Corresponding to the success theory of inductive validity is, of course, a *failure theory* of invalidity. This, too, seems at first to fit quite closely what we ordinarily mean when we call an inference unreasonable or illogical. If an inference technique is conspicuously unsuccessful—if from true premises it leads us more often to false than to true conclusions—we rightly question its validity. Unwillingness to abandon or modify such a form of inference is the mark of a person who is not reasonable. Consider, for example, the child who predicts sunshine in the face of the weatherman's "Nine chances in ten of rain." The child's argument may be: "I want sunshine. Therefore, there will be sunshine." If we point out to him that in most cases in which he wants sunshine and the weatherman confidently predicts rain, it rains, we might regard it as a crucial test of his logical maturity whether he gives up his old way of arguing.

The case for defining inductive validity and invalidity in terms of predictive success and failure can be stated on a more advanced level. It can be argued, for example, that our reliance on a scientific theory depends entirely on the theory's success in generating true predictions about unexperienced reality on the basis of true descriptions of experienced reality. If we can say of a theory, X, that most of the predictions made from it have turned out to be true, we feel justified in using X to form estimates of still other unexperienced reality. If X has failed, in comparison with other theories, to enable us to make successful predictions, we tend to reject it.

1.2. Criticism of the success theory

In spite of the considerations sketched in the last few paragraphs, it would be a mistake to define inductive validity in terms of long-run predictive success. There are at least three drawbacks to the success theory. One is that it is difficult to say what we should mean by the terms "successful in the long run" or "successful in most cases." If we apply these terms to inference forms which have paid off in most cases in which we have *so far* used them, we are simply begging the question of whether the forms in question will help us to estimate realities which we have *not yet* experienced. Notice that the arguments given in previous paragraphs appeal to *past* successes, whereas the success theory seems to promise us inference forms which will help us in estimating future realities. If, however, we apply "the long run" and "most cases" to the whole range of actual and possible experience, past, present, and future, it is hard to see how we could ever be justified in saying that an inference form *is* successful in most cases or in the long run. It would seem as if we would need to apply the form successfully to more than half of all the possible cases in which it might be used before we could say that it was, in the long run, successful. There is no reason to suppose, however, that this has been done for any inference form of much use or interest.

The second drawback of the success theory is that it makes logic a matter of observation of the world, rather than an investigation of formal relations between terms and propositions. If inductive reasonableness is a formal relation between premises and conclusion, we shall be able to judge the validity of an argument without waiting to see whether its premises and conclusion all happen in fact to be true. If we do *not* define validity formally, we shall have to say that a valid argument just "happens" to be valid, that its reasonableness is a contingent matter of fact. While the truth of premises and conclusions may indeed be a contingent matter of fact, it seems at least odd to make their relationship in an argument also a contingent matter of fact.

A success theorist might not be much disturbed by our last criticism. "You can't argue with success," he might say. "If inductive reasonableness can't be derived from formal logic, so much the worse for formal logic." It happens, however, that the "informality" of the success theory is at the bottom of a third drawback, one which even a success theorist should consider serious: we could not *use* inference techniques to guide our *expectations* about reality if we had to "wait and see" before calling a technique valid. There would be no reason for making a specific prediction in the first place if reasonableness had to be judged after the fact. If the logical "following" relationship, validity, is treated as a contingent matter of fact, no *pre*diction can be seen to be more reasonable than any other.

A simple example may put both the strengths and drawbacks of the success theory in a clearer light. Suppose that we are asked to make an estimate as to whether an apparently honest penny will turn up heads each of the next ten times we flip it. It would seem reasonable to say, "No, that's unlikely. It's possible, of course, but highly improbable." If we were asked for reasons in support of our estimate, we might reply somewhat as follows: "This seems to be an honest coin. Hence, the odds of heads on any one flip are about even. The odds of ten heads in a row must therefore be less than even." We shall polish up this inference somewhat later in the chapter. Even after being polished up, however, the argument would be open to the question "Why is *that* a valid argument?" According to the success theory, the answer would be: "Because if you reason in this way, you will be right about most sequences of ten flips of an apparently honest penny." The strength of the success theory lies in the fact that we *do* expect to be right most of the time in such situations if we reason in the indicated way. Let us notice, however, that before we flip the penny we do not know whether our estimate will turn out right. We do not even *know* that *most* sequences of ten flips of the coin before us will fail to turn up ten heads. After the flips are over, assuming that we do not often get ten heads in a row, we can look back, of course, and say, "Yes, it *was* reasonable to make the predictions we made," but this analysis after the fact is of no help whatsoever before the fact. And besides, when are we to say that the flips are over? After a hundred sets of ten tosses, perhaps? But surely the coin will last through several hundred thousand sets of ten tosses. If "valid" means "successful in most cases of all possible cases," we would have to wait through at least half of those several hundred thousand sets of ten flips each in order to verify the reasonableness of the argument concluding that ten heads in a row are unlikely. And even then we would be quite in the dark about the remaining hundreds of thousands of tens of flips. A notion of validity which judges an inference technique by its results may be of some use when the results are at hand, as they are, in a sense, in deductive inferences, but such a notion is of doubtful value when the "results"—the truth or falsity of an inferred conclusion—are not at hand. Hindsight is more accurate than foresight, but the need to make estimates of *un*experienced reality is a need for foresight—a need which simply isn't met by hindsight inference.

1.3. Similarity as a formal principle of inductive validity

We noticed earlier that arguments brought forward in support of the success theory are in fact based on past successes. It is reasonable enough to argue that an inference form is valid because it has worked, or would have worked, in the past, but this way of arguing represents a radical departure from the success theory itself. For notice that we are no longer defining the validity of an inference about unexperienced reality by its accuracy with respect to the unexperienced, but are defining it by its coherence with what we have already experienced. The reasonable expectation is no longer defined as the one which will in fact be fulfilled, but as the one which asserts a similarity between what we have not experienced and what we have experienced. Our major criticism of the success theory was that it gave us no basis for declaring one expectation about unknown reality more reasonable than any other, since, on the success theory, we cannot tell from present inspection of an argument with true premises whether the conclusion "follows" or not. This difficulty disappears if we define validity by reference to the similarity between experienced reality as described in the premises and unexperienced reality as estimated in the conclusion. It would appear that the formal relationship of similarity is what people really have in mind when they think they are being reasonable about the future. In order to get a clearer view of this relationship, let us approach it from another angle. Instead of stumbling across it, so to speak, in the course of criticizing a rival notion of validity, we shall examine it in comparison with certain basic principles of all formal logic, the laws of identity, "All *A* are *A*" and "If *P*, then *P*." Our claim will not be that the basic principle of induction can be *deduced* from such necessary logical truths. We shall argue, however, that the similarity relationship plays the same role in our attempts to deal rationally with the world as does the identity relationship in our efforts to be rational in thought and language: when the laws of identity fail, formal logic in general fails; when the future fails to resemble the past, formal logic fails in its application to the world.

We have noted more than once that in formal logic the relations between terms or between propositions hold good only to the extent that meanings are held constant. In the derivation of Aristotle's term logic presented at the end of the last chapter, it was laid down as axiomatic that "All A are A," no matter what general term expression replaces the variable A. The corresponding law for propositional logic is "If P, then P," where any propositional expression may replace P. But these laws of identity, which cannot be rejected without rejecting formal logic, do not necessarily hold when the expression replacing A (or P) is used with one meaning in its first occurrence and with a different meaning in its second occurrence. "All Cardinals are Cardinals" is false, for example, if the first "Cardinals" refers to birds and the second to baseball players. Constancy of meaning is required if the laws of identity are to hold, and the laws of identity must hold if work in formal logic is to be possible: to state these laws amounts to saying that meanings *are* constant in formal logic.

So long as our aim is merely to organize descriptions of our past experience, or to clarify the implications of what we say or think, we can get along with a formal logic based entirely on principles like the laws of identity: necessary truths, propositions which no possible experience can falsify. To every *de*ductively valid inference, there corresponds just such a proposition, and deductive logic is of inestimable value in meeting the persistent human need for clarity and precision of thought and expression. As we know, however, there is another need which logic attempts to meet, our need to make estimates about reality which we have not experienced. It is this need which inductive inference tries to meet.

The distinctive principle of inductive logic is *like* the principle of identity underlying formal logic in general. It has been stated in various ways, among them the following: "The future will resemble the past," "The reality we have not experienced will be like the reality we have experienced," "There are laws of nature," and, "Nature is uniform or consistent." The parallel with the laws of identity will be plainer if we add yet another formulation to those just given: "Things of the same kind have the same properties." Let us use the symbol S_k to indicate those things of a certain kind, the S kind, which we know, from experience, to have a certain property, P. From statements of the form "S_k is P," we may *de*duce identical statements of the form "S_k is P." Now let S_u stand for those S's whose possession or lack of P is unknown to us. From statements of the form "S_k is P," we *in*ductively infer corresponding but not identical statements of the form "S_u is P." The premise and conclusion of the deduction are identical. More particularly, the subjects of the two propositions in the deductive argument are identical. The subject of the inductive premise is *similar* to the subject of the conclusion, but not identical with it. The things talked about in the premise and conclusion are of the same *kind,* but they are not absolutely the same things. The similarity of the future to the past, the similarity of the experienced to the unexperienced, and the uniformity, consistency or lawfulness of nature referred to in the earlier formulations of the principle of induction may all be expressed in the claim that every valid induction can be stated as an argument of the form "S_k is P; therefore S_u is P."

Formal logic as a whole proceeds on the basis of sameness of *meaning* for specific *symbols:* if no expression could be used twice with the same meaning, formal logic would be impossible. Inductive logic proceeds on the assumption of sameness of *properties* for specific kinds of *things.* If things of the same kind had nothing in common except the properties used to define them as of the same kind, inductive logic would be utterly unsuccessful in meeting our need to anticipate reality which we have not experienced. We assume, however, that things will share not only the properties which lead us to compare them, but others as well: for example that if all known dogs are carnivorous, then dogs which are as yet unknown will be, too.

1.4. Objections to the use of similarity to define validity—and replies

The philosophical reader may here object that our basic principle of inductive logic is not a logical principle at all, but a claim about the world, at best a contingently true statement of fact. Further, and worse, it does not even seem to be a true claim about the world. As we constantly discover, things of the same kind in some respects are not the same in all respects. Not all married men have children, though most do; not all cows are brown: some are, some are not. Indeed, since no two individuals are absolutely identical, we can be sure that any two things "of the same kind" differ with respect to *some* property or other. These objections are by no means superficial. If they could not be met, our own view of inductive reasonableness would come out worse than the success theory examined earlier. Before proceeding to specific forms of induction, we must attempt to answer these objections to induction in general.

The *use* of our principle of induction to make inferences in real life does involve a hopeful claim about the world. As formal logicians, however, we are not actually making this contingently true claim. The laws of identity used in all formal logic are not claims that people do in fact use the same words always, or even usually, with the same meanings. Rather, they are claims that rational argumentation demands constancy of meaning for identifiably similar expressions. In the same way, the principle of induction is not a claim about the world. It is a claim, rather, that the world can be reasoned about only if, and as, identifiable similarities in some respects are reliable signs that things are similar in other respects. To engage in formal logic is to accept the demands made by the laws of identity, though it remains a contingent matter of fact whether anyone does in fact engage in formal logic or accept those laws. To use the principle of induction in forming expectations about the world is to hope that the world can be reasoned about. The falsity of this claim in particular cases no more falsifies the principle of induction—as a logical principle—than the facts of vagueness and ambiguity in ordinary language falsify the laws of identity—as principles of formal logic. *If* our past experience of the world affords us any rational basis for anticipating what we have not experienced, it is by means of resemblances between the experienced and the unexperienced. To the extent that the future *differs* from anything in our past experience, as it often seems to, the past affords us no sound basis for saying what the future *will* be like.

The first objection to "S_k is P; therefore S_u is P" was that it embodied a claim about the world. The second objection was that the claim is a false one. Our answer to the first objection was that our *use* of the principle embodies a factual claim, the claim that the world will be reasonable, so to speak, but that the principle of induction is not itself an empirical proposition. But this answer may seem evasive, for from a practical point of view, the use of the principle is what we are most interested in. The second objection seeks to uncover this evasion: not all things of the same kind *do* behave in the same way, it says, and thus the principle of induction, though it may appeal to our sense of logical propriety, fails us as a means of dealing with the illogical world in which we actually live.

We shall conclude our treatment of inductive validity with three remarks in response to this objection.

At a very general level, we can concede the objection entirely. Life is full of surprising changes and chances. It is by no means a trivial task of the arts and of philosophy to call our attention to this fact, so that we can be responsive to novelty, prepared for the unexpected, ready to admit, perhaps, that there may be things we cannot prepare for but must await in patience. There is surely something lifeless about a person who treats his friends and neighbors as entirely predictable machines, and perhaps we are missing something about the world at large if we view *it* as thoroughly predictable, the same old thing over and over.

Still, the poet and the philosopher who call our attention to creative novelty or to the radical contingency of things do their work in the assumption that regularity also is to be found in the world. A writer expects that his pen will not turn into a peacock feather, and he supposes that the postman will carry his insights to the publisher—basing his expectations in both cases on the past behavior of similar subjects. We should hesitate, therefore, before describing the world as fundamentally lawless. Instead of accepting every irregularity in the world's behavior at face value, we must for some purposes, at least in some cases, hope to discover that such apparent irregularities can be explained as expressions of deeper regularities. Consider the weather, for example. Some days it rains, some days it doesn't. The world is perhaps a more instructive place because of this lack of monotony; the passage of rains and seasons charms the poet, and it may be of use to the prophet. But prophets, philosophers, and poets are often transported by sailors, and they are all fed by farmers—the farmer and the sailor have good reason to wish that the weather may be foretold. Accordingly, and for a quite legitimate purpose, they look for some way of distinguishing those circumstances in which rains, say, or storms seldom or never occur from those circumstances in which they usually or always occur. To the extent that this kind of search is successful, it uncovers regularities beneath apparent irregularities.

It is worth remarking, finally, that the objection itself rests on the principle of induction, the principle it sets out to deny. The argument is that since not all things of the same kind have the same properties, we should not expect the things of tomorrow to have the same properties as the things of today. But this is itself an inductive argument, and thus the objection tends to refute itself as an objection to induction, although it does indeed point out a fundamental difference between two types of induction. In some cases we *do* expect variable behavior from things of the same kind, but even if we cannot explain the variability as the expression of a deeper uniformity, we can use it as evidence for inductive inferences about the future. Some flips of the coin come up heads, some tails. There would be something suspicious about a coin flipping situation in which we *could* predict much more than half the time how the penny will turn up. Still, as we shall see in a few pages, the random behavior of an honest penny can be used as the basis for some quite reasonable inferences. If the objection to induction is dealt with on the level of particulars, the reply would seem to be this: some kinds of things *do* behave irregularly, at least with respect to certain properties; the reasonable inference is that *such* things will pursue the same irregular ways in the future as in the past.

2. Some specifics of valid induction

In the last several pages we have said our piece about inductive validity in general. We shall now get down to specifics. A good way to begin this job is by filling in some gaps in the formula which we have presented as the logical basis for every valid induction. As these gaps are filled in in different ways, different more or less solid inference forms result.

The distinctive formal principle of induction may be stated as "S_k is P; therefore S_u is P." This formula has at least the following gaps. We have not specified (1) how S may be quantified in the inductive premise(s), nor (2) how it is to be quantified in the conclusion of an inductive inference. (3) We have said nothing as to the kinds of general terms which may replace the S variable in our formula, and (4) we have left unspecified the kind of predicate which may replace P. A lot depends on the way in which these open places in the formula are filled in. An inference involving one sort of quantification, for example, may be much more reasonable than an otherwise similar inference in which different quantifiers are used. We shall see that valid inductions have formal differences other than those just indicated, but these four are perhaps most basic.

Through the next few pages we shall often be referring to the six inferences given below. These arguments differ a great deal in the ways and degrees in which they are reasonable. Each represents a different way of filling in the gaps in the formula, "S_k is P; therefore S_u is P."

(1) John's blood circulates.
   Gertrude's blood circulates.

(2) The blood of a large number of human beings circulates.
   Gertrude's blood circulates.

(3) The blood of a large number of human beings circulates.
   Every human's blood circulates.

(4) Humans have circulatory systems.
   Lions, tigers, and kangaroos have circulatory systems.

(5) Animals have circulatory systems.
   Sap circulates in trees.

(6) Blood circulates in animals.
   Some plants have something like a circulatory system.

2.1. Quantity of S_k

One swallow does not make a summer, and the examination of just one individual of a certain kind is generally a poor basis for conclusions about other subjects of the same kind. Compare inferences (1) and (2) on this page for an illustration of this point. So many factors affect one human being which do not affect others that it is usually rash to treat one person, say John, as a perfect representative of all persons. As we seem to learn from experience, some things of the same kind do tend to have the same properties; for other kinds of things, there is considerable variation from specimen to specimen with respect to many properties. If we know about only one individual subject, our evidence cannot *help* being uniform. If we observe only one flip of a penny, for example, we have perfectly uniform, specific evidence for one or the other of these predictions: "Every flip of this coin will turn up heads," or else (if our single observed flip has yielded tails), "Every flip of this coin will turn up tails." Logical prudence suggests that we give our subjects a chance to tell their story more fully. If their behavior in fact tends to be variable, as does an honest coin's behavior, we must give them time to tell us so. If, on the other hand, all individuals of a certain kind tend to have a certain property, then *this* pattern will emerge more clearly as we study more of the subject. An examination of several human beings suggests that a person's possession of a circulatory system is not like a coin's turning up heads. (Notice, however, that some important human traits—sex, for example—vary noticeably from specimen to specimen.)

Although it is better to have examined many individuals than to base our conclusions on experience with just a few individuals, it does not follow from this that a premise reporting on one hundred subjects is anything like one hundred times stronger than a premise describing one subject. Indeed, sheer quantity of subjects often contributes less to the "weight of the evidence" than other factors. If we wish to draw a conclusion about Gertrude, for example, a premise reporting on a few individuals who are very similar to Gertrude will do us more good than a description of a multitude of subjects who resemble her only slightly.

2.2. Quantity of S_u

Now compare inferences (2) and (3) in our list of samples. Since the conclusion of (2) is *de*ductively implied by the conclusion of (3), but not vice versa, (2) is clearly the safer inference. If (3) pans out—if every human's blood *does* circulate, then so does (2); but not contrariwise. The conclusion to (3) claims more than the conclusion to (2), for Gertrude's blood might circulate, even though there were exceptions to the generalization that everyone has a circulatory system. A person who made inferences like (2) could not possibly be wrong in his conclusions more often than a person who reasoned from the same evidence, but along the lines of (3). When conclusion (3) is right, (2) is also right, but (2) may be right in additional cases as well. The impossibility here is a formal one. From the standpoint of purely logical prudence, then, (2) must be judged the better inference.

It may be argued, on the other hand, that failure to draw universal conclusions, like the conclusion of (3), shows a certain lack of logical courage. For after all, the premise common to (2) and (3) is relevant to Gertrude purely and merely because she is a human being, not on account of any of those properties which make her just Gertrude and not someone else. We might therefore substitute some other human being for Gertrude in the conclusion of (2) without lessening the validity of the inference. Suppose now that we did this repeatedly, first inserting Mabel, then George, then George's first grandson, if any, and so on, through all the humans there ever were, are, or will be. The natural end of such a process would be a large *set* of inferences from the same premise, and the conjunction of the singular conclusions of the inferences in this set would be equivalent to the universal conclusion of (3). So why not draw the universal conclusion at once?

This is in fact the usual approach of science. Scientific work normally proceeds on the assumption that the world can be generalized about in *some* way, and that the problem is to find the correct way. The normal procedure of scientists is to allow particular facts to suggest quite general propositions which can then be tested by reference to yet other particular facts. The crucial scientific activity of experimental testing gets its meaning as much from the general theories tested as from the facts discovered in the test.

However, it is important to keep in mind that scientists, in assuming that some generalization can be applied to a situation, *are* making an assumption. The world is composed of individual things, not of general terms. No matter what "kinds" or "universals" we reason in terms of, the world may disappoint our expectations. While we should look for universal conclusions, therefore, we should not be astonished to find that many of the generalizations that we adopt break down. The proper remedy is not to stop generalizing, but to generalize warily, and to abandon generalizations known to be faulty.

2.3. Specificity of S

Some general terms are more general than others (see Chapter 2 1.1.2.). "Animal," for example, is more general than "dog," and this would be so even though every animal happened to be a dog. Hence, we can compare inductive inferences in accordance with the specificity or generality of their terms. If we do so, we discover that inferences concerned with highly specific subjects are stronger than those which concern only generically similar subjects. Compare (4) and (5), for example. To make the comparison clearer, let us rewrite them as:

(4)′ Some animals (humans) have circulatory systems.

Other animals (lions, etc.) have circulatory systems.

(5)′ Some organisms (animals) have circulatory systems.

Other organisms (trees) have circulatory systems.

We judge (4)′ to be more reasonable than (5)′ on the ground that different kinds of animals are more similar to each other—they are known to have more points in common—than are different kinds of organisms; it is thus reasonable to expect greater similarity in *unknown* respects from types of animal than from types of organism.

The principle at work in the previous illustration can also be seen in the solution of a kind of problem which arises in statistical inference. Consider Jones, for example, a thirty-year-old mountain climber. What is the likelihood that Jones will live to be forty, given as evidence that (1) far more than nine out of every ten thirty-year-olds for whom we have information have survived to forty, while (2) fewer than eight out of ten thirty-year-old mountain climbers have survived to be forty? Assuming that we have a tolerably large sample of mountain climbers, it is clear that the probability of Jones's celebrating his fortieth birthday is, sad to say, less than 80 per cent. We are confronted here with a choice of terms in describing Jones. We may describe him simply as a thirty-year-old man, or, more specifically, as a thirty-year-old mountain climber. On the principle that no available evidence should be ignored, we choose the more specific description. The use of specific terms, when possible, *does* always give us "more" evidence, simply because the criteria for applying a specific term to two or more things are always more stringent—the things must have more in common before the description is correct—than are the criteria for applying an associated generic term.

2.4. Specificity of P

Finally, compare (5) with (6). The essential difference between these two inferences is in the specificity of their predicates. In (5) we expect trees to have circulatory systems; in (6) our expectations are less specific. Since the conclusion of (6) can be deductively inferred from the conclusion of (5), but not vice versa, (6) is clearly the safer inference. The same considerations apply here as in the comparison of (2) and (3) (see 2.2.).

Also as in 2.2., there is something to be said for the less safe inference form. Although you may go wrong more often in making inferences like (5), when you are right you are more precisely right than you are with inductions like (6). We sometimes need, and we should always wish to have, the more precise account. If our whole aim in life were never to be wrong, it would be best to give up inductive inference: the person who draws no conclusions draws no false ones. Now to ascribe an extremely general predicate to a subject is like drawing no conclusion about the subject. Calling something colored, for example, says less about the subject than calling it red. While there are more possibilities for going wrong if we expect things to be red, green, yellow, etc., than there are if we predict only that they will have "some color or other," we sometimes need, and we should always wish to have, the more precise account. Accordingly, we should have courage to infer conclusions with specific predicates, while prudently recognizing that such conclusions will sometimes be false.

3. Inferences from mixed evidence: the probability calculus

Although there is an element of uncertainty in all inductive inference, we can divide valid inductions into two classes in accordance with the source of uncertainty involved in each. In some cases the uncertainty arises from the known behavior of just those specific things whose future, unknown behavior we wish to predict. If we are asked whether an honest penny will turn up two heads on the next two flips, the correct answer is an uncertain "no." The uncertainty here is connected with the fact that honest pennies do quite often, though not usually, turn up heads twice running. Contrast this with the "uncertainty" involved in answering "no" to the question "Will this penny turn into a rooster when we flip it?" Here the uncertainty is of a more general kind. No penny we know of ever *has* turned into a rooster. Nothing very much *like* a penny has become a rooster, only eggs have. Indeed, in any use of "certain" you are likely to encounter outside a philosophy book, it is *certain* that the penny will *not* turn into a rooster. Still, there would be no *logical* impossibility in such a transformation: "The thing I have flipped is a penny" does not strictly imply "The thing which lands on the table is not a rooster." If we reflect that strange things do sometimes happen, and if we strain our imaginations to the utmost, we may be able to entertain the idea, if only for a moment, that a penny flipped is a rooster launched. When we have performed these mental exercises, however, we come back to the fact that nothing in the past behavior of pennies supports them. Only by ignoring past pennies can we imagine a rooster emerging from the penny before us. The most specifically pertinent evidence is *uniformly* against the expectation of a rooster. The "two heads" question is different. It is precisely because we *do* pay attention to pennies and their normal behavior that we are uncertain as to whether this penny will yield two heads on the next two throws. Here the most specifically pertinent evidence is *mixed*. We can use the distinction between uniform and mixed evidence to divide the subject matter to be covered in the rest of this chapter. It is worth noting that the distinction is accompanied, other things being equal, by a difference in degree of inductive support. For every argument from mixed evidence it is possible to conceive of a stronger argument for the same conclusion based on uniform evidence. It should also be noted that arguments from mixed evidence with singular conclusions illustrate the general principle of induction in a peculiar way. When the most directly pertinent evidence for or against a single event runs in both directions, the nearest we can come to expecting the future to resemble the past is to weaken or strengthen our *expectations* in proportion as the evidence is more or less equally mixed on the two sides. Either the coin will turn up two heads on the next two tosses or it will not: a single event cannot be mixed. But our expectation about the event can and does reflect the mixture in the evidence. To say that the chances against two heads are three to one may be interpreted to mean that although we do expect at least one tail, we are only 75 per cent convinced that it will turn up.

For our purposes, the probability calculus can be defined as a formal system for making valid inferences from mixed evidence. After a word more on the nature of mixed evidence, we shall present some useful theorems from this system.

Statements of mixed evidence are all of the general form "Some S are P, and some S are not P." However, not all statements of this form are statements of genuinely mixed evidence. In order for the evidence to be genuinely mixed, it must not only be possible to make contrary particular statements about the S-P relation; it must also be impossible to make any useful universal statements about that relation. Consider coin tossing again. The evidence normally available for estimating the probability of, say, two heads in a row is a good example of what we mean by mixed evidence: some (about half) of the flips of this coin, or of coins like this one, have turned up heads, and some flips (again about half) have turned up tails. In most cases, furthermore, we have no basis for saying in advance which flips will be heads and which tails; *all* we can say is that some (about half) have been heads, and some have been tails. For the probability calculus to be strictly appropriate, this second condition must be satisfied. We must be unable to state any universal rule for the occurrences of heads rather than tails on specific throws which would enable us to predict the later throws in a sequence from a report of the earlier ones. It is easy to imagine a situation in which this condition is not met, and if we do imagine such a situation, it will be clear that merely probabilistic reasoning does not apply to it. Suppose that we had a machine to do our coin tossing for us, a precisely constructed machine which not only flipped the coin in exactly the same way each time (exactly the same pressure applied to exactly the same point on the coin's underside, whatever it happened to be, and so on), but retrieved the coin and proceeded to the next flip. Now then, let us assume that our machine flips the coin in such a way as to produce the following sequence of heads (*H*) and tails (*T*):

H T H T H T H T H T H T H T H T H T H T H T H T H T H T H T

This sequence amply satisfies our first condition for mixed evidence: some *S* are *P*, and some aren't; that is, some of the tosses turn up heads, some do not. But our second condition is not satisfied, for there evidently is a universal rule determining the sequence of heads and tails: every head is followed by a tail, and every tail within the series is followed by a head. A person who grasped the rule would be extremely foolish to use the probability calculus in this situation unless he had reason to suppose that the future of this sequence would fail to resemble its past. He could be quite *sure*, for example, that two heads in a row would *not* occur so long as the machine continued to function in its accustomed way. Accordingly, when we speak of mixed evidence from now on, we mean genuinely mixed evidence, behavior which is, so to speak, *ultimately* variable so far as we can describe it. A more usual way of putting this requirement is to say that the order among those *S*'s which are *P* and those *S*'s which are not *P* must be "random" or "chance." Still another way of putting the point is to say that probability calculations are relevant to a set of events only to the extent that each event in the set is "independent" of each of the others. For example, when we toss coins in this chapter henceforth, we shall assume that the result of any one toss is independent of the result of every other toss, meaning by this that the probability of getting heads is exactly the same on one toss as it is on any other toss, regardless of what has come before.

What can validly be inferred from genuinely mixed evidence? Among other things, we can infer answers to the following questions: How likely is it that the next two flips of an honest coin will both be heads? How likely is it that the next two flips will either both be heads or both be tails? How likely is it that the next three flips will include at least one head? These questions illustrate types of problems which can be dealt with rationally with the aid of the probability calculus. The theory of probability applies, of course, to much more complicated and important situations than coin tossing. We can use our honest coin, however, as a model for expounding some ideas basic to all inference from mixed evidence.

3.1. Some symbols

The question *"How* likely is *X?"* suggests that there is a range or scale of likelihoods, and that the likelihood of *X* falls somewhere on this scale.

It is an immense technical convenience to represent various degrees of likelihood in a clear and concise way. Although the principles of the probability calculus can be applied, in a rough way, to situations in which "very unlikely," "extremely likely," etc., are the order of the day, the calculus itself has been developed on a numerical basis. Standard practice here is to represent the two extreme points of the scale as 1 and 0, and to use fractions for the degrees of probability in between. If we wish to assert, for example, that *X* is certain to occur, we write:

The probability of *X* is 1.

Or, even more concisely:

$P(X)=1$

If, on the other hand, we wish to assert that *X* definitely will *not* occur, we write:

X has zero probability.

Or, more concisely:

$P(X)=0$

For representing all the intermediate degrees of probability, we have available an infinite set of fractions which can equally well be written as "½, ¼, ¾ . . . etc.," or as ".5, .25, .75 . . . etc." Thus, for example, if we want to say that *X* is exactly as likely to occur as not to occur, we write:

$P(X)=½$

or:

$P(X)=.5$

If *X* is more likely to occur than not to occur, we use a fraction greater than ½; if *X*'s *non*occurrence is more likely, we say that $P(X)$ is less than ½. Suppose, for example, that out of one thousand thirty-year-old men for whom we have records, 953 lived to their thirty-first birthdays. Then, if all that we know about Jones is that he is a thirty-year-old man, we might reasonably say:

The probability that Jones will live to his thirty-first birthday is .953.

Using *JL* for "Jones lives to his thirty-first birthday," we may condense the preceding to:

$P(JL)=.953$

Since the fraction used is considerably higher than ½, we are saying that Jones is quite likely to live another year.

But, of course, some men like Jones do die young, forty-seven out of a thousand, according to our evidence. Using *JD* for the event of Jones dying before turning thirty-one, we write:

$P(JD)=.047$

Since .047 is much less than ½, we have just asserted that Jones's death, before his thirty-first birthday, is an extremely *im*probable event. (It is worth noting that $P(JL)+P(JD)=1.0$, which is to say that it is *certain* that Jones will be either alive or dead on his thirty-first birthday.)

3.2. *Joint occurrence of independent events*

Let us get back to our honest penny. The first step in tackling the problems laid out earlier is to formulate our evidence in terms of the symbolism just introduced.

Let *H* and *T* stand for the events of, respectively, the coin turning up heads and the coin turning up tails. If we treat *H* and *T* as the only possible outcomes of flipping the penny, we can write:

(1) $P(H)+P(T)=1.0$

This effectively ignores the pennies that land on edge or get lost in dark corners (your willingness to worry about these is a good sign of your taste for philosophical rigor). We are asserting as certain that the penny will come up either heads or tails. If we have an honest penny, we can also write:

(2) $P(H)=P(T)$

If the various flips of the coin are independent events, we can take it that (1) and (2) apply to every flip, no matter how the preceding or succeeding flips turn out. From (1) and (2), we reach the following, which we also take to be true of any and every flip:

(3) $P(H)=.5$
$P(T)=.5$

So much for the evidence. Now, given (3), how likely is it that the next *two* flips of our coin will *both* be heads?

We obtain the answer to this question by using the *product theorem* of the theory of probability. The product theorem states that if two events are independent, then the probability that both will occur is equal to the probability of one of them multiplied by the probability of the other. If we use "*A* and *B*" to mean that the two events *A* and *B* both occur, we can write the product theorem as:

$P(A \text{ and } B)=P(A)\times P(B)$

In the present case we are concerned with the two events, heads on the next flip and heads on the flip after next, which we may refer to as H_1 and

H_2. Now we know from (3) that the probability of heads on any single flip is .5. Accordingly, we can write:

$P(H_1)=.5$

and:

$P(H_2)=.5$

Making use of the product theorem, which we can fill in as:

$P(H_1 \text{ and } H_2)=P(H_1)\times P(H_2)$

we reach:

$P(H_1 \text{ and } H_2)=.5\times.5=.25$

In other words, the probability of two heads in a row is ¼.

But why? What is the basis of the product theorem? A rigorous answer to this question is beyond our scope, but a moment's reflection will make the theorem plausible intuitively. Let us imagine that we repeat the experiment of flipping the penny a great many times. If we group our flips in sets of two, we will have a large number of *pairs* of flips ("flip pairs"), each pair consisting of a first flip (an H or a T) and a second flip (an H or a T). On the basis of (3), we would expect roughly half of our flips to turn up heads. In other words, roughly half of all of our flip *pairs* should *start* with heads. Now, what proportion of *those* flip pairs (half of the total) will have heads as their second flip? The answer is again provided by (3): roughly half, for the probability of heads on the second flip is supposed to be neither increased nor diminished by the occurrence of heads on the first flip. But half of a half is a fourth: one fourth of all of our flip pairs should both be-gin *and* end with heads. The same result is reached if we begin our calculations from the other end. What proportion of pairs which begin with H should end with H? Half. But what proportion of our total pairs should be-gin with H? Again, half. And again, $.5\times.5=.25$.

To make the preceding arithmetic more vivid, we offer the following tab-ulation of a typical hundred flip pairs of an imaginary honest coin:

First flips	50 Heads		50 Tails	
Second flips when the first flip has turned up				
	Heads		Tails	
	25 Heads	25 Tails	25 Heads	25 Tails
Frequency of each possible outcome:				
	25 Heads then Heads	25 Heads then Tails	25 Tails then Heads	25 Tails then Tails

One hundred flip pairs of an honest coin

The product theorem applies directly only to the joint occurrence of independent events. We can gain a better understanding of the assumption of independence if we pause a moment to analyze the *gambler's fallacy*. We shall then be in a position to consider the modifications which must be made in the theorem in order to deal with events for which we know that the assumption of complete independence would not be true.

The gambler's fallacy is committed when a person argues that an apparent departure from chance in one portion of a series of independent events must be compensated for in some other portion of the same series. Suppose, for example, that you have been predicting tails for each flip of an honest coin, and that heads has come up five times running. You commit the gambler's fallacy if you suppose that the probability of tails on the next flip is even fractionally more than .5. If the various flips in the series really are independent of each other, then the occurrence of heads on the first five flips simply has no effect on the likelihood of tails on the sixth flip.

3.3. Joint occurrence of events which are not independent

To see how the product theorem must be modified to deal with the joint occurrence of events which are *not* independent, let us shift from pennies to playing cards. A normal deck of fifty-two cards contains thirteen hearts. Accordingly, if a card is drawn at random from such a deck, the probability is 13/52, or .25, that it will be a heart. What is the probability of drawing two hearts in a row? If the first card drawn is replaced and the deck shuffled before the next draw, the first and second draws are independent events, and the product theorem can be applied without modification:

$$P(H_1 \text{ and } H_2) = P(H_1) \times P(H_2)$$

or:

$$P(H_1 \text{ and } H_2) = .25 \times .25$$

that is:

$$P(H_1 \text{ and } H_2) = .0625$$

In other words, the probability of drawing two hearts in a row, under the stated conditions, is $\frac{1}{16}$.

Suppose now that we vary the conditions of drawing. Instead of replacing the first card before drawing the second, we set it to one side and make our second draw from the fifty-*one* cards remaining. Clearly, this move affects the *independence* of the two events H_1 and H_2. If the first card *is* a heart, $P(H_2)$ will be 12/51, since the fifty-one remaining cards will include only twelve hearts. If the first card drawn is *not* a heart, there will still be thirteen hearts left in the deck (which is now reduced to fifty-one cards), and $P(H_2) = 13/51$. Accordingly, if we wish to calculate the likelihood of drawing two hearts in a row under these conditions, some modification of the product theorem is necessary.

Fortunately, a small change will do the job. If we use the idea of a "draw pair" in the same way as we earlier used the notion of a flip pair, we can start off by saying that one fourth of all draw pairs will begin with a heart. We now ask, "What proportion of *those* draw pairs [the only ones in which we are interested] will end with a heart?" The answer, as given in the last paragraph, is 12/51. Hence in 12/51 of one fourth of all draw pairs, both cards drawn should be hearts. We can generalize this result as follows: the probability of the joint occurrence of two *non*independent events is equal to the probability of one of them multiplied by the-probability-of-the-other-on-the-assumption-that-the-first-has-occurred. In symbols:

$P(A$ and $B)=P(A)\times P(B,$ if $A)$

In the case at hand:

$P(H_1$ and $H_2)=P(H_1)\times P(H_2,$ if $H_1)$

or:

$P(H_1$ and $H_2)=\frac{1}{4}\times 12/51=3/51=.0588$

In other words, the probability of drawing two hearts in a row, under the stated conditions, is one in seventeen. Slightly fewer than six of every one hundred draw pairs should consist entirely of hearts.

3.4. Alternative occurrence of mutually exclusive events

What are the chances that a card drawn at random from a normal deck will be either a heart or a club? To answer this question, we must employ the *addition theorem* of the probability calculus: if A and B are mutually exclusive events, then:

$P(A$ or $B)=P(A)+P(B)$

In the present case, the A and B of the theorem are for "drawing a heart" and "drawing a club." The probability for each of these is .25, since one out of four cards in a normal deck is a heart, and one fourth are clubs. Using H for "drawing a heart," and C for "drawing a club," we can fill in the addition theorem thus:

$P(H$ or $C)=P(H)+P(C)$

$P(H$ or $C)=.25+.25$

$P(H$ or $C)=.5$

In other words, since one fourth of our possible draws are hearts and another one fourth are clubs, *half* of our possibilities will be hearts *or* clubs: any of twenty-six out of the fifty-two cards in the deck satisfies the condition of being "either a heart or a club."

One of our original questions about penny probabilities was "How likely is it that the next two flips will *either* both be heads *or* both be tails?" The product theorem needs help from the addition theorem to answer this question. The *A* and *B* of our new theorem will now correspond to the *complex* events "H_1 and H_2" and "T_1 and T_2." After using the product theorem to calculate the separate probabilities of these complex events (.25 for each), we fill in the addition theorem thus:

$$P[(H_1 \text{ and } H_2) \text{ or } (T_1 \text{ and } T_2)] = P(H_1 \text{ and } H_2) + P(T_1 \text{ and } T_2)$$
$$P[(H_1 \text{ and } H_2) \text{ or } (T_1 \text{ and } T_2)] = .25 + .25$$
$$P[(H_1 \text{ and } H_2) \text{ or } (T_1 \text{ and } T_2)] = .5$$

In other words, the odds are even that the next two flips of our honest coin will both turn out the same way, either both heads or both tails.

If we look again at the tabulation of one hundred flip pairs on page 204, the reasonableness of the preceding result is apparent. As the table suggests, roughly one fourth of all the flip pairs in a long series of experiments should be "both heads." Another fourth should consist entirely of tails. Thus *half* the members of a large set of flip pairs should satisfy the condition of being "*either* 'both heads' *or* 'both tails.'"

The addition theorem applies directly only to the alternative occurrence of *mutually exclusive* events. "H_1 and H_2" and "T_1 and T_2" are mutually exclusive events in the sense that no single flip pair of an ordinary penny can yield both two heads and two tails. "Drawing a heart" and "drawing a club" are mutually exclusive events if you draw but once, because no one card is both a heart and a club.

3.5. Alternative occurrence of events which are not mutually exclusive

The need for modifying the addition theorem to deal with nonexclusive alternatives will be clear from a simple card problem. What is the probability that the next card drawn from an honest deck will be either a club, a diamond, a heart, a face card (king, queen, or jack) or an ace? If we used the addition theorem here without modification, we might start from the following list:

A normal deck of 52 cards includes:

13 clubs
13 diamonds
13 hearts
12 face cards (a jack, queen, and king in each of four suits)
4 aces

If the events we were concerned with were mutually exclusive, we could solve our problem simply by dividing each of the numbers on our list by 52 and adding them all up. This would give us the interestingly impossible result:

P(club *or* diamond *or* heart *or* face card *or* ace)$=13/52+13/52+13/52$
$+12/52+4/52=55/52=1.06$

This result is impossible for two reasons: (1) it says that the probability of a specific event is greater than 1.0, but we have previously defined 1.0 as the extreme upper limit of our probability scale, and (2) it implies that other quite possible events are impossible (drawing the two of spades, for example).

The difficulty arises from the fact that the possibilities on our list are not, like heads and tails, mutually exclusive. One and the same card can be both a club and a face card, or both a diamond and an ace, and so on. In effect, we were counting some cards more than once when we applied the addition theorem to this problem without modification. We need a modification of the theorem which will help us avoid such double counting and its impossible consequences.

We need only *subtract* the probability, if any, that *both* of two alternative events will occur. The modified addition theorem will then read:

$P(A$ or $B)=P(A)+P(B)-P(A$ and $B)$

Now, if we wish to calculate the probability that the next card will be either a club or a face card, we write:

$P(C$ or $F)=P(C)+P(F)-P(C$ and $F)$

or:

$P(C$ or $F)=13/52+12/52-3/52$

that is:

$P(C$ or $F)=22/52=.42$

The reason for subtracting 3/52 is that three cards in the deck are both clubs and face cards: the jack, queen, and king of clubs.

In some cases, more than one subtraction must be made in order to be sure that each possible outcome is being counted only once. To solve our original problem, for example, we must subtract at the end the probability of drawing each of the following:

a card that is both a club	and a face card ($13/52 \times 12/52=3/52$)
" " " " " " diamond	" " " " (3/52)
" " " " " " heart	" " " " (3/52)
" " " " " " club	and an ace ($13/52 \times 4/52=1/52$)
" " " " " " diamond	" " " (1/52)
" " " " " " heart	" " " (1/52)

In other words, the probability of drawing a card which is either a club or a diamond or a heart or a face card or an ace is: $13/52+13/52+13/52+12/52+4/52-3/52-3/52-3/52-1/52-1/52-1/52=43/52=.83$

The probability is high here, but not impossibly high, and there is room to draw the two of spades.

Another method of dealing with such problems is sometimes simpler and will always lead to the same result. We shall conclude our discussion of the probability calculus by using this simpler method to solve the last penny problem stated at the beginning: How likely is it that the next three flips of an honest coin will include *at least* one head?

We are asking, in effect, how likely it is that *either* the first flip will be a head, *or* the second flip will be a head, *or* the third flip will be a head, *or* that more than one will be a head. If we applied the addition theorem without modification, we would reach the impossible result:

$$P(H_1 \text{ or } H_2 \text{ or } H_3) = P(H_1) + P(H_2) + P(H_3)$$

or:

$$P(H_1 \text{ or } H_2 \text{ or } H_3) = .5 + .5 + .5 = 1.5$$

This would mean that we were more than certain to get at least one head in three flips, and also that it was impossible (indeed, impossibly impossible) to come up with three tails in a row. It is this second impossibility which suggests a simpler method for dealing with such problems. Instead of using a modified addition theorem to calculate correctly $P(H_1 \text{ or } H_2 \text{ or } H_3)$, why not use the *product* theorem to calculate $P(T_1 \text{ and } T_2 \text{ and } T_3)$? The only way in which we can fail to get *at least* one head in three flips is by having all three flips come up tails. Now either we will get at least one head or we won't. Accordingly, if three tails is the only way of not getting at least one head, we can write:

$$P(H_1 \text{ or } H_2 \text{ or } H_3) = 1.0 - P(T_1 \text{ and } T_2 \text{ and } T_3)$$

The likelihood of three tails is easily calculated as $1/2 \times 1/2 \times 1/2 = 1/8$; hence, the probability of at least one head is $1 - 1/8 = 7/8$. This method is also usefully applied to the card problem. The only cards *not* clubs, diamonds, hearts, face cards, or aces are numbered spades. The probability of numbered spades is $9/52$; hence, the probability of one of the others is $1 - 9/52$, or $43/52$.

In general, if an event A either will occur or won't occur, so that $P(A) + P(\text{not } A) = 1.0$, we can calculate the likelihood that it *will* occur $(P(A))$ either directly or indirectly. The indirect method, which is sometimes simpler in practice, is to calculate the probability of P (not A) and subtract from 1.0.

4. Inferences from uniform evidence

We remarked earlier that uncertainty about the conclusion of an inductive argument can arise from two sources. Arguments from mixed evidence leave us with an uncertainty based on the known behavior of those specific things whose unknown behavior we are concerned to predict. When our evidence is uniform (when all the S's we know of are P), reasonable uncertainty about the conclusion of an inductive argument can still arise, though not out of the premises of the argument itself. In cases of uniform evidence, reasonable doubt arises from *other* possibly true propositions bearing on the same things as the inductive argument specifically in question. To see how this can occur, we shall take advantage of a point made in Chapter 2. After using this point to rewrite our formula for induction in a more refined way, we shall be able to show both how objections to uniform inductions arise and what sorts of inferences are least liable to such objections.

We argued in Chapter 2 that no one general term is ever uniquely and completely descriptive of an individual thing. If we reflect that the basis in reality for any inductive inference is our experience of individual things and their properties, we can see that the following is a more accurate statement of the general principle of induction than the formula we have so far been using. Let *a*, *b*, and *c* stand for singular terms, designating individuals. We argue, in every inductive inference:

> *a*, *b*, and *c*, which are *S*'s, are *P*.
> ———————————————————
> other individuals which are *S*'s are *P*.

Considerable variation is possible within this formula. Using *J* for "John," *G* for "Gertrude," *H* for "human," and *C* for "possessor of a circulatory system," we can write argument (1) on page 195 as:

> *J*, who is an *H*, is a *C*.
> ———————————————
> *G*, who is an *H*, is a *C*.

If we want to indicate clearly that all known individuals of a certain kind have a certain trait, we can say:

> *a*, *b*, *c*, *d*, and *e*, all the *S*'s we know of, are *P*.
> ———————————————————————————
> (Some or all) other (individuals who are) *S*'s are *P*.

If we wish to represent a typical inductive argument form in the symbolism of Chapter 3, we can write:

$$\frac{(\exists x,\ y,\ z)(S_x \cdot S_y \cdot S_z \cdot P_x \cdot P_y \cdot P_z)}{(x)(S_x \supset P_x)}$$

Our aim in all of these new representations is to stress the fact that the propositions in an inductive argument express some experience of concrete individual things. The premise or premises characterize these things as being of a specific kind and as having a certain property. The conclusion is then drawn that other individuals of the same kind will have that property.

We are now in a position to see where objections can arise to inductions from uniform evidence, for it is sometimes the case that different characterizations of the individuals referred to in the premises support different conclusions about other individuals, like them in some respect but not in others, whose properties we are concerned with predicting. Let us first consider matters in the abstract. Then, and for the rest of the chapter, we shall work from a concrete example.

Suppose that we have an argument of the following form, whose premises we suppose to be true:

(1) *a*, *b*, and *c*, which are *S*'s, are *P*.

other *S*'s are *P*.

Remembering that no general term is uniquely or completely descriptive of an individual thing, we might raise the question "Is there some *other* general term with which we can accurately characterize *a*, *b*, and *c?*" Suppose that there is such a term—call it *Q*. Suppose, in other words, that the same experience which is the basis for (1) serves as a basis for the following:

(2) *a*, *b*, and *c*, which are *Q*'s, are *P*.

other *Q*'s are *P*.

Now suppose, finally, that we encounter another individual, *d*, which is not an *S* but is a *Q*. How reasonable is it to conclude that *d* will be *P?* Other things being equal, the case for *d*'s being *P* is evidently weakened by *d*'s failure to be an *S*. So far as the stated evidence is concerned, its being an *S* and its being a *Q* are both reasons for expecting something to be *P*. Only one of these reasons applies to *d*. Clearly, then, we should have less confidence that *d* will be *P* than we should have had if both reasons applied, if, that is, *d* were both an *S* and a *Q*. But notice, too, that someone who had observed that *a*, *b*, and *c* were *S*'s, but not that they were *Q*'s, would have no reason at all to expect *d* either to be or not to be *P*.

In many situations, reflections like those in the last paragraph would be expressed with the aid of the ideas of causation or explanation. We can give some flesh and blood to our reasoning by using these ideas here, though retaining the symbols *S*, *P*, *Q*, etc., for one more paragraph. Suppose someone observes that *a*, *b*, and *c* are all *P*. "But *why?*" he might ask. Argument (1) suggests that *a*, *b*, and *c* are *P* because they are *S*'s. Argument (2) offers another explanation. "These individuals are *P*," it suggests, "because they are *Q*'s." It is easy to imagine a dispute in which one party claimed that "*S*" was the answer to "Why are *a*, *b*, and *c* *P?*" and insisted that it was purely accidental that *a*, *b*, and *c* all happened to be *Q*'s. So far as the stated evidence is concerned, the other party to the dispute might equally well claim that their being *S*'s was the accident, and that the real reason *a*, *b*, and *c* are *P* is that they are *Q*'s. The *S* and *Q* sides to the dispute would, of course, have very different expectations about *d*. "Of course *d* is *P*," one will say, "for after all, it's a Q, isn't it?" "Nonsense," will be the reply, *"That's no reason to expect d to be a P. Since it isn't an S, we have no basis for expecting it to be P."* Each party has somewhat understated the other's case, but the dispute may be enlightening, nonetheless. Let us bring it down to earth, then, by providing actors and issues.

As a concrete example of the logical situation discussed in the last paragraph or two, consider a dispute between I. M. Smooth, principal of the Hollyhill Hall School, and his most persistent critic in educational circles, G. R. Gruff. Smooth, writing in an educational journal, reports that all recent graduates of his school have done well in college. Therefore, he concludes, we can expect Hollyhill Hall methods of instruction to improve the chances of college success for other high-school students as well. On the basis of this argument, Smooth goes on to recommend important changes in the public school system of his state. In a letter to the editor of the journal, Smooth's critic, Gruff, offers a barrage of counterexplanations to account for the fact that graduates of Smooth's school have been unusually successful in college. "I doubt very much," he writes, "that the methods of instruction used at Hollyhill Hall have a great deal to do with success in college. I consider it more likely that Smooth's students were a selected group to begin with. Perhaps they were all of above-average intelligence, or possibly they came from homes in which scholastic achievement was more strongly emphasized than in the average home. Another possible explanation for the college success of these individuals is that they had had superior educational preparation before Smooth ever laid eyes on them. In any case, the fact that Smooth's students succeed is no proof of the claim that his methods will lead to success in college if they are applied to other individuals."

Gruff has suggested that Smooth's students may have other common characteristics besides being Hollyhill Hallers, and that one or more of such other characteristics may be responsible for their remarkable success in college. Let us symbolize properties, characteristics and students as follows.

C—Successful in college. Being successful in college is the property whose occurrence Smooth and Gruff are trying to explain and predict.

H—Student exposed to Hollyhill Hall educational methods. Smooth's final claim is that persons who are H's will be C. As evidence in support of his claim, he points out that recent graduates of his school, who have been H's, are C.

tdh—Tom, Dick, and Harry, recent graduates of Hollyhill Hall. In fact, there have been several hundred Hollyhill Hall graduates in recent years, but since it would be tedious to list them one by one, we shall imaginatively collapse them into Tom, Dick, and Harry, and then collapse Tom, Dick, and Harry into tdh.

I—Person of above-average intelligence.

S—Person highly motivated toward scholastic achievement.

E—Graduate of exceptionally good elementary school. *I*, *S*, and *E* indicate characteristics which, according to Gruff, are likelier to be connected with college success than *H* is. We can call these the Gruff
factors.

Gruff does not know, of course, whether Tom, Dick, and Harry *were*
exceptionally bright, highly motivated, or well prepared when they entered
Hollyhill Hall. His point in mentioning these characteristics is to show
that Smooth has by no means *proved* that exposure to a Hollyhill Hall
education is the factor which accounts for the college success of Hollyhill
Hall graduates. If Gruff himself had initially been asked to explain the fact
that *tdh* are *C*, he would have directed his attention first to such relevant
factors as intelligence, motivation, and prior education. His suggestion is
that Smooth should have paid some attention to these factors before rushing
into print with his praises of *H*.

To get a clear idea of the logical situation produced by Gruff's speculative
counterexplanations, compare the following three arguments. The first is
Smooth's original argument. The other two take the Gruff factors into account. Their premises indicate what Smooth might have observed if he had
initially asked whether *I*, *S*, or *E* might not be common to *tdh* (and hence
a possible explanation of their being *C*). In argument (2), all of Gruff's
hunches have panned out. Argument (3) represents the other extreme case:
H holds the field as the only characteristic so far mentioned which *tdh* actually have in common. As you inspect these arguments, ask yourself which of
them offers least support, and which most, for Smooth's conclusion.

(1) *tdh*, who are *H*'s, are *C*.
$\overline{\text{other } H\text{'s are } C.}$

(2) *tdh*, who are all *H*'s, *I*'s, *S*'s, and *E*'s, are *C*.
$\overline{\text{other } H\text{'s are } C \text{ (even if they are not } I\text{'s, } S\text{'s, and } E\text{'s).}}$

(3) *tdh*, who are all *H*'s, but *not* all *I*'s, *S*'s, and *E*'s, are *C*.
$\overline{\text{other } H\text{'s are } C \text{ (even if they are not } I\text{'s, } S\text{'s, and } E\text{'s).}}$

Notice that neither (2) nor (3) directly adds or subtracts anything from
Smooth's original statement that some *H*'s are *C*. The quantity and uniformity of the original report on the *H-C* relation are left unchanged. And
yet (3) provides much stronger support for Smooth's conclusion than does
(1), whereas (2) is so weak as to be downright unreasonable or invalid. This
illustrates the point with which we began, that uncertainty about the conclusion of a uniform induction does not arise out of the premises of the argument in question but is based on *other* possibly true propositions bearing on
the same things as the original argument. The "same things" are here Tom,

Dick, and Harry. The "other possibly true propositions" are Gruff's suggested characterizations of Tom, Dick, and Harry as already highly intelligent, motivated, or educated when they entered Hollyhill Hall. If we discover these propositions to be in fact true, we will tend to regard Smooth's characterization of *tdh* as *H*'s as possibly irrelevant to the fact that they are *C*, and this in turn will lessen our confidence in Smooth's prediction that other individuals will be *C*, for the prediction—other *H*'s will be *C*—is in terms of the characterization. But, contrariwise, if no other possibly relevant description fits the individuals under consideration, our confidence in the explanatory and predictive power of the original description is increased.

Thus (3) is stronger than (1). Does (3), then, prove Smooth's conclusion beyond peradventure of a reasonable doubt? No one would suppose, of course, that the conclusion had been *de*ductively proven: to deny "other *H*'s are *C*" is not to contradict the premise *"tdh,* who are *H*'s, are *C."* The question is not whether the conclusion logically might be false, but whether our experience of Tom, Dick, and Harry can afford us any basis for supposing that it actually is false, or is at least not especially likely? Or, to raise an equivalent question, might there be some reason for doubting that their being *H*'s explains the fact that Tom, Dick, and Harry are *C?* We might expect that Smooth's conclusion would be safe if none of the factors mentioned, other than *H,* could be shown to be uniformly associated with *C.* Yet two types of objection can still be raised.

First, it might be the case that each Hollyhill Hall graduate was *either* very bright *or* highly motivated *or* well prepared educationally, so that although no one of these factors could explain all the cases of college success under consideration, all three factors taken together could do the whole explanatory job. Or, secondly, the true explanation of *C* might be some factor not even mentioned so far in the argument. We shall conclude our treatment of inductive logic by discussing these objections. With regard to the first we can give some fairly effective formal advice, though as formal logicians we shall have very little to say about the sometimes very important second objection.

Suppose that about a third of Smooth's graduates are exceptionally bright, that another third are quite highly motivated, and that the rest received first-rate educations before entering Hollyhill Hall. Thus, of the specific factors mentioned, *H, I, S,* and *E,* only one, *H,* characterizes all the individuals with whom we are concerned. But a somewhat artificial generic term also applies to them all: each is "either-an-*I*-or-an-*S*-or-an-*E*." Gruff can argue, then, that *this* is the factor which explains *C.* He might say that there *isn't* any *single* cause of *C,* but that *I* accounts for *C* in some cases, while other individuals are *C* because they are *S*'s, still others because they are *E*'s. It is not necessary to appeal to *H* as an explanation simply because

H is the only specific or single characteristic which Tom, Dick, and Harry have in common.

So long as Smooth bases his argument for *H* only on individuals who are *H*'s, there is simply no answer to objections like the preceding. To apply our point from Chapter 2 once more: no individual is merely and only an *H*. Each of Smooth's graduates will have *some* characteristics not captured in describing him as an *H*. An extremely obstinate Gruff could therefore argue that the cause of Tom's college success is his red hair, that Dick succeeded because he likes pistachio ice cream, and so on. If the factors meant as counterexplanations are spelled out, there is, however, a solution, at least ideally or in principle. What Smooth must look for is a set of subjects who have *not* had a Hollyhill Hall education, but who are *otherwise similar* to Tom, Dick, and Harry. To say that a Hollyhill Hall education leads to college success suggests that Tom, Dick, and Harry *would not have done so well without* such an education, and this in turn implies that individuals like them who have not had the benefit of such an education will not do so well in college as Tom, Dick, and Harry. Smooth's case for *H* will be considerably strengthened, therefore, if he can find individuals (call them the *xyz* group) who have not done well in college but who resemble Tom, Dick, and Harry in intelligence, motivation, prior education, and all other relevant characteristics except attendance at Hollyhill Hall. The following is a rough formalization of the argument Smooth could then present. (We can note that arguments of this form are extremely important in the sciences.)

(4) *tdh,* who are *I*-or-*S*-or-*E*'s and *H*'s, are *C*.
     xyz, who are *I*-or-*S*-or-*E*'s, but not *H*'s, are not *C*.
     _____
     being an *H* is causally related to being *C*.

Ideally, the two groups *tdh* and *xyz* should be identical in every relevant characteristic other than *H*. If, for example, some individuals in the first group are bright, highly motivated, *and* academically well prepared, care should be taken to include an equal number of subjects like this in the second group. If this procedure is followed, we shall have what scientists call a *control group* for studying the effects on Tom, Dick, and Harry of their being *H*'s. The control group will be a good one to the extent that it is similar to the Hollyhill Hallers in all relevant traits except *H*.

A subject or "experimental" group should be similar to its control group with respect to all *relevant* characteristics except the one in question. But what characteristics *are* relevant? This brings us up against the remaining objection to (3).

The objection was that some factor not even mentioned by Smooth or Gruff might be the correct explanation of *C*. Perhaps Tom, Dick, and Harry have (while x, y, and z lack) some important common characteristic which both educators have overlooked or dismissed as irrelevant. Perhaps a group which possessed *this* characteristic but lacked a Hollyhill Hall education would do as well in college as Tom, Dick, and Harry. If such was found to be the case, we would have to conclude that it had been something of an accident that *tdh* were all H's; their being H's would turn out to have been irrelevant at least to their being C.

But what *is* "this" characteristic? We must be careful to ask this question sympathetically, though critically. If the conjectured counterexplanation is left completely unspecified, we cannot, of course, deal with it by any of the devices of ordinary formal logic. Accordingly, if any of the specific factors already brought to our attention *seems* to explain all the occurrences of some property, it is tempting to show contempt for the very idea of there being a better explanation. It would be rash, however, for anyone to claim to have considered in detail every logically conceivable explanation of even the simplest physical event, for such a claim could be justified only if one had a list of all the specific concepts in terms of which that sort of event had been, was, or might possibly ever be described—an extraordinary list, to say the least. And yet only if one had considered all possible explanations could one be sure that there wasn't, somewhere, a better explanation than any currently accepted. So we must be careful to avoid dogmatism when we ask what "this" unnamed better explanation is in any particular case. Someone may name it to us, or it may name itself.

And, of course, we are sometimes forced to look for explanations where none currently exist. Accordingly, we often find ourselves groping for new information or even new ways of thinking, or for terms in which to express fresh insights or novel claims about the world. The frequency with which this occurs is one of the facts which suggests that there is much more to the effective use of reason than is outlined in this and previous chapters. How much there is to the effective use of reason can be indicated only by a study of reasoning as it takes place outside of logic books and logic classrooms. This is the subject matter of the next chapter.

Chapter 5

Rational and Fallacious Thinking
in Everyday Life

At this point the reader has been exposed to many formal rules for good thinking, as well as to extended discussion of some of the problems surrounding these rules. All of this study is, in various ways, good training for the power of reasoning. However, it is noteworthy that the material taught in the first four chapters of this book is not very frequently appealed to in everyday reasoning. It is not altogether common for everyday reasoning to resolve itself into syllogisms, or into the basic forms of reasoning dealt with in the study of symbolic or inductive logic.

In the following pages we shall discuss two broad topics which supplement the material of the rest of the book. One is that of rationality in everyday life. There are many factors in rationality—many more than are likely to be dealt with in traditional logic books. Our remarks about these factors will be intended to illustrate a thesis. This is that the ingredients of rationality are harder to formulate than many writers on logic picture them as being. Not only are the factors involved in rationality diverse; but also, we shall show in the case of many of these factors that excellence cannot be systematized, or made the subject of specific rules on "how to be rational."

The second topic that we shall deal with is that of fallacies. Fallacies are poor types of reasoning. Even though there are an infinite number of ways in which to reason badly, there are certain types of bad reasoning which are very common. We shall discuss these after we have completed our discussion of everyday reasoning. Thus the reader, having been shown the complexity of what counts as good thinking, will be given an account of the most common pitfalls to be avoided.

1. Rationality

When we speak of a man as rational, we may have a variety of things in mind. Sometimes we may merely be praising him for not giving way to emotion. For example, if we say, "Emperor X took rationally the news of the defection of his trusted general," we probably mean that Emperor X did not fly into a rage and immediately order the execution of everyone remotely connected with the general, or fall into an excessive panic. A related sense of "rational" means something like "open to arguments." For example, we may praise an administrator as "rational," meaning that he is prepared to listen to what we say and does not hold his opinions dogmatically.

Usually, however, when we speak of a man's "rationality" we are praising him for an intellectual ability connected with formulating or solving problems. Man, according to Aristotle, is a rational animal, in the sense that it is in the nature of man to have some reasoning ability. But some men have more reasoning ability, or a more highly developed reasoning ability, than others. When we praise a man as "rational" we may mean that he has a better than average reasoning ability. It is this sense of "rational" that we intend to discuss. What are the factors which contribute to a man's having highly developed rational powers? And how are these factors related to what is taught in formal logic? Can we really produce a set of rules which will by themselves enable someone to reason well in everyday life?

In the next several pages we shall discuss six factors which may be involved in one man's having better reasoning ability than another. This list of six factors does not claim to be an exhaustive list of all the factors involved in rationality. It merely refers to what seem like the most important factors. Furthermore the division among skills which is marked by this list is an arbitrary one. The six factors are not intended to illustrate some deep underlying structure of rationality, but merely are intended to illustrate in a convenient way how various the things are that go into rational thinking.

Broadly speaking, there are two areas in which rational thinking can be of high or low quality. One is in formulating problems or answers to problems. The other is in solving problems or judging solutions to problems. The first two factors of rationality that we shall consider are connected with formulation. The third through sixth factors are connected with arriving at or judging solutions.

1.1. Classification

The first factor that we shall discuss is classification. The classifications that a person makes supply his basic apparatus of thought. Someone who classifies poorly is likely to think in a confused way. On the other hand, someone whose classifications are sharp, accurate, and flexible has an excellent basis for beginning to draw conclusions.

By "classification" we understand the process of arranging facts, objects, or names in such a way as to indicate varying degrees of relationship. The most rudimentary act of classification is involved in saying that *"X is a Y."* This involves the implicit claim that X is similar to other things that are Y's, in a way or ways in which X is not similar to things which are not Y's. Statements like *"X is a Y"* put similarities and dissimilarities on our map of the world.

Besides involving a claim, *"X is a Y"* suggests a way of looking at things. It has been pointed out, notably by Benjamin Lee Whorf, that our perceptiveness and the way in which we experience things will be strongly affected by the classifications we make. When we say *"X is a Y,"* we adopt a view of reality in which consciousness is focused on the links connecting X with other Y's, and in which consciousness is focused upon the differences between X and things that are not Y's. For example, we have a single word, "snow," for a whole variety of frozen precipitation, and thus are routinely aware of the similarities among all the things that are called "snow." The Eskimos, who have a number of different classifications for things all of which we classify as "snow," are much more sensitive to differences among types of snow than we are.

The primary source of the classifications that any individual makes is his language. The language that we speak gives us the framework for our *"X is a Y"* judgments. It is because we speak English, for example, that we classify both shops that make bread and shops that make pastry as "bakeries." If we spoke French, we would classify them separately as *"boulangeries"* and *"pâtisseries."* It is because we speak English that we have a different classification for snow than the Eskimos do.

Thus, insofar as classifications provide us with the basic apparatus of thought, a first step in becoming rational is to master one's native tongue. This is not so trivial as it may sound. There is a myth that all people who have reached a moderate educational standard, say graduation from high school or from college, can be assumed to have mastered the English language and to have acquired a basic apparatus of thought. But degrees of mastery can differ considerably, even among college graduates. Someone who speaks English in a casual and sloppy way, and has a low and in-flexible vocabulary, has a considerable disadvantage in thinking rationally.

However, being aware of the distinctions which are embodied in language is only a part of the business of providing oneself with an effective apparatus of thought. An important part consists of being able to hit upon the classification which is relevant to a given problem. Normally a person or object can be classified in a large variety of ways, but not all of these ways provide grist for inference. Thinking of the relevant classification—of the needed word—becomes an important step in producing an inference.

For example, suppose that we wish to prove that Socrates lived in Europe. A first step for such a proof would be to find some characteristic of Socrates from which we could infer that he lived in Europe. Now, as we pointed out in Chapter 2, the "same" being may fit into a number of classifications. If we are classifying persons and objects by size, Socrates would be classified as medium-sized. If we were classifying persons and objects by location, Socrates might be classified as having been in Athens for most of his life. If we were classifying persons and objects according to their biological status, Socrates would be classified as a human being. And so on.

Plainly, if we began our proof that Socrates lived in Europe by saying, "Socrates was medium-sized," it would be hard to see where to go from there. What is needed is not merely a correct classification, but a relevant classification. To say that Socrates was in Athens for most of his life is relevant, since we can then remark that Athens is in Europe, and thus prove that Socrates lived in Europe. If we do not hit upon a relevant classification of Socrates, though, we could say a great many true things about Socrates without being able to prove that he lived in Europe.

Thus there are two aspects to effective classification. One is that of having the knowledge needed for classification, which includes having an adequate and flexible vocabulary which is capable of making important distinctions. The other is that of using this knowledge well: of thinking of the relevant classification in connection with a problem.

1.2. Clarity

Clear formulations of problems and of evidence are an important asset in thinking rationally. Problems which are clearly formulated are much easier to solve than problems which have been given a confused or sloppy formulation. There are three major ways in which a formulation can lack clarity. These are: confused arrangement, vagueness, and ambiguity.

Confused arrangement in formulation can make complicated problems especially difficult. If a great mass of facts is presented as a jumble, it is difficult for the mind to begin moving toward a conclusion. The first step in approaching a problem is to distinguish what is relevant to the problem from what is irrelevant, and to place the relevant things in an order which is easy to work with. (Part of this task overlaps with that of classifying effectively. Effective classification, after all, is, among other things, clear.)

Let us take the example of someone who at 5 P.M. on a weekday is trying to find Jones. He is given the following facts:

Jones is a war veteran.

There is a movie theater near Jones's place of work which is showing a western.

Jones has a cousin named Sally.

Jones's office is rather small and cramped.

Jones leaves work at 4:45.

Jones enjoys playing golf on Sundays.

Jones is an avid cribbage player.

Jones is six feet tall.

Jones wears glasses.

Jones votes Republican.

Jones's best subject in school was English.

There is a pool hall near Jones's office.

There is a post office near Jones's office.

There is a coffeehouse near Jones's office.

There are at least two traffic lights within five hundred feet of Jones's office.

Jones lives alone in an apartment a good distance away from his office.

Jones owns a parakeet.

Jones is very fond of westerns.

Jones reads a newspaper regularly.

Jones likes coffee, especially in the afternoon.

Jones does crossword puzzles.

It is cold.

There were three gruesome murders in Chicago today.

The western starts at 5:30.

The Boston basketball team won its game.

Jones does not like basketball.

The first step in finding Jones is to eliminate from consideration the irrelevant facts. Jones's being a war veteran seems irrelevant, as does the name of Jones's cousin, the basketball results, etc. The most obviously relevant facts are:

There is a movie theater near Jones's place of work which is showing a western.

Jones leaves work at 4:45.

There is a coffeehouse near Jones's office.

Jones lives alone in an apartment a good distance away from his office.

Jones is very fond of westerns.

Jones reads a newspaper regularly.

Jones likes coffee, especially in the afternoon.

Jones does crossword puzzles.

It is cold.

The western starts at 5:30.

In solving the problem of Jones's probable whereabouts, we would be helped if we put the relevant facts in new order, and also stated intermediate conclusions in our reasoning right after the facts that justified them. This would give us:

There is a movie theater near Jones's place of work which is showing a western.

Jones is very fond of westerns.

The western starts at 5:30.

Intermediate conclusion: Jones may well be planning to be at the theater near his office at 5:30.

Jones leaves work at 4:45.

Jones lives alone in an apartment a good distance away from his office.

It is cold.

Intermediate conclusion: if Jones is going to the movie at 5:30, he may well decide not to go home and then come back, but rather to remain in the neighborhood of his office between 4:45 and 5:30.

Jones likes coffee, especially in the afternoon.

There is a coffeehouse near Jones's office.

Jones reads newspapers regularly.

Jones does crossword puzzles.

Intermediate conclusion: If Jones is staying in the neighborhood of his office between 4:45 and 5:30, he may well be in a coffeehouse reading a newspaper or doing a crossword puzzle.

Conclusion: A good place to look for Jones is the coffeehouse near his office.

In deciding where to look for Jones, a good deal of the rational work consisted just of rearranging the evidence. As we shall point out later, there are quite different kinds of problems, in which thinking of relevant evidence is much more important than the factor of rearranging evidence which has already been presented.

The evidence which is presented in the case of Jones's whereabouts was stated fairly precisely. Which is to say that it was not very vague. "Vague" and "precise" are polar opposites, like "hot" and "cold"; and like heat and coldness, vagueness and precision are matters of degree. For example, to say that Jones is very fond of westerns is less vague than it would be to say that Jones likes adventure films; but to say that he is very fond of westerns is still not so precise as it would be to say that he likes westerns in which there is a great deal of shooting (at least five people shot) and not too much psychological analysis.

Vagueness occurs when an expression is used in such a way that it can apply to a wider range of possibilities than we are concerned with or to an indeterminate range of possibilities. For example, if I say, "Several men came up the hill," this leaves open the possibility that the number of men who came up the hill was six or seven, and also leaves open the possibility that the number was twenty or thirty. Thus, "Several men came up the hill" is more vague than "Fifteen men came up the hill," and creates a less definite impression. "Some men came up the hill" would be even more vague than "Several men came up the hill," since the word "some" seems to leave open the possibility that there were only two or three men, and thus leaves open an even wider range of possibilities than does the word "several."

A great deal of our everyday language has some degree of vagueness. In the introductory chapter we cited Wittgenstein's contention that the word "game" could not be satisfactorily defined, and that it could apply to a variety of different sorts of activities. Something like this is true of almost all general terms in the language. In the sentence "Several men came up the hill," for example, the world "hill" has some degree of vagueness. "Hill" can refer to a slight rise in the land or to something which is fairly steep but not high enough to be called a mountain.

Only a pedant would attempt to eliminate all of the vagueness from his everyday speech. Someone could say, "Fifteen men came up that land that has the fifty-foot rise at a thirty-degree incline"; but for most purposes this would be no better than "Several men came up the hill," and indeed it would sound ludicrous. In fact, even though "Several men came up the hill" has a considerable degree of vagueness, normally we would not label it as vague. To call a formulation vague suggests condemnation, and normally means that its degree of vagueness is *too high* for the present context. Consequently the degree of vagueness that makes a statement vague depends on the context. In work in mathematics and physics even a small degree of vagueness exposes a statement to condemnation as vague. In classical biology a higher degree will be tolerated; in historical work a still higher degree usually will be tolerated; and in everyday talk a very high degree of vagueness indeed usually is needed to make a statement what we would call vague.

We can see this in our reasoning concerning Jones's probable whereabouts. A crucial piece of evidence was stated as "Jones likes coffee in the afternoon." This has some element of vagueness: it leaves open all sorts of possibilities as to how much Jones likes coffee (does he like it just a little, or must he have it?), what kind of coffee Jones likes, how much he drinks, etc. For the context, though, "Jones likes coffee in the afternoon" specifies as much as we need to know, and consequently we would not call it vague. "Jones likes to drink beverages in the afternoon," though, would have been too vague: we would have condemned it as vague. It would not have allowed us to arrive readily at the conclusion that the coffeehouse was a good place to look for Jones: we first would have had to know what beverages Jones drank in the afternoon.

If vagueness can spoil a piece of reasoning by not giving us enough specific claims to work with, ambiguity can make reasoning difficult by creating doubt as to which claims are being made. Whereas vagueness occurs when an expression is used in such a way that it could apply to a wide or indeterminate range of things, ambiguity occurs when an expression is used in such a way that there is some doubt about what it means, and there are two or more distinct alternative meanings to choose among.

There are two main ways in which ambiguity can occur. It can occur because an expression has two or more distinct meanings, and is used in a context which fails to make clear which of the meanings is being used. For example, if out of the blue someone says, "I saw a cardinal today," you would not know whether he meant a dignitary of the Roman Catholic Church or a red bird. But if you had been talking about birds, the ambiguity would be eliminated, and you would know that he meant a red bird rather than a church dignitary.

The other main way in which ambiguity can occur involves faulty grammatical constructions. If a sentence is constructed poorly, it may not be clear to whom or what a word or phrase refers. For example, if we say, "Jones was standing near a bull, and he looked exceptionally fierce," it may not be clear who it was that looked fierce, Jones or the bull. If we say, "It is terrible that Jones was winning the game until he made that mistake," it is not clear what is being described as terrible, the fact that Jones had been winning the game or the fact that he then made a mistake.

The effect that ambiguity can have on a reasoning process can be illustrated by going back again to the reasoning concerning Jones's probable whereabouts. Suppose that instead of saying, "Jones is very fond of westerns," we had said, "Westerns are not so popular as mysteries, and Jones is very fond of them." The reasoning process hardly could proceed until it was established which Jones was fond of, westerns or mysteries.

Probably the most important thing to remember about vagueness and ambiguity is that they are problems with language. Reasoning well requires formulations which are unambiguous and which are not vague, and mastery of one's language is required to produce such formulations. It is widely believed that using language well and reasoning well are radically distinguishable skills; but in this section and the previous one we have shown that this is not true, that major factors in rationality require command of language.

1.3. Leaps of reason

We remarked a while ago that the factual statements relevant to a reasoning process usually do not assemble themselves on a platter. A good deal of the job of arriving at a rational conclusion usually requires thinking of relevant evidence, or thinking of something which suddenly makes an assortment of evidence make sense. Given the evidence for Jones's whereabouts that we had assembled, we could see without difficulty that the coffeehouse was a good place to look for him. But for a friend of Jones's, who was just beginning to think about Jones's whereabouts, the whole problem would be very different. For him solution of the problem would require that relevant facts come to mind, rather than irrelevant facts, and that the hypothesis of Jones's being at the coffeehouse come to mind rather than some senseless or misleading hypothesis.

An important factor in this process is what we shall call a "leap of reason." This phrase is modeled on the phrase "leap of faith" that the Danish philosopher Kierkegaard is notable for using. Kierkegaard was making the point that in meaningful religion there is always a gap between what rational evidence justifies and what a believer believes in. In the case of someone who has faith, this gap is bridged, according to Kierkegaard, by a free, spontaneous, and nonrational commitment of the believer to the object of his belief. In somewhat the same way, one can speak also of a gap existing in many purely rational arguments between the evidence and the conclusion. In many arguments the conclusion will involve factors which need not have been mentioned in a competent summary of the evidence. The most important step in getting from the evidence to the conclusion may be that of simply happening to think of these factors. Even though there is nothing outside the scope of reason involved in thinking of factors relevant to a given problem, the process is comparable to Kierkegaard's leap of faith in that it represents a free and creative contribution to something that cannot be solved mechanically.

We can take as an example the problem of a detective who is trying to locate the thief of some valuable paintings. The detective knows what the thief looks like, and in what city the thief is living, but not where in the city the thief is living. He also knows that the thief selected the paintings he stole with considerable discernment, carefully avoiding taking artistically inferior paintings or fakes. His problem is to choose public places in which to look for the thief.

This is not an emotional or spiritual problem, or an invitation to mere caprice. The detective's problem is rational, and whether he can arrive at a list of likely places in which to look for the thief will be some test of his rational ability.

His problem can be broken up into two steps. First, the detective must think of places in which the thief might be sought; and secondly, he must decide in which of these places there would be the best chance of finding the thief. In other words, he must construct a number of hypotheses as to the thief's future movements, and then decide which of the hypotheses are best. We shall discuss the second of these steps later; right now we shall concentrate on the first step.

The first step probably would involve a leap of reason. It would be unlikely for the detective to rely on rules in thinking up hypotheses. It would be difficult to find very general rules for where to look, and in any case the detective is unlikely to recite rules to himself. On the other hand, the detective's efforts are unlikely to consist of a mere haphazard listing of places that come into his head at random. Leaps of reason are not guesses; and just as someone with a trained mind often will make the best split-second decisions, so someone with developed rational powers will have the most plausible things come into his mind. What rises to the surface of the mind, so to speak, depends upon the caliber of the mind.

Faced with the problem of thinking of places to look for the thief, a stupid person might find his mind going blank. An unintelligent person might think at random about street corners that he has passed. A good detective, knowing about the thief's ability to tell good paintings from bad ones, might think of places of culture. For example, it might occur to the detective that a concert of chamber music to be given the next evening might be a good place to look. Also, it might occur to him that the thief might be looking for wealthy and unscrupulous people to buy the stolen paintings. The detective then might think of night clubs and expensive bars as possible places in which to look for the thief.

Good leaps of reason often seem obvious after they have taken place. For example, someone to whom the detective says that he may look in expensive bars might think, "Of course you could infer that from the situation." He may then regard the detective's thinking as being like carrying out an exercise in formal logic. Given the premises, he might think, you could see that certain conclusions follow in a fairly mechanical way. But there is nothing mechanical about the detective's happening to think that the thief's attempting to sell the pictures would be relevant to the problem of finding the thief. This factor probably would not occur as relevant to someone with an untrained mind. The detective's thinking of the factor as relevant is the result of training, just as making good shots in tennis is the result of training and practice; but in both cases the result of training is the right thing being done in a spontaneous way.

The most famous leaps of reason are those which have resulted in great scientific theories. Typically a scientist who is constructing a theory is confronted by a set of evidence and is searching for something general that will imply and explain the evidence. In arriving at a theory he may think of factors as relevant to his problem which no one else would have thought relevant. For example, Einstein connected the concept of simultaneity with problems concerning the speed of light, and thus was helped in arriving at his theory of relativity.

The theory that the scientist arrives at typically is not implied by the available evidence. Indeed the theory will imply things that go beyond the evidence, and thus will have to be tested by means of further observations and experiments. For example, Einstein's theory implied certain predictions concerning the orbit of the planet Mercury; subsequent observations of the orbit of the planet Mercury helped to verify Einstein's theory.

Thus it is particularly appropriate to speak of the scientist as taking a leap from the evidence in constructing his theory. People sometimes speak of this leap, in the case of a great scientist, as involving creativity. In Einstein's case it took not only training and intelligence but also genius to make the leap of reason. But his achievement is like that of the detective, for both arrived at conclusions which went beyond what was implicit in the facts that were presented to them.

1.4. Reasoning from analogy

As the reader will recall from Chapter 4, some implicit reliance on similarity or analogy is at the heart of our reasoning about the world, including our everyday reasoning about the world. In a variety of ways we assume that the patterns which have existed in the past will continue in the future: that cultured men will continue to attend concerts in the future as they have in the past, and that coffee drinkers will continue to visit coffeehouses in the future as they have in the past. If we were unable to rely upon analogies between what we have experienced and what we are now concerned with knowing, our experience would be useless in making predictions.

However, there are some cases in which an appeal to analogy plays an especially prominent role in our thinking. We might, for example, be worried about how Smith, whom we know slightly, will behave in a very risky situation. We might say, "Smith seems to be of the same personality type as Jones and Brown, and Jones and Brown always were extremely cool in dangerous situations; therefore probably Smith will be extremely cool." Or we might be extremely worried about the world situation and say, "The situation of Russia in relation to us is like the situation of Mithridates in relation to Rome: Russia's power cannot long continue."

In a case of reasoning in which very prominent reliance is placed on analogy, the question is bound to arise, "How good is the analogy?" Is Smith really very much like Jones and Brown? Can Russia really be compared to the empire of Mithridates? The question also can arise, "Are the respects in which the analogy is good important ones?" Analogies rarely are entirely successful. There are bound to be some differences, as well as similarities, among Smith and Jones and Brown; and no two historical situations are entirely alike. In judging an analogy, therefore, we have to be conscious of whether the similarities that it points to are more important than the differences.

Consciously or unconsciously we rely on analogies in a great deal of our thinking. For example, it seems that the preparations that nations make for war usually are based on the nature of the last wars that they had fought, even if the last war was quite different from the war that they are about to fight. It could be argued that France spent the 1930s preparing for the sort of attack the Germans had launched in 1914, and that since 1946 we have been preparing for Pearl Harbor. Since most of the analogies that people rely on in their thinking are weak, or are used badly, it is very important in becoming highly rational to use analogies intelligently.

Yet it is very difficult to formulate rules for intelligent use of analogies. Some historians, indeed, have suggested that in dealing with political problems the best thing that we can do is to forget the lessons of the past, since we are more likely to draw misleading analogies than useful ones. One good rule in dealing with analogies is to be cautious. Other rules are harder to formulate in any useful way. Certainly one can say, as we just did, "Be sure that the similarities involved in the analogy are important." But how can one be sure that the similarities are important? We use analogies most frequently in areas (concerning judgments of people or of historical situations) in which there are few or no generally accepted general laws which can give us assurance of the relative weight to be given factors in a situation.

Consequently little systematic treatment seems possible of this important area of rationality. In most subjects experience obviously is helpful in making good analogies, as (arguably) is a well-developed "intuition." The study of logic is not a help, except in enabling the student to become clear about the role of analogies in his reasoning, and thus enabling him to avoid facile jumping to conclusions.

1.5. Weighing evidence

The fifth factor that we shall discuss shades off into the fourth. Weighing evidence can include operations like weighing the value of an analogy that we have just suggested to ourselves. However, it includes the operations of weighing a variety of sorts of evidence. For example, in the case of the reasoning concerned with Jones's whereabouts, we would have to consider whether the evidence for regarding the coffeehouse as a good place to look was really good evidence. In the case of the art thief, we would have to decide whether the evidence for regarding the concert hall and expensive bars as good places in which to look was really good evidence. In the case of Einstein's theory, after the supporting evidence regarding the orbit of Mercury was found, scientists had to decide whether the evidence for the theory was now strong enough so that they could regard the theory as established.

It is this factor of rationality, more than any other, that distinguishes what we would call a sensible person from someone who lacks sense. Anyone who thinks that the evidence that we cited in connection with Jones's whereabouts indicates that a good place to look for him is a pinball arcade lacks sense. Anyone who thinks that the best place in which to look for the thief is in the cheap tavern across from the police station lacks sense.

What is this "sense," though? What rules will tell us that a concert hall is a better place in which to look for the thief than the cheap tavern across from the police station?

To begin with, we might rely on statements of probability. Most thieves stay away from the area of police stations. A large percentage of the people who can tell good paintings from bad paintings also would enjoy concerts, and would want to attend them. In a high percentage of cases, people who enjoy coffee and who have free time in the afternoon will spend this time in a coffeehouse.

Probability statements like these can help us a great deal in judging whether a conclusion has been justifiably drawn. There are cases, however, in which we can get little help from established probabilities. These cases occur especially in connection with the more difficult sorts of judgments of people's character or of historical situations. Let us suppose that we know that Jones belongs to the same clubs as Smith and Brown, holds roughly the same views on all major moral and political issues, and makes a similar personal impression at first meeting. Is someone justified in concluding that he will behave as coolly in a risky situation as Smith and Brown do? Let us agree that there has been a major war in every century of the history of mankind. Is someone justified in concluding from this that there will be a major war within the next hundred years?

Many people feel that difficulties in finding answers to these questions exist because of the relative backwardness of psychological and historical science. (On the other hand, it can be argued that the difficulties are inherent in the subject matter: for material to support such a position, see Sartre's book *Search for a Method*.) But in any event these difficulties exist. Our systematic apparatus for weighing evidence concerning people or historical situations is severely limited. No one can claim to have an indisputable rational basis either for feeling confident that there will be war within the next hundred years or for feeling confident that there will not be war within the next hundred years.

Still, we can expect that if history books are written in the year 2200 about the present period, the authors will say that the few "really intelligent" thinkers of our period were able to gauge the likelihood of war. (It is which thinkers will turn out to have been the "really intelligent" ones that is so hard to predict.) Also it seems (although some psychologists dispute this) that there are some people whose predictions of the behavior of others are unusually successful. These are people who, we would say, are unusually good at "sizing up" people. Very often they are much better at this than are other people who, in objective terms, have had equal experience of personal relations. If we give these "human experts" evidence concerning someone's probable behavior, arguably they will be unusually good at sizing up the evidence.

What we are suggesting is that *perhaps* in some cases there is a good deal more to weighing the rational evidence for a conclusion than could be systematized in rules. In some cases rational evidence is very easy to weigh, and in such cases we might readily produce probability statements which give a complete account of the weight to be given the evidence. But in some cases, concerning people or historical situations, evidence is very difficult to weigh; and it is here that arguably experience and "intuition," of the sort which cannot be distilled into formulas, are important assets in weighing evidence.

1.6. Deductions

As a final factor we can mention that of making or evaluating deductions. This factor plays a secondary role in everyday rationality: most of our thinking is concerned with relating evidence to conclusions which cannot (strictly speaking) be deduced from the evidence. It is rare, for example, that the conclusion that we are trying to arrive at is related to our basis for the conclusion as the conclusion of a syllogism is related to its premises.

Not only does deductive reasoning play a secondary role in everyday rationality, but also most of the deductive reasoning that we do use is not of the sort discussed in formal logic. Inferences of the sort "If Jones is married, he must have a wife" are more common than inferences like "If Jones is a man and all men are mortal, then Jones is mortal." As we pointed out in the first chapter, it is not formal logic that teaches us that if Jones is married he must have a wife. The principle involved is not general enough to be included in formal logic. Instead it is our sense of language that tells us that Jones must have a wife. We know that the word "married" can be applied to a man only if he has a wife.

The chief skill which will aid us in making ordinary deductions, then, is not likely to be a recollection of the rules of the syllogism or of symbolic logic. Instead it is just our general sense of language. Indeed, as we pointed out in the first chapter, even formal logic is intended to reflect our awareness of what certain uses of language imply. The rules of the syllogism, for example, reflect what is implied by a combination of a certain pattern of terms with certain uses of the so-called "logical connectives" ("some," "all," "are," "is," and "not"). The truths of symbolic logic reflect what is implied in the meanings of artificially defined symbols. The meanings of the symbols that the logician uses are intended to correspond very roughly with the meanings of such ordinary English words as "every," "some," etc.

The central point to remember about deductions, whether they take place in a logic book or in the midst of ordinary life, is that they draw their validity solely from what is implicit in the meanings of the words or symbols used. In ordinary reasoning, deductions take place in ordinary words. In ordinary reasoning, then, the only way to arrive at valid deductions, or to judge competently the validity of deductions, is to be aware of the proper use of the words used in the deductive argument.

1.7. Skills to be learned in coming to reason well

At this point we have completed our list of the major factors involved in being rational. As we said earlier, the list does not claim to be exhaustive or to involve extremely precise distinctions: it merely serves to give a picture of the variety of factors involved in the effective use of reason in everyday life. It also illustrates our thesis that these factors are too complicated to be systematized or to be reduced to a set of rules on "how to be rational."

Nevertheless it might be asked, "How can one learn to be rational?" What is the process of education which produces the best development of these diverse rational powers? There is no simple answer; and indeed the factors involved in rationality are diverse enough so that no one would suggest that courses in rationality be included in university curricula. However, there are certain basic skills which seem to play a part in attaining excellence in more than one of the six factors in rationality that we have discussed. Four of these basic skills are especially worth mentioning.

One major skill that someone who wishes to reason well should have is an ability to use his language precisely and flexibly. Someone who has mastered his language will also be able to classify subjects of discussion effectively, and to be aware immediately of the implications of ways in which words are used in descriptions, demands, requests, etc.

A second major skill is that of possessing a sense of relevance. Most everyday rational problems require an ability to size up what is relevant to a problem and what is irrelevant. There are an unlimited number of facts that might have some connection with a given problem. Solving the problem thus requires an ability to grasp immediately the facts to be reckoned with. Someone who totally lacked this ability would never get started in his reasoning processes.

A third skill is that which consists of having, and being able to use, knowledge of the world acquired through experience. A great deal of ordinary reasoning requires an ability to anticipate regularities, estimate likelihoods, etc. There is a philosophical myth that reason and experience are entirely separate in our intellectual functioning. It is indeed true that deductive reasoning does not require any experience other than experience of language, but most of our ordinary reasoning is not deductive. Most of our ordinary reasoning is concerned with connections among facts. This can be carried on only by someone who has the relevant experience of facts.

A fourth skill is the general ability learned in formal logic. There are very few everyday reasoning operations in which this skill would come directly into play. However, the study and mastery of formal logic strengthens many powers which do come into play in most ordinary reasoning. It gives the student an awareness of the aim and nature of his reasoning which prevents basic confusions. Also, mastering the rules of formal logic has the same strengthening effect on performance in informal reasoning that calisthenics have on performance in sports. Since the various sorts of rational problems that we encounter are too diverse to put in a syllabus, this indirect training of our reasoning abilities is the best that is possible.

2. Fallacies

The ingredients of reasoning badly are just as numerous as the ingredients of reasoning well. Clumsy use of language, lack of a sense of relevance, lack of relevant experience, or lack of the awareness provided by training in formal logic all can cause bad reasoning. However, as we said earlier, while there are an infinite number of forms which bad reasoning can take, there are certain very common patterns of bad reasoning. The remainder of the chapter will be taken up with a discussion of these.

A fallacy is a bad form of reasoning. In discussing common fallacies we shall again be illustrating a thesis. This is that often there is not a very sharp contrast between a fallacious line of reasoning and one which is sound and sensible. Fallacies sometimes have their appeal because of genuine resemblances to sound reasoning. Consequently it takes a certain amount of intelligence and flexibility to avoid fallacious reasoning. Avoiding fallacies is in general not something which can be worked out mechanically by means of fixed and precise rules.

We shall survey seven common fallacies.

2.1. Argument from weak analogy

A very common form of bad reasoning consists of seizing upon a slight similarity between two things and concluding on the basis of it that something which is true of one of the things is also true of the other. For example, suppose that we know Jones and know that he comes from Nebraska and is fond of apple pie, and that we know Smith and know that he comes from Nebraska, but do not know his tastes in desserts. It would be argument from a weak analogy if we were to conclude that Smith likes apple pie.

The reader should notice why the analogy in this case is weak. It is weak because there is no reason to suppose a strong connection between the similarity seized upon, that of having come from Nebraska and eating apple pies. There is no reason to suppose that two people who come from Nebraska would have the same taste in desserts. If we wish to infer something about Smith's tastes in desserts, we would have to appeal to facts about him which are more relevant than the fact that he comes from Nebraska.

In order to recognize the Nebraska-to-apple-pie argument as weak, we have to know certain facts. We have to know that there is not an extreme uniformity in eating habits in any given state in the union. Thus it takes more than just logical acumen to recognize the Nebraska-to-apple-pie argument as weak. It takes some experience, or knowledge derived from the experience of others.

We can see this by contrasting the Nebraska-to-apple-pie argument with another argument which sounds very similar. Suppose that we meet X who comes from country A in eastern Europe and who is fond of sausage of type S—a meat for which country A is famous and which is consumed in large quantities there. We also meet Y who comes from country A and whose taste in food we do not know. We then might, on the basis of the similarity of national origin, infer that Y also likes sausage of type S.

The analogy underlying this argument probably is not very strong, but seems stronger than the analogy underlying the Nebraska-to-apple-pie argument. That is, it would seem that we have a somewhat better basis for concluding that Y likes sausage of type S than we had had for concluding that Smith likes apple pie.

The reason for this is factual. We know that there is more uniformity in tastes in sausage in a given eastern European country than there is uniformity in tastes in desserts in a given state of the union. Consequently, if we are given the facts that X and Y come from the same eastern European country, and that Jones and Smith both come from Nebraska, it seems more likely that Y shares X's tastes in sausages than that Smith shares Jones's tastes in desserts.

In the case of neither argument was our conclusion either certain or necessarily false. It is possible that Smith likes apple pie, and it is quite possible that he does not. It is quite possible that Y likes sausage of type S, and it is quite possible that he does not. But the chances that Smith likes apple pie are little better than they would be if Smith were someone who did not come from Nebraska, which is why the Nebraska-to-apple-pie inference is so weak. The chances that Y likes sausage of type S, on the other hand, if we are given the fact that he comes from the same eastern European country as Y, seem rather good.

The point that we have been getting at is twofold. First, that knowledge of the world is necessary in order to construct arguments from good analogies and to avoid arguments from poor analogies. Secondly, that a fallacious argument from weak analogy may at first glance look very much like a strong argument from a good analogy. Indeed in some cases it may be an open issue as to whether a given argument is a fallacious argument from weak analogy or is a strong argument.

Perhaps the most famous example of this in the history of philosophy is an argument for the existence of God presented in Hume's *Dialogues Concerning Natural Religion*. The argument begins from the observation that the universe in many ways seems ordered and smooth running, just as a machine is ordered and smooth running. Machines, of course, have been created by craftsmen. Therefore by analogy we can conclude that the universe also has been created, by a craftsmanlike god.

One of the characters in Hume's dialogue immediately objects that the analogy which underlies this argument is pitifully weak. There is not much similarity, he says, between the universe and an artifact. There is about as much similarity, in fact, as between a vegetable and a human being; and those who looked for circulation of sap in vegetables similar to the circulation of blood in human beings were sadly disappointed.

The opinion of readers of the Hume *Dialogues* always has been divided. Many people look at the design of a snowflake, or the perfect running of the solar system, and claim then to be impressed by a very definite similarity between the world and an artifact. Others are struck by plagues and famines, and natural disorders of various kinds, and claim to find a dissimilarity between the universe and well-made artifacts.

The point to be made here is that no logician has a pre-eminent claim to judge the validity of this argument. Just as the Nebraska-to-apple-pie argument depends on the factual assumption that people who have in common the fact that they come from Nebraska also generally have their tastes in desserts in common, so also the argument in the *Dialogues* depends on the factual assumption that things which share the general characteristics of order which the universe has, and also the differences from artifacts which the universe has, will generally have been created. No logician has any special competence to judge this assumption. For that matter, it does not seem in the realm of science either to confirm or to disconfirm the assumption. After all, the only member of the class being generalized about that we know is that universe; and it is precisely whether it has been created that was the disputed point.

2.2. The fallacy of post hoc, ergo propter hoc

The fallacy of *post hoc, ergo propter hoc* (which means "after this, therefore because of this") occurs when an investigator assumes that an event which preceded a given event is thereby the cause of that event. For example, if the Smith company hires Jones as sales manager and sales drastically improve during the following twelve months, executives of the Smith company are liable to assume that Jones's hiring is the cause of the increased sales. This *may* in fact be the case. But the major cause also may turn out to be something different: an improvement in the quality of Smith company products, or a growing familiarity of buyers with the merits of Smith company products. The Smith company executives, in assuming that Jones's hiring was the cause, would be committing the fallacy of *post hoc, ergo propter hoc*. A comparable reasoning to theirs was produced by Smooth, in Chapter 4, in inferring the efficacy of a Hollyhill Hall education.

Any event is preceded by a very large number of events, some of which may catch our attention and some of which may not. Often it will turn out that an event, such as an increase in a company's sales, is caused by a large number of preceding events, each of which contributes something to the result. Often also it will turn out that an event is caused by a preceding event or events which had not caught our attention.

Viewed in this perspective, the fallacy of *post hoc, ergo propter hoc* is really just the fallacy of jumping to a conclusion about the cause of an event. It is a fallacy involving mental laziness. In general someone who commits the fallacy of *post hoc, ergo propter hoc* is guilty of assuming that some event which preceded a given event and which caught his attention is the cause of the event, instead of investigating the possible causes more thoroughly.

An important thing to realize is that someone who reasons this way will not always go wrong. Some hasty judgments are correct. The cause of an event will indeed be a preceding event or events, and very often it will indeed be the case that the preceding event which had caught our attention is the cause. Someone whose reasoning is of the *post hoc, ergo propter hoc* variety may well be right as often as he is wrong.

However, such a person will not be right in as high a percentage of cases as he would be if he took time to examine a large number of possible causes of an event. Someone who reasons carefully will be more likely to be right than someone who reasons hastily. Also, someone whose reasoning is of the *post hoc, ergo propter hoc* variety, just because he will be right in many cases, is liable to be blindly dogmatic in cases where he is wrong.

A final point is that there is no very sharp line between the *post hoc, ergo propter hoc* fallacy and good sound reasoning about causes. Normally any inquiry, no matter how careful, concerning causes cannot go on for a very long time. Of the very large number of events preceding an event, any one of which conceivably could have been a contributory cause, not all will be examined. Consequently the haste of an inference concerning the cause of an event is a matter of degree. A high degree of haste may lead to reasoning which would be labeled fallacious, especially if the problem is complicated. A low degree of haste normally would result in sound, careful reasoning. Most of us, in our everyday reasoning concerning causes, are in moderate haste, and fall somewhere between the two extremes.

2.3. The fallacy of affirming the consequent

This fallacy consists of affirming a conditional statement, affirming the consequent of the conditional statement, and then on the basis of this affirming the antecedent of the statement. For example, someone might say (a) "If the Red Sox won their game yesterday, people in Boston would look very happy," and (b) "People in Boston look very happy," and conclude from these that (c) "The Red Sox won their game yesterday."

The form of this fallacy then is as follows:

$$\text{If } X, \text{ then } Y$$
$$\underline{Y}$$
$$\text{Therefore } X$$

As the reader knows, if we are given "If X, then Y," and also X, we could legitimately infer Y. A thoughtless person who knows this could easily confuse the legitimate inference from "If X, then Y" and X to Y, with the illegitimate inference from "If X, then Y" and Y to X. However, we can easily imagine cases in which both "If X, then Y" and Y are true, without X being true. It may be true that the Red Sox's winning their game would make the people in Boston very happy, and it may be true also that they are very happy; but this may be for some reason other than anything connected with the Red Sox. Even if it is true that if you light several matches you start a fire, and that there is a fire now raging in the Jones warehouse, that does not imply that someone had lit several matches in the Jones warehouse.

The fallacy of affirming the consequent is usually the result of mental carelessness. However, there are occasional cases in which someone's reasoning might appear to be of the form

$$\begin{array}{c} \text{If } X, \text{ then } Y \\ \underline{Y} \\ \text{Therefore } X \end{array}$$

and is not fallacious, and in fact is fairly good. These are cases in which we would be justified in adding the premise "X is practically the only thing which could bring about Y." An inference of the form

$$\begin{array}{c} \text{If } X, \text{ then } Y \\ Y \\ \underline{X \text{ is practically the only thing that could bring about } Y} \\ \text{Therefore probably } X \end{array}$$

is entirely sound.

Therefore, in cases in which we are given the fact that "If X, then Y," and also are told that Y is the case, we must ask ourselves: "Is X practically the only thing that could lead to Y, or are there many things other than X that could lead to Y?" If the answer is that there are many things other than X that could lead to Y, then to conclude "X" on the basis of the evidence given would be falling into the fallacy of affirming the consequent. On the other hand, if X is practically the only thing that could lead to Y, "X" may represent a sound conclusion. The reader may easily imagine borderline cases: i.e., cases in which there are only one or two things, which are rather uncommon, other than X which could lead to Y. In such a case it may be very difficult to decide whether it would be sound or fallacious reasoning to conclude "X." This illustrates again the point that avoiding fallacies cannot be regarded simply as a straightforward matter of following rules.

2.4. The fallacy of denying the antecedent

This fallacy consists of affirming a conditional statement, denying the antecedent of the conditional statement, and then on the basis of this denying the consequent of the statement. For example, someone might say (a) "If the Red Sox won yesterday, people in Boston would be very happy," and (b) "The Red Sox did not win yesterday," and conclude from these that (c) "People in Boston are not very happy."

The form of this fallacy then is as follows:

$$\text{If } X, \text{ then } Y$$
$$\frac{\sim X}{\text{Therefore } \sim Y}$$

This fallacy is very similar to the fallacy of affirming the consequent. Both center around misuse of the "If . . . then" form. Both read "If X, then Y" wrongly, as if it said that X was a necessary condition for there to be Y.

Consequently our general remarks about the fallacy of affirming the consequent apply equally to this fallacy. If we were able to assume that X is practically the only thing that could bring about Y, then a form of reasoning which concluded $\sim Y$ from "If X, then Y" and $\sim X$ would be fairly good and not fallacious. On the other hand, if the answer is that there are many things other than X that could lead to Y, then to conclude that Y is false on the basis of the evidence given would be falling into the fallacy of denying the antecedent.

2.5. The fallacy of equivocation

The fallacy of equivocation consists of using a word with two or more meanings during the course of an argument while at the same time conducting the argument as if the meaning of the word was being held constant. We showed one example of this fallacy in the first chapter. The argument "The hall was full of good citizens; good citizens are people, therefore the hall was full of people" is invalid. That is because the phrase "full of" in "The hall was full of good citizens" has connotations of "predominantly containing," which would enable us to speak of the hall was full of good citizens if the hall was only half full but it was very notable that everyone there was a good citizen. "Full of" in "The hall was full of good citizens" thus has a slightly different meaning than that of "full of" in "The hall was full of people."

Another example of the fallacy of equivocation would be the following:

Humanity is the property of being human.
Among the qualities for which Jones was prized, besides his wisdom, were his generosity and humanity in dealing with the poor.

Therefore, just as we prize Jones's humanity, we should prize the humanity of X—, even though X— is a mass murderer.

This argument plays on a double meaning of the word "humanity": one meaning in which all men have the attribute of humanity, and another meaning in which the quality of humanity is the (not altogether common) quality of being able to share and appreciate the feelings of others. The sense of "humanity" in which we prize Jones for his humanity is *not* the sense of "humanity" in which to be a man is to have the attribute of humanity.

A point worth remembering is that arguments involving equivocation are seldom completely outlandish, and occasionally have considerable wit to them. In the example that we have just given, for example, the play on the meanings of "humanity" does serve to remind us that being able to appreciate the feelings of other men is a virtue, and that mass-murderer X—, too, is a man. The play on words in this case, however, is, in our opinion, not enlightening enough to make the argument a good one.

Cases can be given, however, of arguments involving equivocation in which the equivocation creates considerable suggestive force for the argument. W. K. Wimsatt has pointed out, for example, that the puns in the poetry of Pope are successful because they point to a genuine relationship between meanings that normally are thought to be separate. When Pope speaks of a character as losing "her heart, or necklace, at a ball," he of course is using the word "lose" in two different senses. However, an argument of the form "Miss X has a strong tendency to lose things; therefore it is probable that she sometimes loses her heart" seems to have considerable strength. It seems to be true that the sort of person who chronically loses things usually falls in love at least as often as does a careful, meticulous sort of person.

This should make us realize that the fallacy of equivocation, like other fallacies we have discussed, in some cases can bear a close resemblance to intelligent reasoning. No hard-and-fast rules will enable us to realize in which cases use of a word in more than one meaning represents merely sloppy thinking, and in which cases it suggests something witty and true.

The intelligent thinker will be sensitive enough to nuances in language, and aware enough of connections between different meanings of a word, so that he will be able to distinguish the occasional cases in which equivocation represents wit from the more frequent cases in which equivocation represents a crude fallacy.

2.6. The black-or-white fallacy

The black-or-white fallacy is the error in reasoning involved when someone refuses to recognize a difference between two things because the difference is a matter of degree. For example, in the United States someone who holds views hostile to the established order is likely to suffer unpopularity and possibly ostracism. In totalitarian countries someone who holds views hostile to the established order is likely to suffer imprisonment. Fuzzy thinkers sometimes seize upon the fact that in all cases someone who has views hostile to the established order will suffer, and say: "The United States is really just like a totalitarian country." This is an example of the black-or-white fallacy. It ignores the difference in degree of suffering between unpopularity and imprisonment, and concentrates instead on the fact that both involve suffering.

Another example is a defense sometimes given of Nazi war crimes. "After all, in war there always are some innocent people killed." Often someone who takes this line will point to our bombing of the German civilian population. Again the fallacy in this line of thought lies in not taking account of a very important difference in degree.

The black-or-white fallacy gets its appeal from a tendency we all have on occasion to be purists. The world of the adolescent in which everything either is or is not X is a much easier world to think in than the world of the adult, which is complicated by matters of degree, circumstances, and qualifications. In addition, it is always tempting to impose an extremely high standard on the facts of life. We might like to think of a society in which no one with unpopular views suffers the slightest discomfort. Or we might want to insist that there be no civilian casualties in war. It is easy, if this sort of desire is thwarted, to reject anything short of our ideal as equally bad. This is how the black-or-white fallacy originates. Mature thinking, however, even if it does cherish ideals, will recognize that there are variations in degree of falling short of the ideals, and that the variations in degree can be extremely important.

2.7. The fallacy of begging the question

The fallacy of begging the question consists of assuming in an argument the very thing one intends to prove as a conclusion. For example, suppose that a philosopher is arguing that our senses are reliable guides to reality. He might argue that, after all, our senses seem usually to give us correct information. But if we ask him how he knows that the senses usually give us correct information, his only answer would be to appeal to the evidence of the senses: e.g., that things usually look at one moment as they had at a previous one, thus indicating that the testimony of the senses at the previous moment is not to be disregarded. The philosopher's argument that we can rely on our senses thus boils down to:

The evidence of our senses tells us that our senses usually give us correct information.

Therefore the evidence of our senses is to be taken as reliable.

The reader can see that this argument assumes what it sets out to prove. The ultimate basis of the philosopher's argument for the reliability of the senses would collapse if we did not assume the reliability of the senses.

In everyday arguments the fallacy of begging the question usually occurs in a modified form. That is, often only part of what is to be proved is assumed; but the part of the question that is begged is an important step toward the conclusion. For example, someone might argue that:

General unkindness to one's family is a much more serious fault than stealing an automobile.

Stealing an automobile is punishable by one year in prison.

Therefore general unkindness to one's family ought to be punished by more than one year in prison.

Here it is not the case that the whole question is assumed: i.e., nowhere in the premises is it assumed that general unkindness to one's family ought to be punished by more than one year in prison. But in order to believe that general unkindness to one's family ought to be punished by more than one year in prison, one must believe that all faults, even those of a private nature, should be subject to the criminal code. That is the real issue. The arguer is tacitly assuming that if general unkindness to one's family is a serious fault, it ought to have a place in the criminal code. This key step in the argument is not stated. Consequently the argument represents a modified form of the fallacy of begging the question.

The best way to avoid this common form of the fallacy is to be very clear about just what one is assuming in an argument. The cure, in other words, is extreme intellectual self-consciousness. It helps, in spotting one's hidden assumptions, to try to imagine how someone might object to one's line of reasoning. The points that someone might quarrel with are very often the points in one's reasoning that one has been least clear about or has taken for granted.

Something that complicates the task of avoiding begging the question is that many pieces of good reasoning have features very comparable to those of reasoning which involves the fallacy. Take, for example, the following argument:

Kidnapping is much worse than stealing an automobile.

Stealing an automobile is punishable by one year in prison.

Therefore kidnapping ought to be punished by a sentence much more severe than one year in prison.

Most people would agree that this is sound reasoning. Like our previous example, though, it contains a key unstated assumption. In this case the key assumption is that if one crime is much worse than another it ought to draw much the severer penalty. In addition, the argument assumes that, as we all know, both kidnapping and stealing an automobile are crimes. It also assumes that the present punishment for stealing an automobile is roughly appropriate. The full argument, with these assumptions stated, would read as follows:

Kidnapping is a crime which is much worse than the crime of stealing an automobile.

If one crime is much worse than another, it should draw much the severer penalty.

Stealing an automobile is punishable by one year in prison, which is an appropriate penalty.

Therefore kidnapping should be punished by a sentence much more severe than one year.

Why did this argument as it was first stated, with all its assumptions left unstated, not involve the fallacy of begging the question? Why was it, even as first stated, a sound argument, whereas the argument about general unkindness to one's family was fallacious?

The answer is twofold. First of all, in ordinary discussion we do not speak like logic texts; and it is quite natural, and ordinarily permissible, to leave some of the assumptions of our arguments unstated. But, secondly, the assumptions that we normally may leave unstated are the ones that most people would not challenge, that genuinely can be taken for granted. Most people would consider it obvious that if one crime is much worse than another, it should draw much the severer penalty. Consequently this assumption does not need to be stated. On the other hand, a great many people would question whether private faults should be subject to the criminal code. Consequently, someone arguing that unkindness to one's family should be punished by more than one year in prison would be expected to explain the controversial basis on which his argument really rests. If he does not state this basis, but glibly pushes on with his argument, then he will be accused of begging the question.

Here again we see that a thin and indistinct line lies between good reasoning and fallacious reasoning. In this case the distinguishing factor is the obviousness of the assumptions left unstated.

2.8. Concluding remark

What we have mainly tried to do in discussing fallacies is to loosen up the reader's picture of reason. There is so much of a ritual element in formal logic that we all need reminding that in everyday life ordinary alertness and flexible good sense are important in avoiding fallacies and in reasoning well.

Even in those cases in which we apply formal logic very directly to problems of everyday reasoning, as we have shown repeatedly throughout the book, alertness and flexible good sense are needed in order to avoid mistakes. Consequently this book, or any logic book, should be regarded as a point of departure on the road toward becoming highly reasonable, and not as a compendium which contains all that is needed.

Answers to Exercises

CHAPTER 2

ANSWERS TO EXERCISES ON PAGE 32, SECTION 1.1.1.

I. Distinct terms are separated by slashes (/); expressions which are not terms are omitted.

1. Roses/red.
2. Roses/red/violets/blue.
3. Roses/violets/flowers. This sentence can be taken as shorthand for "Roses are flowers, and violets are flowers."
4. Roses/violets/have attractive fragrances.
5. Roses/white.
6. Rose in the southeast corner of Aunt Jane's garden/white.
7. Roses/red/those (roses) in Aunt Jane's garden/white. "But" indicates some sort of opposition between two statements, both of which, however, are put forth as true. It is not a term but is somewhat like "and." "Those" (and other pronouns) normally function in the same way as abbreviations for specified words or phrases.
8. Bushes elsewhere in Aunt Jane's garden/have yellow roses. "On the other hand" is like "but" in the previous exercise. "Three" functions in this statement somewhat as "some" functions in the previous exercise. It tells us how much of a subject is being talked about, but not what the subject is.
9. This (flower)/fragrant flower. "Ah me" and "indeed" contribute to the meaning of the statement, but not, it may be argued, as terms. "Ah me" seems to express the feelings or reaction of the person making the statement; it does not mention any feature of the flower he is describing. The decision as to whether "indeed" should be counted as part of a term is not so clear-cut. If it is meant as a synonym for "very" (so that "indeed a fragrant flower" is equivalent to "a very fragrant flower") it should indeed be counted as a term. If it is meant

to emphasize the speaker's conviction as to the truth of the whole statement, it should not be counted as part of a term. "A" is more like "some" or "three" than like a term.

10. Three/prime number. In this statement "three" is a term, though those who have thought most about the question disagree as to the sort of reality numbers possess.

11. This (exercise)/difficult exercise/profitable one. "One" acts here as a pronoun.

II. Choice of code letter is arbitrary, so long as the rules at the beginning of the exercise are followed.

1. *(Ro are Re)*
2. *(Ro are Re)* and *(V are B)*
3. *(R are F)* and *(V are F)*
4. *(R are A)* and *(V are A)*. Treating "have attractive fragrances" as equivalent to "are things which have attractive fragrances" allows us to display the logical similarity of this sentence to the last one.
5. (Some *R* are *W*)
6. (Every *R* is *W*)
7. (Most *Ro* are *Re*) but (Some *Rg* are *W*)
8. On the other hand, (three *B* are *Y*)
9. Ah me, indeed, *(T is an F)*
10. *(T is a P)*
11. *(T is a D)* but *(T is a P)*

ANSWERS TO EXERCISES ON PAGE 35, SECTION 1.1.2.

I. 1. General.
2. Singular.
3. General. The Yankees are the only team to which the term correctly applies, but this is a matter of fact, not of logic.
4. Singular in most contexts? When baseball fans argue as to who was the best center fielder in baseball, they argue as if there can be at most one center fielder who was "best" without qualification. Such an argument may end in a draw, of course, in which case each candidate may be described as "one of the best" center fielders in all baseball.
5. General.
6. Singular.
7. General.
8. Singular.
9. General? It might seem reasonable to take "the elephant" here as an abstract singular term, on the order of "three" in item 6 in this exercise, or "autumn" in number 8, but in order to avoid confusion with "the

elephant" in 10, some logicians would classify our present example as a general term, a sort of shorthand for "all elephants," arguing that "The elephant is a mammal" means the same as "All elephants are mammals."

10. Singular. The term fails to do its job if there is more than one elephant in the zoo in question.

II. 1. Contraries.

2. Contradictories.

3. It depends on what you are classifying and what you mean by the terms themselves. As applied to living things of more than microscopic size, "animal" and "plant" are roughly contradictory. As applied to everything, these terms are merely contraries. In the game of Twenty Questions, for example, "mineral" is sometimes used as a coordinate category with "animal" and "vegetable."

4. Contradictories. Of course, sticks and stones are neither true nor false, but what if we restrict the application of these terms to statements, propositions, beliefs, and the like? These are generally regarded as either true or false, those that are "partly true" being classified as false. There are, however, "three-valued" systems of logic in which "true" and "false" are merely contraries, even when applied only to such things as statements and propositions.

5. Contraries. We simply may not know whether a statement is true or not.

ANSWERS TO THE EXERCISE ON PAGE 43, SECTION 1.2.2.

1. **O.** Men who fly through the air/pilots.
2. **O.** Men who are flying/pilots.
3. **E.** Animals who are not men/pilots.
4. **A.** Passengers/animals.
5. **I.** Passengers/men.
6. **I.** Animals who are not men/passengers.
7. **I.** Passengers in airplanes/poodles.
8. **E.** Passengers/cases of crackerjacks.

ANSWERS TO EXERCISE ON PAGE 50, SECTION 1.2.3.

1. **A** men/by nature desire to know.
2. (**A**$_8$ Gruff/was in the room) *and* (**E**$_8$ Gruff/laughed) *and* (**A** persons in the room other than Gruff/laughed).
3. **A** men who are truly free/wise.

4. (I men/went up the mountain) *and* (I men/came down).

5. A man/rational animal.

6. A people/funny? The effectiveness of this proposition partly depends on its indefiniteness.

7. A times when Jones likes to take a vacation/times when Jones can take a vacation.

8. E_s Jones/takes vacations.

9. E times/times when Jones takes vacations.

10. (A_s his mother/gave Johnny an apple) *or* (A_s his mother/gave Johnny an orange).

11. (A_s Johnny/likes apples) *and* (A_s Johnny likes oranges) *and* (A Johnny's brothers/like apples) *and* (A Johnny's brothers/like oranges).

12. A cats and dogs/enemies. It might be argued that "I cats and dogs/enemies" is better. The important point to notice is that "enemies" is here a relational predicate.

13. I women/prefer mink.

14. (I cases/cases in which the cost of excellence is high) *and* (E cases/cases in which the cost of excellence is too high).

15. I man/walked into the house next door.

16. A men who pay attention to the evidence/likely to draw the right conclusion.

17. (I swallows/had left by December) *and* (O swallows/had left by December).

18. E_s the man who walked into the house next door/had companions.

19. (I swallows/had left by December) *and* (O swallows/had left by December).

20. *If* (A_s Jones/comes back soon), *then* (A_s Smith/will be surprised), *but if* (A_s Smith/will be surprised), *then* (E_s Green/won't pay back Black) *or* (I geese/will turn purple).

ANSWERS TO EXERCISES ON PAGE 59, SECTION 2.1.

1. 1-EAE	8. 1-AEE	15. 3-EIO
2. 2-EAE	9. 4-AEE	16. 1-IEO
3. 2-AAE	10. 1-AEA	17. 3-AAI
4. 3-EAE	11. 1-IAI	18. 2-OOA
5. 1-AAA	12. 4-EAO	19. 4-EIO
6. 1-EEE	13. 3-AII	20. 2-AOO
7. 2-AEE	14. 4-AOO	

ANSWERS TO EXERCISES ON PAGE 66, SECTION 2.2.1.

I. The following can be reduced by the steps indicated. Numbers skipped refer to syllogisms which either are in the first figure already or are invalid.

   2. Convert "(No) mules are horses" to "No horses are mules," to reach Celarent.

   7. To reach Celarent, convert (1) "Undertows don't crest" to "Nothing which crests is an undertow" and (2) "Undertows aren't waves" to "No waves are undertows."

   9. Convert "No well-informed person is a professor" to "No professor is a well-informed person," to reach Celarent.

   12. To reach Ferio, (1) convert "No tigers are lions" to "No lions are tigers," (2) substitute "Some lions are animals" for its superaltern, "All lions are animals," and (3) convert this to "Some animals are lions."

   13. Convert "Some boiling water is salty" to "Some salty things are boiling water," to reach Darii.

   15. Convert "Some canoes have sails" to "Some sailboats are canoes," to reach Ferio.

   17. To reach Darii, (1) substitute "Some steaks are delicious" for its superaltern, "All steaks are delicious," and (2) convert this to "Some delicious things are steaks."

   19. To reach Ferio, convert (1) "No one who is playing the piano wears mittens" to "No one wearing mittens plays the piano" and (2) "Some of those who wear mittens are cold" to "Some who are cold wear mittens."

   20. Indirect proof through Barbara: denying the conclusion "Some Hungarian is not English" is tantamount to asserting, "All Hungarian is English," which, with the premise that all English is Indo-European, implies (by Barbara) that all Hungarian is Indo-European, which contradicts the other premise of the original inference.

II. In addition to numbers 12, 15, and 19 in part I (which are, respectively, fourth-figure **EAO**, third-figure **EIO**, and fourth-figure **EIO**), the following moods can be reduced to Ferio as indicated. From Festino in the second figure we reach Ferio by converting the major premise. If the minor premise of Ferio is both converted and strengthened, the result is Felapton in the third figure.

III. 1.   Eb/c

       Ia/b

       ‾‾‾‾‾

       Oa/c

Denying the Ferio conclusion **O** *a/c* gives us **A** *a/c*. But if this is combined with the major premise of the syllogism, we reach the contradictory of the minor premise. That is, from **A** *a/c* and **E** *b/c*, we infer **E** *a/b*. Since this result is reached by a syllogism in Celarent, we must either reject Celarent or accept Ferio, for accepting Celarent and denying a conclusion in Ferio has led us to a contradiction.

2. (a) Disamis

Some existing thing is beautiful.
All existing things are good.

Some good thing is beautiful.

Denying the conclusion yields "No good thing is beautiful." This and "All existing things are good" can be used as the premises of a syllogism in Celarent with the conclusion "No existing thing is beautiful," which contradicts the other premise of our Disamis.

(b) Festino

No good things are beautiful.
Some existing things are beautiful.

Some existing things are not good.

Denying "**O** existing things/good" yields "**A** existing things/good." This, with, "**E** good things/beautiful," leads, by Celarent, to "**E** existing things/beautiful," which contradicts the minor premise of our Disamis.

It is interesting to notice that our examples of Celarent, Disamis, and Festino depend on the fact that the following three propositions cannot possibly all be true:

(1) All existing things are good.
(2) No good things are beautiful.
(3) Some existing things are beautiful.

If we affirm the first two (as in Celarent), we must deny the third. If we accept (1) and (3) (as in Disamis), we must reject the second. If (2) and (3) are true (Festino), (1) must be false.

ANSWERS TO EXERCISE ON PAGE 72, SECTION 2.2.3.

3. Rules 2 and 7 are violated: since the conclusion is negative, one premise should be negative, and the middle term should be distributed.
4. Illicit minor.
6. Rules 1 and 3 are violated.
8. Illicit major.
10. Rule 1 is broken.
11. Undistributed middle. Beware of confusing inferences like this with inferences like number 5.

14. Undistributed middle.

16. Illicit major.

18. Rules 1, 3, 4, 5, 6, and 7 are all violated by this horribly invalid syllogism, which is included as further illustration of the point that true premises and a true conclusion do not show that the inference form connecting them is valid.

ANSWERS TO EXERCISE ON PAGE 82, SECTION 2.2.4.

 1.

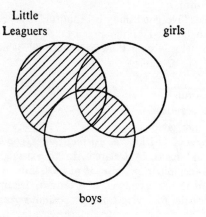

Little
Leaguers   girls

VALID

boys

2.

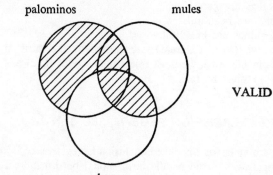

palominos   mules

VALID

horses

3.

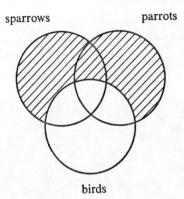

sparrows parrots

birds

INVALID

4.

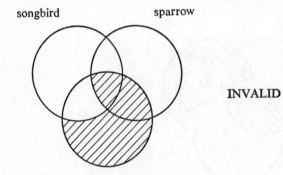

songbird sparrow

nightingale

INVALID

5.

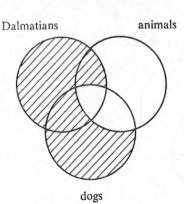

Dalmatians animals

dogs

VALID

6. brave men   fight

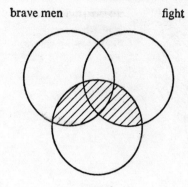

INVALID

cowards

7. undertows   waves

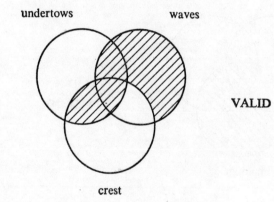

VALID

crest

8. well-informed   college professor

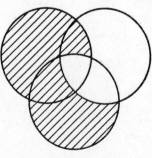

INVALID

really absent-minded

9. well-informed   professor

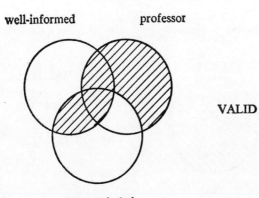

VALID

absent-minded

10. dogs   animals

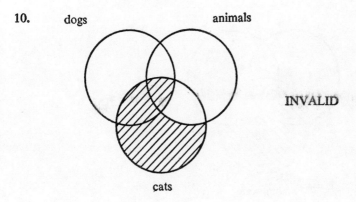

INVALID

cats

ANSWERS TO EXERCISE ON PAGE 86, SECTION 2.2.4.

11. collies   animals

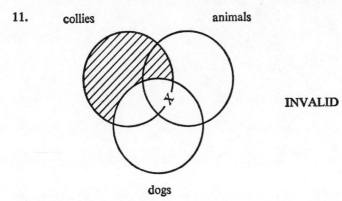

INVALID

dogs

12.

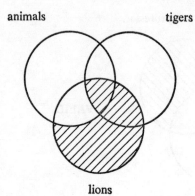

animals   tigers

lions

INVALID on the Boolean interpretation of "All lions are animals," though valid on the classical interpretation.

13.

salty   bubble

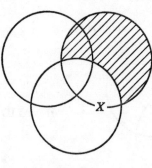

boiling water

VALID

14.

men   English novelists

novelists

INVALID

15.

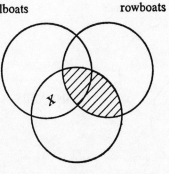

sailboats   rowboats

X

VALID

canoes

16.   birds   flounder

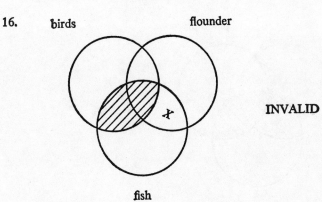

INVALID

fish

17.   delicious   expensive

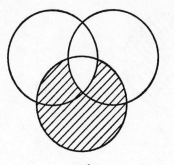

INVALID on the Boolean interpretation of "All steaks are delicious," though not on the classical interpretation.

steaks

18.

dogs   animals

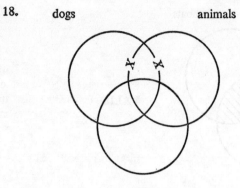

INVALID

collies

19.

cold   piano players

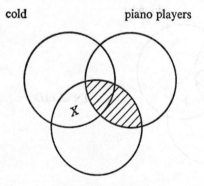

VALID

mitten-wearers

20.

Hungarian   English

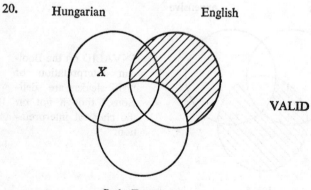

VALID

Indo-European

ANSWERS TO EXERCISE ON PAGE 90, SECTION 3.3.

1. Every responsible person is a voter. (If you feel uncomfortable with this, it is because "nonvoter" applies best to persons who could or should vote but do not. It may be that some responsible persons are ineligible or otherwise unable to vote. This does not make them "nonvoters" in the best (that is, the worst) sense.
2. Some of his listeners were not convinced by his arguments.
3. A few cherry trees were not without blossoms by Easter.
4. At least two of us were absent from the meeting.
5. His argument was invalid.
6. You've always had it not so good?

ANSWERS TO EXERCISES ON PAGE 91, SECTION 3.3.

1. a. True (the converse of the subaltern of "A nightingales/birds").
   b. True (the obverse of "A nightingales/birds").
   c. False (the contradictory of the converse of the obverse of "A nightingales/birds").
   d. Undetermined. This might be either true or false.
   e. True (the obverse of the converse of the obverse).
2. a. Undetermined.
   b. True (obverse of the converse of the obverse).
   c. False (contradictory of the converse of the obverse).
   d. Undetermined.
   e. False (contradictory of b).

ANSWERS TO EXERCISE ON PAGE 95, SECTION 3.4.

1. First order, missing the major premise "All expensive mink coats are good ones." With this proposition counted in, the argument is a case of Barbara. This is perhaps the commonest type of enthymeme. Notice, however, that if we use as a premise the more plausible proposition "All good mink coats are expensive," we do *not* come up with a valid argument.
2. Second order. All we need add, in order to get a case of Disamis, is "I roses/red," a true proposition. The false proposition, "A roses/red," would serve as the minor premise of a syllogism in Darapti.

3. First order, missing the major premise "**E** what has failed me in the past/to be trusted now." With this premise, the argument is valid, though not, perhaps, entirely sound, since the missing premise may be liable to criticism.

4. Third order. If the writer means to defend his friends by presenting evidence for the conclusion "**E** my friends/scoundrel," he has not done a good job. Not even "**O** my friends/scoundrel" follows from the stated premises. The most that can validly be had from these premises is "**O** scoundrels/my friends," and even this does not follow from a Boolean reading of the premises.

5. First order. So long as we restrict ourselves to the two quantifiers "All (None)" and "Some," we must demand for our missing major premise the rather strong proposition "All who have grown up among automobiles are able to fix their cars when things go wrong with them." Only with this implausible premise will the inference be valid.

ANSWERS TO EXERCISE ON PAGE 96, SECTION 3.5.

1. Babies cannot manage crocodiles.
2. *Your* presents to me are not made of tin.
3. My poultry are not officers.
4. No comet has a curly tail.
5. Puppies that will not lie still never care to do worsted work.
6. All the gluttons in my family are unhealthy.
7. An egg of the Great Auk is not to be had for a song.
8. When you cut your finger, you will find Tincture of Calendula useful.
9. No bird in this aviary lives on mince pies.
10. No pawnbroker is dishonest.
11. No kitten with green eyes will play with a gorilla.
12. These sorites-examples are difficult.
13. All my dreams come true.
14. No heavy fish is unkind to children.
15. No badger can guess a conundrum.
16. I cannot read any of Brown's letters.
17. I always avoid a kangaroo.

CHAPTER 3

ANSWERS TO EXERCISES ON PAGE 132, SECTION 1.2.2.

A.1.

P	Q	(~Pv~Q)vPQ
T	T	T
T	F	T
F	T	T
F	F	T

2.

P	Q	P⊃~(Pv~Q)
T	T	F
T	F	F
F	T	T
F	F	T

3.

P	Q	R	(P⊃QR)⊃PQ
T	T	T	T
T	T	F	T
T	F	T	T
T	F	F	T
F	T	T	F
F	T	F	F
F	F	T	F
F	F	F	F

4.

P	Q	~((~Pv~Q)v(P·~Q))
T	T	T
T	F	F
F	T	F
F	F	F

5.

P	Q	(P⊃Q)v(~Q⊃~P)
T	T	T
T	F	F
F	T	T
F	F	T

6.

P	Q	(~Q⊃~P)v(P·~Q)
T	T	T
T	F	T
F	T	T
F	F	T

7.

P	Q	$PQ \cdot (\sim Pv \sim Q)$
T	T	F
T	F	F
F	T	F
F	F	F

8.

P	Q	$(PvQ) \supset PQ$
T	T	T
T	F	F
F	T	F
F	F	T

B.   1 and 6
C.   7

ANSWERS TO EXERCISE ON PAGE 136, SECTION 1.2.3.

1. False	5. True
2. True	6. True
3. True	7. False
4. True	8. False

ANSWERS TO EXERCISES ON PAGE 145, SECTION 1.3.1.

A.1. Yes	6. Yes
2. Yes	7. No
3. No	8. No
4. Yes	9. No
5. No	10. Yes

B. Q
C. $\sim P \cdot Q$ and also $\sim (Q \supset P)$

ANSWERS TO EXERCISES ON PAGE 151, SECTION 1.3.2.

A.1. $Qv \sim Q$ (the expression is tautologous)
  2. PQ
  3. $PQv(\sim P \cdot \sim Q)$ or alternatively $(P \supset Q) \cdot (Q \supset P)$
  4. $P \cdot \sim Q$
  5. PvQ
  6. P

B.1. Formula 3 tells us that $\sim\sim P \equiv P$. We substitute $\sim\sim P$ for P in $P \vee Q$. This gives us $\sim\sim P \vee Q$.

We now use formula 4, letting $\sim P$ stand in for P and Q stand in for Q. This gives us $(\sim P \supset Q) \equiv \sim\sim P \vee Q$.

Thus we arrive at $\sim P \supset Q$.

B.2. We can begin by applying formula 3 to PQ. Formula 3 allows us to replace P by $\sim\sim P$ and Q by $\sim\sim Q$.

This gives us $\sim\sim P \cdot \sim\sim Q$.

We now use formula 2, letting $\sim P$ stand in for P and $\sim Q$ for Q. This shows us that $\sim\sim P \cdot \sim\sim Q$ is equivalent to $\sim(\sim P \vee \sim Q)$.

If we use formula 4, letting P stand in for P, and Q for Q, we get $P \supset \sim Q \equiv \sim P \vee \sim Q$. We can apply formula 24 to this. Formula 24 states that "If $X \equiv Y$, then $\sim X \equiv \sim Y$." Thus, if $P \supset \sim Q \equiv \sim P \vee \sim Q$, then $\sim(P \supset \sim Q) \equiv \sim(\sim P \vee \sim Q)$. Thus we see that $\sim(\sim P \vee \sim Q)$ is equivalent to $\sim(P \supset \sim Q)$. But $\sim(\sim P \vee \sim Q)$ is equivalent to PQ. Therefore PQ is equivalent to $\sim(P \supset \sim Q)$.

ANSWERS TO EXERCISES ON PAGE 155, SECTION 1.3.3.

1. Formula 4 allows us to transform $P \cdot (\sim Q \supset \sim P)$ into $P \cdot (\sim\sim Q \vee \sim P)$. Formula 3 allows us to write this as $P \cdot (Q \vee \sim P)$. According to formula 11, this is equivalent to PQ. Formula 19 allows us to write this as QP. Formula I.1 shows us that PQ implies Q, and formula I.2 shows us that Q implies $Q \vee \sim P$. Therefore, by I.6, PQ implies $Q \vee \sim P$. Therefore, again by I.6, $P \cdot (\sim Q \supset \sim P)$ implies $Q \vee \sim P$.

2. Formula 2 enables us to transform $\sim(\sim(P \vee Q) \vee Q)$ into $\sim\sim(P \vee Q) \cdot \sim Q$. Formula 3 enables us to write this as $(P \vee Q) \cdot \sim Q$, and formula 19 enables us to write it as $\sim Q \cdot (P \vee Q)$. According to formula 11, this is equivalent to $\sim Q \cdot P$. Formula 19 allows us to write this as $P \cdot \sim Q$. I.1 shows us that this implies P. Thus, by I.6, $\sim(\sim(P \vee Q) \vee Q)$ implies P.

3. In transforming $P \cdot (\sim Q \supset \sim P) \cdot (\sim R \supset \sim Q)$, we can first use formula 4 to replace the $\sim Q \supset \sim P$ component by $\sim\sim Q \vee \sim P$, and the $\sim R \supset \sim Q$ component by $\sim\sim R \vee \sim Q$. Formula 3 allows us to write these as $Q \vee \sim P$ and $R \vee \sim Q$. This gives us, as equivalent to the original expression, $P \cdot (Q \vee \sim P) \cdot (R \vee \sim Q)$. Formula 11 enables us to replace the $P \cdot (Q \vee \sim P)$ component by PQ. Thus we have $PQ \cdot (R \vee \sim Q)$. Formula 21 allows us to write this as $P \cdot (Q \cdot (R \vee \sim Q))$. We can apply formula 11 to the $Q \cdot (R \vee \sim Q)$ component, replacing it by QR. Thus we have $P \cdot QR$, which formula 21 allows us to write as $PQ \cdot R$. Formula 19 allows us to write this as $R \cdot PQ$. We can use I.1, letting R stand in for P and PQ stand in for Q. This tells us that RPQ implies R. Therefore, by I.6, $P \cdot (\sim Q \supset \sim P) \cdot (\sim R \supset \sim Q)$ implies R.

4. In transforming $P \cdot (Q \supset P)$, we can first apply formula 4 to the $Q \supset P$ component. This allows us to replace it by $\sim QvP$, giving us $P \cdot (\sim QvP)$. According to formula 10, this is equivalent to P.

We can transform $\sim Q \supset P$ also by use of formula 4. This gives us $\sim \sim QvP$, which formula 3 allows us to write as QvP. Formula 20 allows us to transform this again to PvQ.

I.2 tells us that P implies PvQ. Since we already have stated that PvQ is equivalent to (i.e., mutually implies) $\sim Q \supset P$, I.6 allows us to infer that P implies $\sim Q \supset P$. Since we already have stated also that $P \cdot (Q \supset P)$ is equivalent to P, I.6 allows us to conclude that $P \cdot (Q \supset P)$ implies $\sim Q \supset P$.

ANSWERS TO EXERCISE ON PAGE 164, SECTION 2.1.3.

1. Letting F stand for being a fish, G stand for being green, and H stand for being a parrot, we have $(x)(Fx \supset Gx) \cdot (x)(Hx \supset Gx)$.

2. Letting F stand for being a fish, G stand for being green, and H stand for being a whale, we have $(x)(Fx \supset Gx) \cdot (x)(Hx \supset \sim Gx)$.

3. Letting F stand for being a plum, G stand for being ripe, and H stand for being edible, we have $(\exists x)(Fx \cdot Gx) \supset (\exists y)(Hy)$.

4. Letting F stand for being a huge forest, G stand for being in California, and H stand for being in Nevada, we have $(\exists x)(Fx \cdot Gx) \cdot (\exists y)(Fy \cdot Hy)$.

5. Letting F stand for being a person, G stand for being able to read Hittite, and H stand for being in the room, we have $(\exists x)(Fx \cdot Gx) \cdot (x)((Fx \cdot Hx) \supset \sim Gx)$.

ANSWERS TO EXERCISES ON PAGE 170, SECTION 2.2.1.

1. If we apply formula 4 to the $Fx \supset Gx$ component, this allows us to write it as $\sim FxvGx$. This makes $\sim(Fx \supset Gx)$ read $\sim(\sim FxvGx)$. According to formula 2, this is $\sim \sim Fx \cdot \sim Gx$. Formula 3 allows us to write this as $Fx \cdot \sim Gx$. Thus we have $(x)(Fx \cdot \sim Gx)$.

We can now apply formula 29, letting Fx stand in for P, and $\sim Gx$ stand in for Q. This gives us $(x)(Fx) \cdot (x)(\sim Gx) \equiv (x)(Fx \cdot \sim Gx)$. Formula 26 enables us to conclude that $(x) \sim (Fx \supset Gx)$ is equivalent to $(x)(Fx) \cdot (x)(\sim Gx)$.

2. We can begin by using formula 27, letting $Fx \supset Gx$ stand in for R. This gives us $(x)(Fx \supset Gx) \equiv \sim (\exists x)(\sim(Fx \supset Gx))$.

Formula 24 allows us to conclude that $\sim(x)(Fx \supset Gx) \equiv \sim \sim (\exists x)(\sim (Fx \supset Gx))$. We can now apply formula 3, letting $(\exists x)(\sim Fx \supset Gx)$

stand in for P. This shows us that $\sim(x)(Fx \supset Gx)$ is equivalent to $(\exists x)$ $(\sim(Fx \supset Gx))$.

By the same method that we used in answering exercise 1, we can replace $\sim(Fx \supset Gx)$ by $Fx \cdot \sim Gx$, which leaves us with $(\exists x)(Fx \cdot \sim Gx)$, which therefore is equivalent to $\sim(x)(Fx \supset Gx)$.

3. We can begin by using formula 28, which tells us that $(\exists x)(FxvGx)$ is equivalent to $\sim(x)\sim(FxvGx)$.

Formula 2 tells us that $\sim(FxvGx)$ is equivalent to $\sim Fx \cdot \sim Gx$. Thus we have $\sim(x)(\sim Fx \cdot \sim Gx)$, which is equivalent to $(\exists x)(FxvGx)$.

4. We can begin by applying formula 27, letting $\sim(\sim Fx \cdot \sim Gx)$ stand in for R. This shows us that $(x)\sim(\sim Fx \cdot \sim Gx)$ is equivalent to $\sim(\exists x)$ $\sim\sim(\sim Fx \cdot \sim Gx)$.

Formula 3 allows us to write $\sim\sim(\sim Fx \cdot \sim Gx)$ as $\sim Fx \cdot \sim Gx$.

This gives us $(\exists x)(\sim Fx \cdot \sim Gx)$ as equivalent to $(x)\sim(\sim Fx \cdot \sim Gx)$.

ANSWERS TO EXERCISES ON PAGE 173, SECTION 2.2.2.

1. We can begin by rewriting the $FxvGx$ component of $(x)(FxvGx)$. Formula 3 enables us to write it as $\sim\sim FxvGx$. Formula 4 shows us that this is equivalent to $\sim Fx \supset Gx$. Thus, $FxvGx$ is equivalent to $\sim Fx \supset Gx$. Formula 30 allows us to conclude from this that (x) $(FxvGx)$ is equivalent to $(x)(\sim Fx \supset Gx)$.

We can now use I.8, letting $\sim Fx$ stand in for P, and Gx stand in for Q. This shows us that $(x)(\sim Fx \supset Gx) \cdot (\exists x)(\sim Fx)$ implies $(\exists x)$ $(\sim Fx \cdot Gx)$. Formula 19 allows us to rewrite $\sim Fx \cdot Gx$ as $Gx \cdot \sim Fx$, and formula I.1 tells us that this implies Gx. Formula I.11 allows us then to assert that $(\exists x)(\sim Fx \cdot Gx)$ implies $(\exists x)(Gx)$, and formula I.6 allows us to conclude that $(x)(FxvGx) \cdot (\exists x)(\sim Fx)$ implies $(\exists x)(Gx)$.

2. If we apply formula 27, letting $Fxv\sim Gx$ stand in for R, we see that $(x)(Fxv\sim Gx) \equiv \sim(\exists x)(\sim(Fxv\sim Gx))$. Formula 24 then tells us that $\sim(x)(Fxv\sim Gx)$ is equivalent to $\sim\sim(\exists x)(\sim(Fxv\sim Gx))$.

Formula 3 allows us to rewrite this as $(\exists x)(\sim(Fxv\sim Gx))$.

Formula 2 allows us to rewrite the $\sim(Fxv\sim Gx)$ component of this as $\sim Fx \cdot \sim\sim Gx$, and formula 3 allows us to rewrite this as $\sim Fx \cdot Gx$. Formula 31 then enables us to conclude that $(\exists x)(\sim(Fxv\sim Gx))$ is equivalent to:

$(\exists x)(\sim Fx \cdot Gx)$

Formula I.1 tells us that $\sim Fx \cdot Gx$ implies $\sim Fx$.

Formula I.11 enables us to say then that $(\exists x)(\sim Fx \cdot Gx)$ implies $(\exists x)$ $(\sim Fx)$. Formula I.6 enables us to conclude that $\sim(x)(Fxv\sim Gx)$ implies $(\exists x)(\sim Fx)$.

3. Formula 29 allows us to rewrite $(x)(Fx) \cdot (x)(Gx)$ as $(x)(Fx \cdot Gx)$. Formula 19 allows us to rewrite the $Fx \cdot Gx$ component as $Gx \cdot Fx$. Thus, according to formula 30, we can write:

$(x)(Gx \cdot Fx)$

I.1 tells us that $Gx \cdot Fx$ implies Gx. I.2 tells us that Gx implies $Gx \mathsf{v} \sim Fx$, which formula 20 allows us to write as $\sim Fx \mathsf{v} Gx$. According to formula 4, $\sim Fx \mathsf{v} Gx$ is equivalent to $Fx \supset Gx$. Thus $Gx \cdot Fx$ implies $Fx \supset Gx$. I.10 allows us to conclude from this that $(x)(Gx \cdot Fx)$ implies $(x)(Fx \supset Gx)$. I.6 allows us to conclude, finally, that $(x)(Fx) \cdot (x)(Gx)$ implies $(x)(Fx \supset Gx)$.

4. I.7 tells us that $(x) \sim (\sim Fx \supset Gx) \cdot \exists x$ implies $(\exists x) \sim (\sim Fx \supset Gx)$. Formula 28 tells us that this is identical with $\sim (x) \sim \sim (\sim Fx \supset Gx)$. Formula 3 allows us to rewrite $\sim \sim (\sim Fx \supset Gx)$ as $(\sim Fx \supset Gx)$. Formula 30 tells us that $(x) \sim \sim (\sim Fx \supset Gx) \equiv (x)(\sim Fx \supset Gx)$. Formula 24 allows us to conclude from this that $\sim (x) \sim \sim (\sim Fx \supset Gx)$ is equivalent to $\sim (x)(\sim Fx \supset (Gx)$. Thus, by I.6, $(x) \sim (\sim Fx \supset Gx) \cdot \exists x$ implies $\sim (x) (\sim Fx \supset Gx)$.

Index